And the Trees Clapped Their Hands

Stories of Bahá'í Pioneers

compiled by

Claire Vreeland

For you shall go out in joy
and be led forth in peace;
the mountains and the hills before you
shall break forth into singing,
and all the trees of the field shall clap their hands.
Instead of the thorn shall come up cypress;
instead of the brier shall come up the myrtle,
and it shall be to the Lord for a memorial,
for an everlasting sign
which shall not be cut off.
Isaiah 55: 12–13

GEORGE RONALD
OXFORD

GEORGE RONALD, Publisher
46 High Street, Kidlington, Oxford OX5 2DN

*A Cataloguing-in-Publication number
is available from the British Library*

ISBN 0–85398–378–x Pbk

Cover painting
The Roaring Silence
by Ken Carter

Printed and bound in Great Britain by
Biddles Ltd, Guildford and King's Lynn

Contents

Introduction

When I was a child, I never liked to take giant strides forward in the playground game because that brought me to the goal too quickly. That same thinking kept me from becoming a Bahá'í sooner. Part of my reluctance was because I wondered what it was I could do to help the Faith. All Bahá'ís teach on the homefront or as pioneers going out to other countries. I did not think I could do either.

But something had propelled me to declare and would not allow for further procrastination. So when I did become a Bahá'í, I was amazed at my temerity. Now what had I done? What would happen next? I really thought I might wake up some morning to discover I was at a pioneering post in some uncomfortably tropical country, working in a bush hospital next to a reptile-infested swamp, surrounded by people whose language I was slow in comprehending. My mission, whether or not I cared to accept it, would be to hand-scour the bed pans.

I had also read and heard of Bahá'ís who found their faith severely tested soon after declaring. So I braced myself for an immediate succession of major calamities such as only my excessively fertile imagination could contrive.

When I did find out what it was I was to do, my relief was considerable. And premature. Three weeks after declaring, it was suggested to me, because of my work and location (I was on the editorial staff at the *Register-Citizen*, a daily newspaper published in Torrington, Connecticut, birthplace of Horace Holley, 1887–1960, a Bahá'í instrumental in the development of the Bahá'í Administrative Order) that I research Holley's life, especially his early years. Researching and writing are the tools of my trade. Before long, I had begun to write a biography. Well, now, this was more like it! Doing the things I loved best. My happiness soon turned to chagrin as I discovered the magnitude of the task. I had a lot to learn about the art of presenting a biography. Somehow, I had been fooled into taking not one or two but several giant strides!

There were yet greater and longer strides to come. For 30 years I had enjoyed a perpetual love affair with my work, that of recording and writing about the history of north-western Connecticut, on a daily basis, as it happened. Often I wrote feature stories about past history. I achieved a panoramic view of all of it and of the people involved, generations of them. My first inkling of trouble with all of this was when I began wanting to write it up, not as a news report, but in the manner of a novel, showing the interplay of characters and the reasons for their behaviour. I had felt I could just go on forever, in my comfortable niche, working for the newspaper. Now my interest began to pall. The work began to seem repetitious, sometimes even boring. Then, as I got more and more involved in developing the Holley life story, I began to resent the hours on the job, hours that took my time and sapped my energy. It was apparent that I could not work at a demanding newspaper job and give the full power of concentration and energy needed for this other task.

I retired to devote my full time to the Holley biography. Two weeks later, I was on a plane for Chicago, thence to Wilmette and the archives at the Bahá'í centre. Friends and neighbours could not understand this strange mode of retirement, a mode that required a daily commitment to this new task.

Meanwhile, another inspiration arrived! The big story is in the massive pioneering movement of thousands of Bahá'ís, entire families, grandparents, and even quite elderly single people to remote regions of the globe, to live in circumstances they never would have dared imagine, to tell receptive souls about the new World Order prescribed by a Manifestation of God many have never heard about. The most difficult thing for many people to accept is the 'strange' name of this prophet, Bahá'u'lláh.

The tenets of the Faith are a different matter. Many souls are receptive to the idea of a new World Order that promotes the brotherhood of man, elimination of racial and religious prejudice, equality of men and women, that fosters the means of using global solutions to the world's environmental and economic problems, that challenges people to find a spiritual reality that enables humankind to live in a peaceful society.

This massive Bahá'í pioneering movement is of tremendous historic significance. There has truly never been anything like it. Scholars and historians will write about this in the future. Meanwhile, the story of how individual Bahá'í pioneers manage to work effectively within divergent cultures is useful knowledge for all who will work on a global basis in the twenty-first century.

This realization was triggered when I received a copy of a letter sent to Estelle Johnson of Jensen Beach, Florida, from Happy Dobbs, pioneering in Grenada. Estelle loaned the letter to our daughter, June, who copied it for me. Thus began the germ of an idea for yet another book and a growing certainty that my work had been chosen for me.

The 'first' pioneer in the Bahá'í Faith was Bahá'u'lláh's eldest surviving son, 'Abdu'l-Bahá, who after 40 years of imprisonment with His father for Bahá'u'lláh's teachings,

went at the age of 67 on historic journeys to Europe and
North America to proclaim the Word of Bahá'u'lláh. He
told how all previous religions brought the Word of God in
a series of progressive revelations and that Bahá'u'lláh was
the promised one mentioned in all the holy books of earlier
religions, the Manifestation of God who would bring God's
Word about the establishment of a new World Order and a
time of lasting peace. World rulers, statesmen and scholars
as well as thousands of ordinary people listened to the
message presented by 'Abdu'l-Bahá, who was renowned
worldwide for His humanitarian work. 'Abdu'l-Bahá was
knighted in 1920 by the British government for His efforts
for the relief of hunger in Palestine during World War I.
But His primary work was in the promotion of the Word of
Bahá'u'lláh and the bringing of many believers into the
new world religion, the Bahá'í Faith.

Since 'Abdu'l-Bahá's time, no Bahá'í has ever been
discouraged, because of age or any other consideration,
from pioneering to the far corners of the earth. This book
brings stories of present-day pioneers of all ages, living now
in many lands, told in their own words – stories of courage
and perseverance in the face of seeming disaster, told with
poignancy and humour.

The young geologist whose sport was mountain climbing, who was jarred into recognition of reality when he fell
from a high mountain peak in Alaska, a family living in
Kathmandu where their nearest neighbours were a band of
rabid monkeys living in an abandoned Hindu temple, the
retired school teacher who drove 3,600 miles from her
home in Michigan to Belize in a station wagon pulling a
house trailer to deliver seeds for Operation Bootstrap –
these and many others present their stories.

Frank Jordan writes how he had earned a degree in
anthropology which he found about as useful 'as a loose
frog in a bed' once he got to Surinam. Ted and Joan

Anderson were adopted by Tlinget Indians and given new names during their pioneering adventure. One man who had worked on the United States space programme found himself piloting rickety DC–3s over the perilous mountain peaks of the Andes to support himself and his family while pioneering.

The stories in this book illustrate how 'The issues of human existence turn upon the axis of education. Education alone can overcome the inertia of our separateness, transmute our creative energies for the realization of world unity, free the mind from its servitude to the past and reshape civilization to be the guardian of our spiritual and physical resources.' World unity, prerequisite for lasting peace, must be the goal of moral, political and religious effort in these times. In this lies the only hope for survival of the human race. How this may be achieved is contained in the teachings of Bahá'u'lláh. It is the work of Bahá'í pioneers to see that the peoples of the world are given the choice of knowing about this great Prophet-Teacher, of knowing what each individual can do to help achieve world unity. No awakened soul, living on earth in these chaotic times, can assume that others will take responsibility for the achievement of world unity and lasting peace. It is up to every person to answer this call in his or her own way.

Claire Vreeland

Acknowledgements

Soon after the book proposal for *And The Trees Clapped Their Hands* was received by the publisher, I received a list of names and addresses of pioneers who would have good stories to relate. I sent out a series of letters and waited for a response. One of the first respondents was John Kolstoe, who with his wife, Beverly, pioneered in Alaska. I felt I knew John because I had read and liked a book he had written called *Consultation*. This book belongs in every business manager's office, in school and home libraries. Although John was busy updating the material in this book to include a new segment for teaching young people this valuable art, he soon sent a script along with scripts from Earl Redman, Sharon O'Toole and Galen Insteness. He also supplied names and addresses of pioneers in other countries. Thus began a network of respondents, each of whom supplied yet more names, creating links in an ever-lengthening world chain. Even established writers whose works-in-progress were at such a critical stage they could not write for *Trees* sent heartening letters of encouragement.

But it was John Kolstoe's first bundles of scripts from Alaska, received when I was wintering in Florida, that lent impetus to the work, and for this I am most grateful.

I am grateful to the publishers of the following works for permission to reprint them here. Timothea Sutton's story 'The African Bees Were Aggressive' first appeared in *Herald of the South*, vol. 23, April–June 1990 under the title of 'Thoughts of a young girl in her first year of pioneering'.

Sue and David Podger's story 'Kabu of the Purari' first appeared in *Herald of the South*, vol. 1, no. 1, Autumn BE 131 under the same title. Both are reprinted here by the kind permission of the publishers. Barry Clatt's 'Pointers for Pioneers' first appeared in *Pioneer Post*, vol. 13, no. 1, June 1990, published by the International Goals Committee of the National Spiritual Assembly of the Bahá'ís of the United States and is reprinted here by its kind permission. I am also grateful to the International Goals Committee for its permission to reprint selections from its letter to returning pioneers. The passages from the booklet *The Good Message*, published in 1941, are reproduced here by permission of the United States Bahá'í Publishing Trust.

I would also like to thank all those pioneers and former pioneers whose stories could not, for one reason or another, be included. I am very grateful to them for their support of this project and their efforts in the pioneering field.

Grenada's Lovely! Wish You Were Here!

Happy Dobbs

July 17, 1989

Warning! If the only thing you'll read is a letter, this is a letter. Otherwise, for a letter it is obviously moderately long. A diary? A journal? Mind flotsam. For those of you who are not ambitious enough to read all of this, and for my semi-literate friends, I will summarize here. Grenada's lovely. Wish you were here.

Dear Ones:

How you ben keepin'? We ben keepin' good. It's rainy season again. I can tell. I just dried my face on a towel that smells like wet dog. The sofas do, too. The fridge is sweating. My hair generally looks like I just got out of the shower. Jessica came out with the stick of Rose Clay deodorant. 'Look, Mom, the deodorant is sweating!' The thermometer says it isn't so hot, only reads 85 to 87 degrees, but it sure is humid.

Ironically, when the rains come, the tap water goes. Filters jam up. No water for four days last week, except for the deluge outside. When we do have water, we are more likely not to have electricity. A public service to keep the population from becoming soft and complacent? This allows us to be consciously grateful for things that we might otherwise take for granted.

Since I last wrote, we have gone from orange foliage, African tulip trees, Barbados Pride, to purple lilacs, crepe myrtle, orchids on very tall stems and the vines season and now are coming back into orange as the flamboyant trees begin their spectacular show. Hummingbirds in the flowering vines.

Living in Grenada provides just enough Indiana Jones to write home about. The termites did their annual air raid this week. The house, the streets, everywhere fills up for a couple of hours with these flying insects. Cover your mouth or breathe them in. Screens, called 'netting' here – and we're about the only ones in St Andrews to have them – have no effect. They come out of the walls or at least it does seem that way. I don't know what happens to the insect part, but they leave behind their wings. Wings everywhere. The strange thing is, here are all these wings, but there are no bodies. Then there are the fruit flies and the ants. Tiny, barely visible ants that appear from a different dimension. They exist in this visible world only around certain substances, usually something you were going to eat. Remove the substance, is gone dey gone.

We don't study food we're eating. Black dots, moving or not, are automatically identified as cardamon, nutmeg or pepper, according to the nature of the dish. No questions. Don't look, eat!

Congorees. Hard, red centipedes, exactly the colour of the bathroom floor. They have an affinity for laundry, attracted by the scent of laundry soap, I guess. They are everywhere in the rainy season, usually on the soap or in your clean clothes, sometimes in closed drawers, kitchen cabinets.

Officially, there is nothing poisonous in Grenada. Now Trinidad, well, Trinidad has so many poisonous things that it's amazing anyone lives there. Trinidad, something bite you, you gon' die. When we enquire on a case-by-case basis, we are told almost everything is poisonous, depending upon whom you ask. Most everyone in Grenada is an expert on almost anything. There's a story about when President Reagan was here. Said he wanted some Grenadians as astronauts for the space programme. Forty applied, all with previous experience.

Always shake clothes, towels, shoes, etc. before you use them. Scorpions favour shoes. I cut the labels out of my clothes, might sprain something twisting around wildly because a label is tickling my back. But look before you swat. You really want to brush stink bugs and blister bugs off before you squash them.

A tarantula the size of Rason's hand was wandering among the smaller insects and lizards on our ceiling, making them appear insignificant. That's why I noticed him. Generally I find it more comforting not to study the ceiling. I thought at first this tarantula (Hairy Mygalomorph, according to the spider book) was a very sick bat. We decided we did not want him up there. Threw a dishrag at him, to Jessi's sounds of aversion from the porch. He fell in slow motion, to the side of the basket holding Scrabble cubes. The cat was sleeping beside the basket. Rason directed me to bring a Cool Whip container. (If you plan to move to a third world tropical place, start now eating things in wonderful reusable containers and save them. Here they are valuable, plus it will give you lovely memories of products that used to be available to you.) Rason's plan was to pick up the basket, have me capture the spider in the container, slide it off the basket while sliding the cover over it. Good plan! But it didn't work that way. The Scrabble cube basket is shaped like a flower pot. The spider, being no dummy, simply slipped around to the other side when he saw the Cool Whip container coming down on him. Unfortunately, Rason's hand was on the other side too. For a brief moment the spider was covering his entire hand. Then it started up his arm. Alphabet blizzard. Even the cat showed uncharacteristic agitation and joined Jessica in her chorus on the porch. The Hairy was found wandering dazed on the floor among the Scrabble cubes. Now it was easy to catch him with the Cool Whip bowl and he was so big I was able to scooch the bowl around so I didn't have to capture any Scrabble cubes when I slid the cardboard under. Rason was studying his hand and arm with grim fascination. We brought out the *Spiders and Their Kin* book. The Hairy was known for its ability to occasionally catch birds, lizards or small snakes. The hairs on the abdomen shed easily and are very irritating to human skin, we read. I got out the ammonia, my cure for anything that stings. The pharmacy sells it by the ounce. Bring your own bottle. No pro-blem! Grenada's great! 'No pro-blem' is the national saying just as 'Have a nice day' was in the States. We put Hairy outside. Later we were told the local name for this spider is 'Four o'clock'. 'If he bite you, you is dead by four o'clock.'

I don't feel comfortable with any spider that eats birds.

Grenada's got centipedes and millipedes and Carol Channing bugs with long, fringed eyelashes. Lightning bugs with headlights instead of tail-lights. Four-inch long grasshoppers. And on our ceilings and walls, tolerated because they eat bugs, are chameleons, tiny, thumb-sized tree frogs and geckoes, who make jungle sounds at night. They can hop across the ceiling upside down without falling. Can cause insomnia if you're lying in bed under them. But most days the only insects we notice are the perpetual sand flies. De san fly dey fret we, fret we, eat we body up to down. I still read in bed after everyone else is asleep so I gather every insect in the house around my head.

Mango season is back. Dropping off the tree outside the bedroom window. All along the side of the roads. I heard someone had a car accident sliding on them. They come in several varieties, all are delicious. The citrons have passed. They are big knobby lemon-like things. Limes are back. French cashews, a red fruit that tastes like roses, as do pomme rose, which are hard to find and so good you wonder if you only imagined them. Pigeon peas are finished. Breadfruit has returned. Christophe, which peel you as you peel them, until someone advises you to peel them under running water. Tamarind. Tart and extremely sticky. I love the jelly of the waternuts (immature coconuts). Passion fruit and guava, several flavours. Soursops, sweet and slimy. We make a drink out of soursop. Other popular local drinks are coconut water, lime squash, ginger beer, mandarin, Ribena (black currant concentrate), sea moss, Peardrax, Cidrax and Malta, as well as Quench-Aid. It's all referred to as juice. It's rare to find fresh juice in a restaurant. Canned or bottled only.

We eat lots of veg-jet-ta-ble food. Meat is generally referred to as 'flesh'. The lack of refrigeration and skill on the part of the butcher, whose training was apparently cutting brush with a cutlass, promotes vegetarianism. If you have the stomach to make it through the pig snouts, ears and various offal surrounding the butchers' stalls at the market, you can buy prime meat for the same price as feet. The thing is, you can't choose. Flesh is flesh and parts is parts.

The local chickens are tasty, but, as with all local flesh, must be stewed, never roasted or fried. The longer they are stewed, the better. These chickens were literally road runners. Rubber muscles.

What to add to the stew? Green papaya. Yams, which are white inside and can be as big as your leg. By the way, here 'foot' is 'leg'. No one here speaks of legs. Just foot, rhymes with boot. The yams have a woody bark on them and are delicious hash-browned. There's tannia but I would prefer to peel the bark off a tree. I just do not have the knack of dealing with tannia yet. There's dasheen, breadfruit. Like Al Capp's shmoo, breadfruit can be whatever you want it to be. Takes on the flavour of whatever its cooked with. Potatoes, dumplings (Grenada dumplings are like bullets, compacted papier mache). Carrots, peppers. The peppers here are wonderful. Celery, smaller than we were accustomed to, with thin stalks. Jessica calls it 'Ethiopian celery'. Fresh rosemary and thyme. Onions. And a local liquid mixture of herbs and spices, known simply as 'seasoning'. Rason calls it 'bug juice'.

Other available foods. Land crabs. Little kids walk around with strings of them, like strung garlic. Possums are called 'manicoo' and are held by the tail (dead) and waved seductively at us as we drive past. I hear they are such a local delicacy they are becoming an endangered species. There are also a few armadillo, called 'tattoo'.

The local equivalent of McDonald's hamburger is roti (ro-tea), a curried chicken. Rotis are very good. Unfortunately, the chicken is never boned and the bones are usually shattered making them more difficult to eat than bony fish. Then there's lambi (conch), or beef stew in a crepe-like thing made of mashed lentils. Imported meats, juices, etc. are sometimes available in St George's but are expensive. It is not just a rumour about third world dumping. Sandwich meats, canned goods, cereals, even the shelf-type yogurt, cream and milk are all several months out of date. Or from funny batches. White grape juice the colour of tea, toothpaste tubes that open at the seams after two squeezes.

Shipping takes its toll and adds to the cost. Rare, imported chocolate chips appear in solid form. One melted, white-blotched chunk per 12 oz. package. Jessi makes her own from local chocolate balls. They have never made it to the cookie stage yet. As soon as they cool, is gone dey gone. Local guava paste, guava cheese and jelly are great. Nutmeg syrup and jelly are also available, made from the fruit, like a peach, not from the seed.

I have finally learned to make pie crusts. Previous attempts made good substitute 'flip chips' for the dogs, with possible less benefit to their health. On my first try, Rason would not let me throw it out to the dog. Meat pies, apple and cherry pies from fillings from cans bought in St George's taste wonderful. Jessi and Rason are both great cooks, so we never go hungry, which is all too apparent. Aunt Ginny's famous fat test keeps me conscious of making no fast stops. Her test: you jump up and down and what's still moving minutes after you stop is fat. Jessi concentrates her skills on desserts and Rason makes the best rice and beans with coconut you've ever tasted.

We save a lot of money by having no cosmetic expenses. Perfume draws insects. Simple polka dot rashes become paisley overnight. Makeup slides. Mousse plasters hair into a helmet. These things can be done for free with sweat. After a shower, I take a cornstarch bath. I feel secure in the knowledge that all whites look alike to the locals. So simply pick out any pretty white girl and I look like her, except she probably is not clutching her underwear because the elastic is all washboarded out.

Country music is popular on the radio here. Wonderful to have access to such immortals as 'Since You've Lost Your Love Handles, I Feel You Slipping Away', 'Drop Kick Me, Jesus, Through the Goal Post of Life', 'I'm Just a Bug on the Windshield of Life'. Some of the lyrics are just too profound: 'I'd give my right arm to hold you in my arms.' The real local music is 'tos'. It's the essence of monotony like 'rap' gone flat. It's played at full and distorted volume on speakers larger than most of the family homes in Grenada. Periodically, the Holy Innocents Anglican School on the mountain opposite us makes a 'joyful noise', a lot of noise unto the nation, until two or three a.m. The speakers are aimed at us, hurling deafening and tangible sound through the night. Holy Innocents. Not wholly innocent. Religious persecution takes on a new meaning.

Rason fantasizes owning a military tank for smashing the 12 foot tall speakers. They're everywhere. You don't dance to the music, you're mauled by it. Drive up, rumble, rumble, smash, drive off. Aah, silence! Who was that bald white man? Here bald, is 'ball'. 'He have a ball head.'

Another fantasy is of owning a portable pressure hose to put out the neighbours' charcoal fires. They make charcoal quarterly, I think. For four or five days they burn, fires smouldering under sand. Our home is the chimney. We're uphill and the wind brings it directly through our bedrooms. It's as I would imagine living in the chimney of a wood-burning stove would be. Fuliginous torture. Headaches, coughing, runny eyes.

Otherwise, our neighbours are great. We have been made to feel welcome in La Digue. Wish it were closer to a nice beach. Rason is building a 21 foot catamaran sailboat, so we can visit islands near here. His 'near' and my 'near' are not the same. To me, visible is near when I'm planning an ocean trip on a small boat. His 'near' simply means somewhere in the same hemisphere. He's going to name it *Spice* because, for me, a little goes a long way. Also Grenada is known as the Spice Island.

Jessi is delighted to be out of school. There is no evidence that she expects to miss Sister Propriety, Sister Homunculus or Sister Inhibitor next year. Actually, towards the end of her time in the convent school, things got a little better. An English teacher came who was so universally disliked that she created a previously lacking unity among her suffering students. Jessi is wildly excited about our upcoming trip to the States and about beginning at Maxwell International Bahá'í School on Vancouver Island, B.C., in September.

We've been here for 13 months now. It's becoming very familiar. The culture shock phase, swinging from 'What am I doing here?' to 'What's not to love?' seems to have mitigated. I'm here. Loving what I am doing. Sometimes wishing I could do more, better and faster. But not somewhere else.

There is only one speed limit sign on the island, on the way to the airport, to impress the tourists, maybe? It's a standard speed limit sign, except it's blank on the mph. There was a stop sign too. We saw a man prying his van out of the ditch with it. He'd knocked it down on his way into the ditch. The constantly changing one-way streets are never marked. Every vehicle has its own number. It must be displayed on the rear. How you do that is up to you. Rason has carved our licence number into the new greenheart bumper. The rest is rusted off.

There's at least one shop in each village. Seven-eleven gone West Indian. Usually called 'rum shops'. Evidently they are required to post a liquor licence number. Beautifully hand-lettered white-on-black background signs: 'Licensed to sell intoxicating beverages' or 'spiritous liquors' and my favourite: 'Licensed to sell intoxicated liquors'. On all of them, at the bottom, is 'License # ---'. Always blank. Like the speed limit sign.

A quick vocabulary lesson:

I deh	I'm here
doh	don't
so-shall	social
tief	thief 'He tiefed we mango.'
en	isn't

in a monkeypants	in a real mess
walk with it	bring it
maycase	make haste
leggo beasts	untethered animals
brapps	suddenly

Challenging to a person who grew up in the land of the good ole bawy (Sumbitch, sumbuddy screwed up sumese words). Southern American has the advantage of being spoken at half-speed whereas Grenadian is spoken at double speed. I'm awed at the Grenadians' ability to say so many syllables without pausing for breath and with such a pretty rhythm. 'Youwansumspysis, Mama? I giveyoucheapbah-gain.'

Here you don't honk your horn. You hoot your hooter. One does not hoot at people conversing in the street. 'Ain' you got no man-nahs? You can' see we haven a con-vaah-say-shun?'

Plurals and possessives as we know them are not used. 'She wear she dress. It be the girl bes' dress.' Innovative use of verbs, too. Repetition is used for emphasis. 'He fret me, fret me, vex me plenty, plenty.' Archaic words add a real flair to conversation. Even ordinary offensive graffiti takes on a simple charm. 'Foc u', for instance. Who says phonetic spelling is not effective?

Adult literacy classes are a wonderful experience. Using the Laubach books. The people I'm working with are thrilled about learning to read. Official statistics show that Grenada enjoys 95% literacy. The criterion must be the ability to write one's name. Even in a culture where reading and writing are not a high priority, adults who can't read suffer low self-esteem. We work on English as a second language. Laubach teaches 'th', which does not exist in Grenada. 'Th' equals 'f', 't' or 'd'. 'We doin' our ting, bofe of us.' 'Dey finish dey wuk.'

The Bahá'í youth classes continue to be a major source of enjoyment and stimulation for us. Try teaching Bahá'í consultation to people who have grown up in a culture that considers verbal abuse and exasperation a way of life, the greatest art form. 'But, Hah-pee, if he idea stew-ped, muss say is stew-ped.'

Or marriage and family life in a nation with rampant illegitimacy and abandonment. To live with a natural parent here is so unusual it is a source of pride. 'My name is Desley. I live by my mother and my father.' Weddings are so few and far between that funerals are major festive social events. Seems there are two or three a week around here, and still the population grows. Obviously a friendly and loving group of people.

Kids who were quiet and shy are researching and reading scripts for the radio. 'I don' wan say "kindness". I wan say it right. Ben-ev-o-lence.' And speaking up fearlessly. Learning to use the computer. Becoming jaded old hands with such miracles as the printer. Jude was convinced it manufactured its own paper as needed. And the copier. 'It shouldn't have copied the stain.' Seeing themselves as part of a larger world. It is good.

Grenada may be the first nation in the world to require in all the schools in the country the teaching of the oneness of mankind and the elimination of all forms of prejudice. This was proposed by the Bahá'ís to the Minister of Education. He is eager and enthusiastic. So are we.

I'd love to show you Grenada. The scenery is striking. The same filter vision that allows me to completely overlook the mess in my own home now allows me to see the flowers in a yard and filter out the rusting moto-cah beside them. What I previously perceived as squalid homes now look homey. Lacy or crocheted curtains tied in a knot at the bottom or strips of coloured vinyl flapping in the breeze. Swept dirt. Steps carefully hacked out of the mud

paths. Hedges of hibiscus, oleander, bougainvillaea, peri-
winkles. Laundry drying on lines in the sun, under the
houses, on rocks, bushes, bridges and porches. If nothing
were blooming, the laundry alone would make things
colourful. Brightly painted wooden homes built on stilts.
Shutters propped open from the bottom with a stick rather
than glass windows. These must be the original mobile
homes. Neighbours vex you? Take the house apart and
move it. Explains how a hurricane can leave 85% of the
population homeless. You can't pass the houses when they
are laid across the truck in front of you, going 3 mph up the
hill. The overhang is very hard on the sheep and goats
grazing on the side of the road and on the people bathing at
the public faucet. The house is wider than the road, you
see.

Here and there are the remains of old rock windmills
with huge trees wrapped around them. Like some mythic
mediaeval tree house. Full moon on the tropical mountains,
silhouetting royal palms and banana fringe. Bright stars.
Tall fluffy bamboo. Kids swimming while the women wash
clothes in the river. Rastamen with their long, matted
'dreadlocks' usually worn stuffed up in an enormous
crocheted cap with a bill, yellow, green and red stripes. The
Rastas must have copied their hairstyles from the Barbados
sheep. There's a Rasta shop in Grenville called Roots. In
the window is a picture of the Last Supper. One of those
black velvet pictures. Everyone attending this version of the
Last Supper is a Rasta.

The basic atmosphere here is that of a huge summer
camp. Public bathing and washing. Roadside personal
grooming. Braiding, trimming, curling. Children everywhere, day and night. 'Sidewalks', a euphemism for the
war zone beside the streets in town, are for vendors.
Popcorn, sugary candy, tamarind balls, vaseline, pins,
shoes, garlic. Everything that moves, moves on the street,

not on the 'sidewalk'. 'Queen' shows. They're obsessed with beauty pageants here. Amazing and bizarre costumes. Cricket games in the road and on the beaches. If it's happening in Grenada, odds are it's happening in the road. Everything is public. Yet the people are quite modest.

Smells: Citrus blossoms, frangipani, urine, oleander, smoke, cinammon, diesel exhaust, fish, nutmeg, fermenting cocoa, ocean air.

Sounds: Roosters, people, struggling unmuffled vehicles, tree frogs, insects, birds, donkeys, sheep, babies, 'tos', and the rain when it hits the tin roof in our kitchen, it is the only sound.

Some things I've learned this year:

1) Do not eat salt fish in any form.
2) Don't buy a transparent brush. It gets lost wherever you put it down.
3) I'd rather be patient.
4) Squalor and beauty can co-exist.
5) I'd rather they didn't.
6) Adventure and insecurity co-exist.
7) Ditto no. 5.
8) Ignorance and intelligence are rarely mutually exclusive.
9) Scarcity of money is not poverty.
10) I'm glad I can read.
11) I have ambiguous feelings. Is there something I am not ambiguous about? No, yes, sometimes. Except salt fish, roaches and itchy skin. I don't like them, at-tall, at-tall, at-tall.
12) Putting rice in salt shakers does not keep salt dry. It douses your food when you move the lid to get at the salt.
13) English defies logic.
14) I'm immensely grateful for friends and family.

This was not Happy's only pioneering post. Her irrepressible spirit, her fascination with exploring inner and outer frontiers, and her strong desire to spread the Word of God was to bring her new pioneering adventures. She wrote:

Immediately after I married Rason, we moved aboard a 42 foot trimaran sailboat, *The Wind Rose*, with the two children, to travel teach in the Bahamas. This was a lot better in theory than in practice. A great deal of our energy went into hanging onto the last shreds of sanity. All our worldly possessions were on this boat. We had no permanent address. Rason had never had children. We were both novice sailors, and newly married. Jessica was conceived the day we moved onto the boat. We did not do much teaching in our seven months on the boat, but we did learn a lot about ourselves. I still haven't recovered from some of the things I learned about myself. Elizabeth and Rob did Calvert School, first and third grades. This was probably the best part of the whole experience. They heard the quote from 'Abdu'l-Bahá, 'Bring them up to work and strive, and accustom them to hardship' so often, they would both tell me that 'Abdu'l-Bahá said lots of other things and that the 'ship' in hardship was not to be taken literally.

When I wrote to Happy for permission to use her letter, I submitted a list of questions, conducting a journalist's interview via the mail. In concluding her answers to the questions, she wrote:

What an interesting exercise this has been! I've never sat down and looked at my whole adult life before. I tend to review isolated segments when I review at all. Life is such a multi-dimensional experience. It's good to flatten it out on paper and look at it now and then. For almost twenty years, I have tried to make my life a gift for Bahá'u'lláh. But looking at it spread out before me today, it comes across like a pre-schooler's gift of a fingerpainting. No one is sure what it represents, but they'll hang it on the fridge simply because it's given and accepted with love.

Q. How did you become a Bahá'í?

A. In 1969 my sister attended a party where she met Dizzy Gillespie. Soon after, she was visiting me in Ridgefield, Connecticut, and she related the things Gillespie had told her of his religion. Surprisingly, neither of us was drawn to religion at that time. Yet what I heard impressed me enough that I felt truly saddened that this was a 'black' religion and I would be deprived of it. By 1971, I had moved to Sarasota, Florida. In the paper was a picture of a white woman with the caption 'Bahá'ís believe that work is worship'. Remembering this phrase as part of Dizzy Gillespie's wonderful religion, I phoned this lady. I went to my very first fireside that very next night. I don't remember that I ever doubted the truth of Bahá'u'lláh's message. It was truly a matter of love at first sight, of intuition over intellect. But the intellect was satisfied as well with the wonderful answers in the books I began reading: *Bahá'u'lláh and the New Era, Release the Sun* and *The Chosen Highway*. It took me three weeks to declare because I thought there must be some initiation phase for one to become worthy. I declared March 2, 1971.

My unsuspecting mother was on a tour of the Greek islands at this time. When she returned, she found her formerly 'sophisticated' daughter had given up smoking, drinking and, temporarily at least, during certain hours of the day, even eating, it appeared. She asked, 'Wait a minute! You don't drink, you don't smoke, and now you don't even eat. No wonder it's a religion with a small following!'

Q. Was this your first pioneering experience?

A. I went to Tanzania from June 1972 to June 1973, the last year of the Nine Year Plan. I went with my first husband and two small children, Rob, six, and Elizabeth, who was only three. My main work was to develop and administer a correspondence course for East Africa, as well as regular pioneering things like speaking in high schools, children's classes, serving on committees. It was ironic. The great adventure in Africa and I often spent 18 hours a day at the typewriter!

Q. What is the most important thing your pioneering experiences have taught you?

A. Recently, I've come to the conclusion that it might not be what I do for Bahá'u'lláh that matters. Maybe it's what I do with Bahá'u'lláh. Switching that preposition has changed my perspective a lot.

2

Our Creole is Coming Along
Alanna and Paul Vreeland

Paul and Alanna Vreeland pioneered in Haiti in the early 1980s. They left for their new post just days after they were married. Their letters reveal many of the difficulties they experienced while simultaneously adjusting to a totally different culture and to their marriage. For Paul, a workaholic of the first order, adjusting to the slow pace of life in Haiti presented many frustrations at first.

November 29, 1982

Dear Ma and Dad:

This will be a hurried note. Whenever we learn that someone is going to the States or Canada, everyone writes hurried notes to give them to mail. With the holiday coming, the mail from Haiti will all but stop until after Easter.

I've had little time for writing. I'm now working 'full-time'. Full-time here is half a day. I teach at the Caribbean American School from 8 a.m. to 1 p.m., observe a class at the Haitian American Institute from 3 to 4 p.m. and teach there from 4 to 6 p.m. So, with commuting up and down the mountain, my day goes from 6 a.m. to 7:30 p.m. and I tire much more quickly in the heat and noise of Port-au-Prince. On Wednesdays I take a regular class at the Caribbean and will take the students through June, grades

1 through 5, all together in one room. Some speak English, others French and yet others only Spanish. Thank goodness the class is small, from eight to ten students. Those at the Haitian-American are adults, paying tuition to learn English as a second language.

Alanna and I are still living out of suitcases, camping out in other people's homes. With luck, we'll have our own house and maid this week. We've had little privacy. When did we ever?

Catching a camionette, a Peugeot station-wagon crammed with ten to twelve people, can be difficult at 7 a.m. or at 6 p.m. Aggression is the only answer. Competing with twenty to thirty people at the curb for a seat gives one a sense of victory when able to board and secure a seat.

Well, folks, I am not writing this letter just to tell you how life is here. The big news is that Alanna is nine weeks pregnant. Now, how can I wait and let that be Page Two news, you might ask? The thing is, it is the big news, it is momentous, but it seems almost secondary to our problems to adapt here. It's difficult to feel comfortable here at all yet. I feel stripped of my self-identity, especially when it comes to language. My Creole is coming along, slowly. Our emotions run Latin; the mood swings are dramatic. There are great days or pits of depression, so many profound changes to go through . . . We're feeling a lot of stress, but then, so do most 'blancs'. With or without difficulty, we are able to share this. We're satisfied with the choices we've made, the decisions, and we know why we are here. Without that, all would be meaningless.

Appreciated your letter, photos! I hope I will be able to write more regularly and with greater depth when my routine is more settled.

Love,
Fuzz

December 31, 1982

Dear folks:

We had a nice rest in Cap-Haitien. We slept on mats on the floor which had a camping feeling to it, especially since we could hear the surf of the ocean and also since the mosquitoes were so bad. It was really the first time we were able to unwind since we got married. We found ourselves laughing and joking a lot.

Sunday, January 2, 1983

Paulie went off one morning in Cap-Haitien and got a haircut. It was so very short and he did not like the way it looked at all. I think it's great. He looks just like Donald Sutherland (one of my teenage movie heroes).

Not long now before I'll be taking off on pilgrimage. Paulie is a bit nervous about running the house by himself, doing the shopping, supervising the maid, plus we have two people staying in the downstairs apartment so must make certain there is food on the table for them. It's nice to have a big house. It allows us to provide hospitality to those passing through. Also, we finally have some privacy because our bedroom and office where we both work is at one end of the hall away from the main part of the house.

Love,
A.

February 3, 1983

Dear Claire and Paul,

You know I was having such a wonderful rest and enjoying myself so much visiting you, I wasn't at all sure I was ready to come back.

There is a church across the road where fervent adherents congregate four or five times a week to celebrate their praise by loud singing which all too soon turns into the most horrible wailing. We could put up with that when it was in the evening but lately they've started having services two or three times a week starting at 5a.m.! Linda, who has been staying in the apartment downstairs, finally decided she had enough and would call the police. She looked up the number in the book under POLICE. It rang and rang with no answer. So she dialed the POLICE EMERGENCY number. It rang and rang and rang. No answer. Paulie thought this was hilarious.

All our love,
Paul and Alanna

The telephone lines between Connecticut and Canada were kept busy during Paul and Alanna's sojourn in Canada awaiting the birth of their child in June 1983. Then in July, they visited in Connecticut, showing the grandparents the brand new grandchild, Sonjel Claire. One week later all three were off to Haiti.

August 8, 1983

Dear folks:

Sunday I took Sonjel out in the morning, put her in the little pouch, walked out to the road and took the camionette downtown. I started getting paranoid wondering why they all seemed to be giving me such disapproving looks. Today our doctor explained all that. She's Haitian and was educated in the US. She said people do not like to see Sonjel in that pouch because that's an African custom, carrying babies tied to you like that, and the Haitians turn away from everything African. They think it's old-fashioned and have decided also it is probably harmful to the infant.

I am so impressed with our doctor I asked Paul to come along with me to meet her. We left the doctor's office feeling

greatly reassured. She gave the baby a thorough examination and said she was perfect. She now weighs ten pounds.
Her first flu shot will be given on Sept. 3. This doctor has a
marvellous system where we pay her ten dollars a month
and can go to see her as often as we like. It's like an
insurance, really. The doctor acts as if she has all the time
in the world, which gives me time to air all my concerns. I
do like her so much. I had been worried about taking Sonjel
into the crowded camionettes because of all the germs
flying around but the doctor assures me this is no problem.
She has a five-month-old baby herself and says she's always
taken her everywhere. She did caution us to boil the bath
water, which we were doing anyhow. She said if we have a
maid looking after her, the maid should be immunized
against TB. At her suggestion, we have decided to wait
until Sonjel has all of her shots before allowing anyone else
to look after her.

Love,
A.

August 31, 1983
Dear folks,

Hurray! I can scarcely believe it but Sonjel has been
sleeping all through the night! I am no longer so tired and
find I can really enjoy her more. She smiles at me quite
often but not as much as the books had led me to expect.

Paul and I have decided we will try to get out on Sunday
evenings to eat in a restaurant. Last night we got all ready,
got the baby all dressed up and just as we were ready to
leave, the rain came. The lights went out for short periods
about three times. We finally gave up the idea of our little
expedition and ate some canned Chinese food the Lords
had left with us. [*The Lords had been pioneers in Haiti before*

Paul and Alanna came.] It was an enormous treat. You can't buy that kind of food here.

Paulie gets enjoyment from his favourite radio station. He has learned the range of radio stations we can get. His favourite is Radio Metropol. They play fairly good stuff, George Benson, Chuck Mangione, Andre Gagnon. Paul seems to have given up listening to short wave altogether. The longer we remain here the more content we seem to be just to let the rest of the world look after itself.

Love,
A.

September 17, 1983
After Midnight

Dear Claire,

I don't know if I am actually going to mail this to you, but I am writing because I need company. I'm so lonely. I got up soon after I went to bed as I could not sleep. Paul is right. I am over-caffeinated. It was only three cups of coffee today, but that's too much after all those months of not drinking it. Paul is both here and not here. He's working very hard. Our financial situation is pretty gruesome and he is concerned with doing everything he can about that. We both are trying to do our best to contribute to the Faith and there is simply no time for us to just do things together. I guess that sounds pretty silly since in our isolation here we are together most of the time. There is a saying in the Bahá'í Faith that one should sacrifice one's life to the Cause as a candle when it burns, drips away and sacrifices itself, to create light. I really feel we are doing that right now and thank God it is for a cause we believe in. But, at times, like tonight, I feel a little crazy and really overburdened. I'd like to cut back our Bahá'í efforts a bit. Maybe I'll phone

Adele and tell her we can't bring cookies to the meeting for the United Nations Day, tell the youth they can't have their friends here on Saturday evenings anymore.

If only we could see that the sacrifice is worth something. So often it simply seems that it is not. The Saturday firesides, for instance, do not seem to be yielding any results.

Oh dear, this letter has taken a different direction than I thought when I started. But writing it has helped to clear my thinking, satisfied my need for a nocturnal talking companion. I've been so preoccupied with how. How can we ever get into this culture? How can we be effective in our teaching? Suddenly I realize the answer is you have to love the people you're dealing with. Too often I feel aggravation or frustration with the misunderstandings. But feeling love and appreciation for them is the answer. It's the missing piece (peace) for which I have been searching.

With much love,
Alanna

Alanna's Journal
September 29, 1983

Paul and I have arrived at the same realization today that we've really had enough, that things are really rotten here, that we both feel like giving up. So, what do we do? We tossed that around for a while and realized there is nothing we can do but endure. How come deciding that made us feel so much better? What can we do now to feel better about ourselves and our efforts here?

In my own life I feel the need for more organization so I can get to sewing projects, decorating our house, writing, etc. It has become essential to have a place for everything. So, that is what I shall do today.

September 29, 1983

Dear Claire:

Your letter came at just the right time today. I was having such a bad day that I began imagining how great it would be to just give all this up and start somewhere else all over again.

But I began reading your letter and all those ideas you planned to use in your creative writing course inspired me. Wish I were taking it. Those sort of exercises in letting your imagination go are fun. We did a lot of similar things in music therapy training but in a different context. Music was the medium, but the reality of it was the same, finding the poetry in the humdrum.

Our lives are so humdrum these days. We like to create, to imagine, to theorize, to philosophize. But because of the heat and the constant effort it takes just to survive, there seems little time for mental exercises. How I hunger for it! You wrote of buying the first apple cider of the fall season, and the brilliance of the weather. It all makes me homesick for North America. I miss the things we can't have here: a little house in the country like the house in Baltic, with fields to roam in, a river to look at, neighbours like Darby and LaVerne. I miss having a favourite restaurant to hang out in, and oh, the pleasure of having a car! But I know that I could not just leave this place and resume the life I had in North America. It just would not be the same.

We've been seeking things to love here, little places to go and things to do, but have never really found them. Could it be we must learn to live without those things too? At least one can still write, no matter where or with what circumstances. The problem here, and this is more on Paul than on me, is that we have to do so many things just to survive, things we do not particularly care to do. In his case, it is teaching and for me, running the house with so many handicaps, but at least I do get somewhat of a chance to structure my day a bit to my liking, more so than can Paul.

I used to think my life was quite interesting. I know Paul felt that way about the things he was doing. Now it seems to be only a constant struggle to carry on. I guess it's not by accident that when you live in a country where millions have to struggle, you too have to share in that struggle. It's all for a purpose, I guess, but I wish I could understand it.

Housekeeping continues to be a hassle. I discovered that we have been spending as much on food as we did when we had two more adults eating here. Started to notice other things; a missing towel, a sheet, a few dishes. Nothing really valuable except that we need these things. I had to start doling out food on a daily basis.

Love,
Alanna

October 21, 1983

Dear folks,

We took Sonjel with us to the beach yesterday. We went with another couple which was great because two of us could swim while the other two watched the baby. They introduced us to snorkeling which is quite something in tropical waters. I was astonished at the underwater beauty so close to the shore. Paul and I were thrilled to discover this new, inexpensive form of entertainment. Finally, a diversion we can afford and one that isn't bad for our health.

November 23, 1983

Dear Folks,

A short note as I want to take advantage of quick mail service to the US via Woody Lord who has paid us a visit

. . . Paul told you that Sonjel and I were out in the countryside the last time you phoned. Sonjel did marvellously well, charmed all whom she met and did not even get a touch of diarrhoea. We slept in the house of a resident Bahá'í. The house had no electricity or running water but was immaculate. The lady of the house had ten kids and knew all about them as you can imagine. We exchanged a lot of information with the local women about pregnancy, childbirth and childcare. Fascinating! Having a baby in this country is a big plus. You are one of the women then, and much less of an oddity than single women with no children.

The Big News is that Paul has quit his job. It's rather scary but I am behind him all the way. It was torture for him to continue in a job that seemed almost a farce at times. We will, no doubt, move to a smaller house in the countryside and he will find some other kind of work. Please pray that he finds it soon.

A.

January 15, 1984

Dear Claire and Paul,

Thank you, thank you for sending the pictures. We pored over them like a couple of new parents. I am enclosing the new address for when we will be moving to Jeremie after the first of February. Don't send anything valuable there. We do not know how the mail service will be there as yet. You could use our old address in Port-au-Prince, the box number, as we will be going there from time to time to pick up mail that may come there. But don't stop the letters. We save every one and from time to time reread them.

I think I mentioned on the phone that we met Darby Brown's cousin in Jeremie and like him a lot. Perhaps you will get a chance to meet him when you come. We have some ideas for when you come. Paul has a clear idea about this but since it is not certain how soon he will be writing I'll mention it briefly. Very often we come across articles in the American press about Haiti. They are most often negative and one-sided in viewpoint. It almost appears like a conspiracy to do Haiti in. Tourism has almost ceased to exist here. We thought it would be interesting for you to do an article or two describing the other side of Haiti, maybe even pointing out the destructive effect that the American press is having on a country whose people already have enough problems. If you come (please don't chicken out), bring plenty of film. You can use my camera. You might even bring two or three rolls for us and we will reimburse you. Film is ridiculously expensive here. Oh, but if you really are coming, don't worry about bringing anything but yourselves. If I actually have an opportunity to go to the airport to meet you, I shall die from excitement.

The past two weeks I have been taking an intensive course on pre-school education. The course is about total stimulation for children 3 to 5 years old. The programme is sponsored by the Haitian government Centre for Special Education and UNICEF. Given the fact that out of one thousand children who enter school in Port-au-Prince at age six, only 150 make it to grade 13, they have concluded there is something seriously wrong with the educational system. They have decided the children are, even before they ever enter school, way behind because they get no stimulation. I know there are programmes in North America that address this problem, as well such as Operation Headstart, but it is hard to imagine the degree of lack of stimulation that exists for some children here. Can you imagine a child who has never had a shirt to put on his back, let alone a toy to play with? The idea behind this new programme is to establish centres through the countryside for pre-school children, the poorest of the poor children, with programmes so enriched that by the time they enter school they are bound to succeed. One of the instructors said, 'A child who has had the stimulation needed to develop up to the age of six is a saved child.' Otherwise he never will be able to develop up to full capacity. This training programme is geared to train girls and women throughout the country how to set up this programme in centres so that as many children as possible can be reached. The course is based on a checklist developed in Portage, Wisconsin, and is divided into five developmental areas: language, socialization, knowledge, independence and psychomotor skills. Point by point, they outline each skill taking it back to from age six months to the end of the first year and so on. The programme stimulates the development of appropriate skills for three-, four- and five-year-olds using songs, games, stories, poems and an array of materials that would make most kindergartens in Canada look pathetic. The materials are organized in four corners: 'kwen kay' set up like a little playhouse with a table, a bed, dishes, dolls; 'kwen konstriksyon' which means building blocks and coloured cubes, wooden cars and trucks, all either handmade or manufactured in this country. Puzzles are called 'je pasyans' (patience games) and have paintings of the same type Haitian artists paint. The third corner, 'kwen sians', has all the games which require thinking, je pasyans, pyramids, triangles, squares and circles and colours that are stacked on different pegs teaching children size, shapes and colours. The last corner, 'kwen belte' (beauty corner), has prints, papers, crayons, drums, maracas, etc.

The training gives a broad range of songs, theatre, poetry writing, drama, Haitian proverbs and riddles. What a thrill that my Creole is good enough to allow me to participate!

We learned activities that will develop the children's motor skills and socialization.

Next week we will spend mornings observing one of the country's leading experts on child development working with a group of children. We saw her first session this morning. She is excellent. During our observation sessions, we will be given two or three things to watch for. I am so impressed with the organization of this process, of the entire programme. Not a minute goes to waste, just as in the planned schedule for the child's day. What an opportunity this has been for me!

Obviously I could not take a traditional college or university programme in education at this time as I want to spend most of my time with Sonjel. Now I am convinced that I am learning much more here than I would ever get had I decided to take, say the B.Ed. programme at the University of Prince Edward Island. I have never seen such a practical programme as this. Not even my music therapy course was so impressive.

So, what happens when the programme is finished? Graduates are expected to set up little pre-schools somewhere in the countryside, by whatever means we can. Perhaps I can go to the Methodist Mission in Jeremie and once I can show I have a group of children enrolled, UNICEF will send materials. I could run such a little school in my home if I am willing to serve as a volunteer.

How, you ask, have I been able to do this course? Well, I took Sonjel and the maid with me every day. The maid sat outside the classroom with Sonjel and whenever Sonjel needed to be fed or I heard her crying, I just went out and got her.

I'm really excited about all this. This whole approach to teaching is radical for this country where mostly they still learn by rote and have a very rigid approach.

January 26, 1984

Dear Ma and Dad,

While the packing boxes are strewn throughout the room and we panic that we won't be ready to move in time, we are very excited about your coming. We want you to experience some of Haiti; something that you can't get anywhere in the US. It is difficult to imagine Africa and North America all rolled up into one where the agrarian, industrial and high-tech revolutions are all taking place at the same time.

We've updated our needs list. In order of priority:

plastic pants for the baby, size 13 and up
diaper liners
Sonjel's passport which Alanna's Mom will mail to you
disposable diapers
a cheap Timex watch, not digital
3 or 4 long fiction paperbacks
recent women's magazines
2 rolls of colour films for prints
two G-13 or LR-44 batteries for the travel alarm clock
Planter's Mixed Nuts
dried fruit and nuts
two short sleeve white shirts, collar 15½ medium

None of these things are life-and-death items. It's probably more important that you keep your luggage to a minimum. Deplaning in Haiti is not deplaning in New York. Your experience in Port-au-Prince will *appear* to be chaotic. Suggestions: Since it takes time to unload the plane, *do not* rush to get into the luggage claim and customs area. You will come into one room where officials will check your passports and issue a visitor's card. There are chairs in this room. Use them while everyone else stands in line and

waits. I think one line is for visitors only and this line does
move more quickly. But you do not want to get through this
area only to have to stand and wait in the baggage area.
There are no chairs in that room. Do not lose your visitors'
cards as you will need them to get out of the country. The
baggage claim area is more chaotic. Here, too, do not be in
a rush. Conveyors bring the baggage around and everyone
piles everything on the floor. There are usually too many
pieces for available floor space. It can be difficult to move
around. This will be your first experience with Haitian
crowding. After you get all of your bags, take them to one of
the lines where another group of officials will open all of
them. This is routine and implies nothing. Once you get
checked through, there are usually men willing to help take
your bags out. If you are carrying more than two or three
easily manageable pieces, let one. Don't pay more than 50
cents. We will be waiting for you right outside the door.
Overall, if you are expecting Bradley or JFK standards,
this can be a miserable experience. If you go with the flow,
however, it can be endured.

I haven't written in some time and I still don't have time
to put my thoughts in order. Since leaving the job in
November, it seems there is even less leisure time.
Somehow we harbour the illusion that when we get to
Jeremie we will have a lot of time before we find a house
and a job. Yet whenever we think we are going to have the
time, it seems to disappear. We've just taken the prayer
book to the printer. We worked and revised the translation
about 15 times over the past four months but have decided
to just go ahead and publish it rather than to spend another
whole year making improvements. I'm to go down to the
printer today to inspect the pages before they assemble the
books. They were so impressed with the camera-ready copy
we produced with the word processor that I expect I will
spend an hour or so explaining how to use the features of

their newly-acquired system. We also have a meeting with the national assembly this afternoon. We need their approval for the series of 12 new radio spot announcements we have produced, and for a deepening cassette and our plans for continued work in Jeremie.

Paul

April 23, 1984

Dear folks,

It's been over two weeks since you left. I had to stay in Port-au-Prince for four days to get Sonjel straightened out. It was good that I went when I did. The doctor suggested a soybean formula as a replacement for milk. Sonjel's thriving.

John Currelly had offered to fly me back to Jeremie but unfortunately his plane was out of commission when I was ready to leave Port-au-Prince. So we had to take the bus. It turned out to be a pleasant ride with Sonjel and me having the front seats to ourselves. We both managed to get some sleep and more or less enjoyed the trip. We arrived in Jeremie at noon and hired a guy to carry our bags and started that awful climb up the hill. Before we reached home we met Paulie heading down to do some shopping. What a welcome sight!

Our friends Fred and Laurence arrived in Jeremie the same day I returned. They are now living in Gibeau, the other side of the bridge, remember, where we visited that day with the Bahá'ís? We saw a lot of Fred and Laurence as they took their meals here while they were settling in. They provided us with stimulating company but now have gone back to Port-au-Prince for a week, leaving us their motorcycle and their bicycle. What a treat! Yesterday when the baby settled down for a nap, we left her with

Marianesse and went to the beach. The water was perfect, not too rough and we had a wonderful time.

We have been busy with Bahá'í activities. Turns out that many of the original Bahá'ís that have been here since 1979 are interested in resuming studies. We had a meeting which over 60 people attended, and elected the Local Spiritual Assembly of Jeremie of which Paul and I are members. Now the real work begins!

Alanna

May 5, 1984

Dear folks,

Time is creeping by what with each day the same as the one before, the weather always the same, the sun always setting early.

Sonjel has taken her first few steps. She and I will go to Canada in June so my mother can see her. Paul will stay behind. His new job is set up to begin in July, we think.

I have been teaching English and Paul has been typing up materials for the Audio Visual Committee. But he will not be himself again until he has a full-time paying job. If the promised contract (foreign aid food distribution) does not come through, we may have to go back to Canada. Paulie feels the only thing that can possibly make this work is for him to stick it out and see if the contract comes through. It seems the only solution given the circumstances.

The Bahá'í community here is developing nicely. Recently they had a birth and a naming ceremony for the baby girl here at our house. We have Feasts regularly with 30–50 people in attendance. We are talking now about the possibility of building a Bahá'í centre here in Jeremie. One of the Bahá'ís would rent land for about $20 per year and the cost of the building would only be about $200. The community itself will have to contribute funds for it.

Love,
A.

Paulie will add to this letter now:

Maurice lives in Morne Beaumont, a sub-district a few miles up the mountain road from Gibeau. Alanna and I were taken there to teach one Sunday by Emile and Eric who live next door to Maurice's hut. A few months later, at a Feast held in Fred and Laurence's house in Gibeau, I met Maurice again. He and his wife asked me if I would be godfather to their nine-month-old girl, Rissa. I had no objection to this as long as I did not have to support the family. A few Sundays later, I got up early, feeling grouchy and out-of-sorts and really not well at all. But I rushed around to prepare a naming ceremony (a Bahá'í substitute for baptism and not an official public event), packed the camera, the necessary certificates, prayer books and the obligatory gifts for the father and godmother (in my haste the best I could do was slip a few dollars into a couple of envelopes) and set off for Morne Beaumont. A dozen or more people gathered, most of whom were members of Maurice's family, who lived in the village. Simple and short, a brief talk, a few prayers, the reading of a couple of the Writings, the signing of the documents and it was over. I kept feeling progressively worse. I really wasn't up to this and now, in retrospect, can see ways in which I could have added to the formality and dignity to the decorum. But I was so sick at the time all I could think about was getting home and to bed. It was a full two-hour walk in noonday heat. As I approached the bridge, my coffee vendor saw me and called to me. I had wanted to avoid greetings and conversations with all those I knew along the way so as to get home as fast as I could. Yet it is an insult if you ignore or don't acknowledge a friend. I stopped, descended to the hut and had a little visit, and welcomed the offered cup of coffee. Earlier this Madam, knowing how much I like coffee, most especially as I had told her, 'Yes, I drink a **lot** of coffee!' on each of my weekly coffee-buying expeditions, thought she'd have a joke with me. So, on one of my expeditions she had asked me if I would like to drink some coffee she had prepared.

'You do like to drink a *lot* of coffee, don't you?' she had asked.

'Yes, of course I do.'

She went to the frond-covered shelter at the side of the hut, a simple, fragile structure commonly used for cooking. In the meantime, her husband came out of the hut with a small tray, a demitasse cup and another larger aluminum cup. I picked up the larger quart-sized cup and jokingly said it was the right size. Little did I know her plan. She returned with the hot pan, poured out the thick, concentrated Haitian coffee, laced heavily with sugar, into the demitasse cup for Alanna, a cup which satisfies most Haitian's morning with a coffee that is quickly downed so that the short fibrillation of the heart acts as a good-morning slap to groggy consciousness, the equivalent to the American's waking to the first sour taste of morning citrus. She then began pouring coffee into the large cup. I now began to see her joke. What was I to do? I could not drink that whole cup. It would kill me. Or at the very least I would not sleep for a week. She poured, putting in about six demitasse cupsful. Thank God she did not fill it. She likes a joke. I had to play along, must get the upper hand. I drained the cup quickly and asked her where the rest was. It provided a good laugh for all. But on this day, by the time I got home and into bed, I was dehydrated and feeling quite ill.

A few weeks ago, Maurice stopped in on his way to Morne Beaumont. He had been in the country where his relative lives, planting this season's crop. He crossed the mountains to descend by way of Carrefour Sanon. That's at the top of the mountain on which we live. Our house is a two-hour walk down from the top. I don't know how many hours it would take to walk up. He paid us a short visit and apologized for not coming earlier, explaining that he'd been out in the country. His mother, he explained, was still disconsolate after the death of one of her sons earlier this spring. I mentioned that I was interested in visiting her and seeing his gardens. Maurice, Fred and I arranged a time to go.

When that day arrived, I waited in front of the Avant-Poste for Fred, trying to squeeze into the shade of an almond tree. I went to look at the monument in back and the soldier in charge told me of the October 1935 flood when peasants left their huts to take refuge on the bridge, a high point above water level, and hundreds lost their lives at the moment that the bridge went out. He said between three and four thousand Haitians lost their lives in this event. The monument is for them.

Fred arrived right on time and I climbed on back of his motorcycle. We headed up along the river toward the village of Moron. We expected that the house was not far from there. A half hour later we were crossing a small stream when we heard voices commanding us to stop. Maurice was there. He had been waiting since early morning. He waved for us to continue up a path of water-rounded loose stones, probably the old stream bed. Maurice said to continue on and he would meet us at the church up there. The path was longer and much steeper than we had anticipated. At each bend, we thought we were finally coming to the top. First gear all of the way. Fred had to stop to let the bike cool off. Maurice walked

behind us at a steady pace which took neither the wind nor
the sweat out of him. How many miles a day he must walk
by habit! We found a hut in front of the church, parked the
bike in the shade of a grapefruit tree, talked to the madam
and then continued to walk on foot. The trail was beautiful.
Flowering poinsettias drooped over the rustic fences. The
houses here were much larger, cleaner and spread out with
great woodland distances between them. The path was
demanding, exhausting even, and while the exercise kept us
bathed in sweat, we had a feeling of leaving one world and
entering another. We could look down several thousand
feet to the Grande Anse River snaking through the narrow
banana and coconut plain between two ridges of mountain.

The high horizon of the ocean was revealed between two
peaks fifteen miles to the north. There were clear skies there
while to the east beyond the plain, grey cumulus were
perched here and there upon isolated summits, dropping
rain like wispy strands of wool cording. Fronting us, across
the ravine, were two flags rising above the trees, single
squares of black and red cloths. Maurice told us, 'That's
the hougan, medicine man.' Higher and higher we climbed,
sometimes having to descend into a ravine before climbing
again. We came upon a group of men beating the bush for a
mongoose. We continued to climb, up and up. My feet
began to understand the Haitian proverb, 'After the
mountains, more mountains.'

Just as I felt certain I was about to collapse, we arrived
at the family home. Maurice motioned for us to enter. It
was a simple two-room hut. The mud walls in the front
main room were whitewashed and decorated with pages
torn from an old Sears catalogue. Pages advertising flannel
shirts, snowmobile outfits and girdles popular ten years
ago. We have seen this quite often in rural homes. This 6 by
10 room contained a bed and a table. Here we were given
chairs and were introduced to the mother. She was dressed

for the occasion in a spotless white dress. There were more shared greetings from other family members. Sitting, trying to catch our breath, while shaking yet another outstretched hand, and then Maurice handed me a towel he had just perfumed, to dry my sweat-drenched face. The family is poor, yet they know how to lavish a cultured formality and enjoy it.

We talked with the mother and from time to time were introduced to more cousins, aunts, sisters, nephews as they arrived. It's like Prince Edward Island in this, as much a village as it is one extended family. The mother explained about the death of her son; how sad she was, how she had not been able to go out, how it had affected her health. Fred and I talked a little bit about life after death and offered several prayers for the departed and for the family. Maurice then gave a short speech telling the dozen or so who crowded into the room, and the others who leaned in through the window, who we were and then asked Fred and me to speak. It was all so formal. Maurice, who orchestrated this visit as if we were political dignitaries, then ushered the other relatives out of the house.

The table was set for Fred and me alone, while he brought a towel, a basin of water and soap for us to wash our hands. We were served scraps of chicken in a sauce and the rice and beans which are standard Haitian fare from the Holiday Inn to the poorest of huts. The others retired to another room to let Fred and me eat in privacy, custom forbidding them to watch others eat. After lunch, Maurice took us on a tour of the grounds to be planted. These are not laid out in neat plots with straight rows of single vegetables. Here, among rocks, trees and the houses of relatives, grows a cluster of mangoes; manioc grows there; and close to the house, protected by a ring of stones, anise and shallots. Higher up, several varieties of peas. Maurice took pride in them as a man rich in earth and labour. Passing from cluster to cluster we passed the houses of his relatives and again went through the ritual greetings. After our tour, we returned to the house for a final cup of coffee and a round of parting speeches. Maurice told us how happy he was, adding a few words I did not understand, which the family applauded. Fred and I took our turns at telling everyone how happy we were to have come. The whole afternoon seemed to have been a continuous round of speeches in which everyone repeated and repeated expressions of their happiness. No one needed the Toastmasters' Club here.

We left, Maurice leading, directing us through a confusing network of paths as we made our descent. When we reached the bike, the woman came out of the house to speak to us. Giving us a bag of grapefruit from the tree and a large papaya, she told of Hurricane David in which all of the houses and churches in the area were blown away, except for her house, the only one left standing. She told this with the excited joy of owning a miracle. Another round of partings and we were on the road again.

Within minutes we had a flat. Fortunately Fred is experienced in travelling here and brought patch kits, a tyre pump and tools. A group of twenty or so crowded around us, admiring Fred's mechanical ability, although some offered to sell us a tyre or do the work for a price. The young girls teased us with bawdy invitations while the more serious children were intent on watching the progress of the work. Other motorcyclists stopped, asking if we needed help. A half hour later we were underway again and then within minutes were removing the tyre tube. When we had the third flat, it was too dark to do the work. We waited.

We stopped a rack-bodied transport truck. Several men helped lift the bike aboard while we tried to find a place among the sacks of grain and other market commodities, and the 50 or more passengers. Most of the group joined in enthusiastic renditions of Christmas carols – a committee of joyful strangers brought together for the moment on a trip to town. The driver made a special detour to take Fred and his bike to his gate and then refused to be paid. I rode on into Jeremie, travel-dirty and weary.

Aftermath: This trip was an exciting event for both Fred and me. We felt that we had seen another, more pleasant aspect of Haiti which is hidden away in the hills out of reach of the foreigners who come and work in the cities. In the mountains, we had enjoyed a break from our routines and went as casual participants on a holiday. Coming back down meant coming back down to real life.

A few days ago Maurice stopped by. He brought gifts of grapefruit, fresh peas and a bunch of sweet, miniature, thumb-sized bananas. He told me he had been sick and had stayed in the mountains. We had some small talk and then he asked me if I wanted to go in with him for a couple of mamits of beans. I would buy the seeds, he would do the work, and we would divide the harvest. I said I would think about it. More small talk and after we spoke of how to prepare the peas, he asked for 'ti kob', a little money. 'I can't fast, I must eat.' I gave him a couple of gouds (40 to 60 cents.) On parting, he asked for a cigarette or two. I nodded. He took five or six.

The visit upset me for the rest of the day. I was uncomfortable with the feeling that I had been taken advantage of and that a very great distance separated me from Maurice. No, I hadn't given him too much. The fruit and vegetables he brought made a relatively fair exchange. It was not that. It's what I perceived as an unconscious rejection of who and what I am.

North Americans come to a country like Haiti and begin to learn a difficult lesson. You cannot trust anyone. This is not just a foreign perception of how bewilderingly backward these people are. Haitians will advise you of this too; something they see and acknowledge as part of their culture. I know other countries share this maxim, countries which have had similar histories of colonial exploitation and which now maintain wide gaps between the poor and upper classes. We learned it first when we discovered how much the maid was taking or giving away when we lived in Port-au-Prince (about $150 a month in foodstuffs). At first we took this as a personal offence and then learned that this is to be expected. We learned that we were the ones at fault for providing the temptation and allowing it to happen. We learned to do what more experienced people do. We had to lock up everything and dole it out in small, daily quantities. We learned not to confront a person for stealing. No one will ever admit it even if it means the fabrication of the most incredible stories to explain the missing items. We learned it is a serious offence to accuse a person of stealing. You can be sentenced just for the accusation unless the thief is caught in the act and there are witnesses present, enough proof to put the person in prison. You learn you can never trust anyone who works for you. This creates an employer/employee relationship where there is a class distinction. It creates formalized, paid slavery.

Thievery: I've learned that if I am alone in the house and working upstairs, I must close the downstairs doors. Once someone entered the house in the middle of the day and stole our dishes. If we are downstairs, we must close the upstairs doors. One night a thief climbed a tree, jumped onto our balcony, entered the house and stole the watch off the bed table twelve inches from my face, while we were still awake. The lesson: Don't trust anyone. Take every caution to minimize theft. Thievery thrives on class difference; the have-nots feeding on the haves, on the surface. Many see that the haves deliberately manipulate society so as to keep the have-nots from advancing. This happens not only in under-developed countries. As much as I am angered and frustrated by a theft in the house, I can accept the difference that exists between me and an unknown person, the assumed separation between us, the abstract difference in class.

Beggars: I hate it when a beggar approaches me. When he asks me for five cents or a pair of shoes he is saying, 'Look, there is a wide gap between us. You are the rich foreigner and there will never be anything shared between us except my demands. You're different from me, so give.' It's a subtle form of rejection. And who can blame the beggar when the-powers-that-be who hold the purse strings have not created other opportunities for the poor? One of the most irritating approaches is when the beggar beckons with, 'My friend', and worse yet, 'mon blanc'. How can you beg from me and expect that anything of mutual friendship could ever develop? You're not asking your Haitian friends, but a white stranger. I am not your friend by your own exclusion and this exclusion angers me. Difference in class again.

The poor: Most of our associations are with the poor and keeping in mind the lesson, we exert a great deal of energy in being suspicious. We are always on the alert to see what it is the person expects to get from us. Sooner or later, that person whom we know, everyone we know, is going to come with a request. Maurice is a case in point. He exemplifies all the others we have known. Sooner or later, these people confront us with our differences and proclaim, 'You will never bridge the gap. You are who you are and we are who we are.' This doesn't mean that confidences cannot be shared or that friendships can't be established; but it certainly seems to minimize the opportunities. Of course, it's unconscious. How can the average Haitian expect anything different after 400 years of reinforced expectations that the rich will milk the poor and the poor will come on servile knees asking for a handout from the pretence of the benevolent master. And the missionaries came. 'Yes, master.' And the aid programmes came, 'Yes, master.' The servile knee is bent in pretence, 'I'll take what I can from you if you're stupid enough to give, because it's you who comes with the condescending smile and says, in essence, "You're dependent. You can't do for your own selves, you're an emasculated race, impotent. Here, let me help you stay that way." ' Building on our differences. Class is such a powerful force driving people into generations of behaviour patterns which are almost impossible to break. You can't trust anyone.

I am not a development worker or a missionary or a representative of foreign aid handouts. And I hate the expectation that I'm not truly interested in you or the way you live; the expectation that I'm to fulfil a role devoid of the personality of who I am; the expectation that you will take whatever you can from me. Yet the history of the classes and the national past experience puts me, unwillingly, into that position. In the two years we have been here, no Haitian has taken a sincere interest in us as individuals. No Haitian has ever asked about us, who we are, what we are about. No one has offered to befriend us. Rather it is, 'What organization are you with?' (What can you give me?) No one has tried to bridge the difference. The constant expectation of a handout of money has robbed us of the only gift we can offer: the act of giving itself. A most insidious form of class prejudice, beyond the superficial issues of human rights, as pervasive as the cement which holds this society together. To bridge the difference would mean a toppling of that society. To cross those gaps would mean denying the sources of material benefits and a whole code of ingrained behaviour. It would mean a loss of identity for everyone. Who is going to be stupid enough to commit cultural suicide in that way?

Perhaps this is a pouring out of frustrations at our personal ignorance. Perhaps I even bring these actions on by not knowing something as simple as giving a spoon when I serve coffee. Perhaps token gestures of 'ti kob' are expected with the formality of a visit. But my gut feelings tell me 'no'. Our personal frustration goes deeper than those caused by class difference. It's frustrating that there is such a disparity between who I think I am and who others perceive me to be. And if these two images are not the same, how can the foundations for any true relating be established? Friendship assumes that *some* basis has been established. There is some sharing of self-image and the more meaningful and intimate relations are those in which a constant dialogue is supported to share ever-changing selves; the ever-present disparity creating a tension which two people work to eliminate and thereby gain a deepening knowledge of the other. But here, a culture is foisting upon us a definition with which we disagree. It's almost like being labelled a 'criminal' and having to live with the condemnation. In this position we cannot tell others who we are should there ever be those who would listen.

The frustration, too, is one of my expectations. I have yet to accept that this is the culture and that my dislike of it is not going to change it.

Should I be a developer, a missionary or an aid programme representative, I'm sure all this would change to some extent. Then I truly would be in one of the expected roles and would have to function as such. Position would remain persona.

When I look at those who are more successful in rendering service I see a conditional generosity and selflessness which insulates them against these frustrations. The key, I guess, is to find detachment. Yet detachment usually is accompanied by a confidence in self-identity, an identity which transcends the egocentric, the greater Self. The confidence and security I once felt in Canada has not been re-established. I'm still struggling to regain a sense of identity as one living in this country. Perhaps when I become more secure, I will be less stingy. We are in a state of transition between the losing of the old life and the finding of a new one. That transition is the struggle of life itself. Coming to a country as foreign as this is one of the quickest routes to having the old life stripped away. It is as painful as the fast jerk which rips away the bandage on the hairy scar of a sensitive ego. When that is done, one is left starkly confronting the awesome demands for self-transformation.

So much of this; it will take years to work out. These pensive moments happen often when I sit with my coffee on the balcony and gaze at the ocean horizon and watch the people mounting and descending the mountain. Yesterday I watched a group of eight men carry a hardwood beam that must have weighed several hundred pounds up the mountain. Another group accompanied them by counting the pace song and beating out the rhythm on sticks. It was the only way the eight men could coordinate their steps. When the music stopped, they stopped. Later, toward evening, I watched another four men carry down a litter on their shoulders with a pregnant woman aboard covered in a blue sheet, her straw hat flapping as the jerky motion of the men's progress snapped her back and forth. Perhaps the trip down was worse than what lay ahead at the hospital.

Paul

May 1985

Dear Ma and Dad,

Michael Bannister breezed through Jeremie for his job and left a half dozen dearly appreciated books; not the ones I would have chosen, but books, nonetheless. So I had my first taste of Le Carre and will push him to the unwanted side of my plate with the canned peas when he's served

again. *Farewell to Arms*, ho hum, and a coupla Len
Deightons, OK, so he can't write but he can tell a story. I
bought *Different Seasons*, Stephen King, while in Port-au-
Prince, devoured it at one sitting, cried for more. Let's hear
it for a written articulation of that down-home, down-east
style of yarning. A real Maine-iac; how can I not think of
Bruce Farmer and those quick stops for coffee and donuts
in Bangor/Brewer while on the way elsewhere? Alanna
bought back *Pet Semetary* and I had another pig-out the
other night. Little details. 'Let the wild rumpus start!' Yes,
Sonjel's got that book, where he tells us that bugged-eyed is
something real – when the rush of fear-induced adrenalin
pushes against the eyes, they pop out.

On the way down the mountain to town, I rounded the
bend by the convent and passed by a man with his eyes
bugged out. My eyes snapped the shutter just as the shock
occurred; at one second he was just a pedestrian as
common as dust and at the next, a man paralysed by fear.
Instinctively, my gaze shifted across the street. A soldier in
khaki made a hesitating step forward; his hand thrust to
unstrap the holstered pistol. I kept on going, not looking
back.

Little details. Why is it that during the twenty-minute
linger between the first cup of coffee and full-blown
consciousness, the most insignificant of memories swims
by?

Life here is often like that twenty-minute linger; a
twilight zone between the fantastic illusion and the other
fantasy we call real. As unknowing as sleep we try to
understand, the guys in the basement of the mind
machining fine concepts from a rough stock of imagination.
And in the end it's the concepts with which we decorate the
interior and prefer over a more boring, or in this case, a less
understood street world.

Did you ever see Willy? He's a Haitian, a Jeremienne,

wears double-breasted suits, pant-leg cuffs turned under midcalf nylon hose in the manner soldiers wear their fatigue cuffs to balloon at the boot tops. Carries an orange coloured fishnet shopping bag, cigarette dangling out of his mouth. Every day he wanders from one end of town to the other, speaking to himself and begging. I often see him in the morning sitting on a bench in the bank as if awaiting the bank president. When he comes to me asking for forty cents or a cigarette I force him to switch to the clear California English he speaks. He claims he spent twelve years in America and others say he served in the US Army in Vietnam. OK, so there's Willy walking down the street, and we say he is real, knowing so far, that he didn't crawl out of an abstract existentialist drama by some well-known French playwright or a *Juliette of the Spirits* film by an equally well-known Italian director. Willy. What we dream of him is what we want to keep of him, or rather *how* we want to cage and define and *keep* still that something which is too uncomfortably undomestic.

And while on the subject do you remember taking us to the zoo? The Bronx Zoo and once with Elaine and Dave to the Catskill Game Farm? Why is it that I know what went through my mind then, or is this fabrication too? The animals seemed more real, more alive in the gum-backed photos torn out of the colouring size books and pasted onto the proper square next to the two-paragraph blurb. Strange, we thought those photos were taken in darkest Africa and didn't suspect at all that they were taken in the zoos. Take the information from the blurb and add a little imagination and there was real life. Life at the zoo, on the other hand, had a funny quality about it. It didn't fit the lick-it, stick-it concepts. The zoo was animal limbo. They were just hanging out until they were dead. They were bored. They didn't see the endless stream of kids sitting on their fathers' shoulders, the father pointing here, there and everywhere, trying to engage Timmy's interest, a Timmy who was more intrigued by the way the cotton candy stuck to Daddy's hair, and they didn't see all the clingy Clarissas, 'I wanna soda. I wanna a hotdog. Gimme a box of popcorn to feed the pigeons. I wanna feed the pigeons.' And the lions, tigers and whatnots were not quite asleep and not quite awake. Animal limbo; today's rerun of the past blank days. A funny quality about life. Of all the images that I remember, and there are not many, what I remember is the animal dung. Don't forget what the child knows comes from those stick-em pictures, and what's in the child's head while he's at the zoo is the fascinating discovery 'That's real camel dung! That's honest-to-goodness zebra dung! Now if you were walkin' through Africa, that's what you'd see.' And the stool smells were a hundred times more exotic than the animals (all fowl and monkeys excepted). And fresh. After all, they had those guys with the cheap white uniforms and shovels. The Bronx Zoo Broom and Groom Squad. I remember walking the wide-paved sidewalks (no vehicular traffic allowed) with those wire trash bins every ten paces, and all that animal dung. And now, I walk along the dusty hard-packed bumpy clay roads of Haiti and head down averting the blinding sun and ever careful of my step, I see all the goat dung, the burro dung, horse dung with all their odours baked out of them. There are no uniformed men with shovels and none of the paddies have fallen from giraffes or kangaroos but it's enough to remind me, to tell me, there's a funny quality about life here. The concept is more exciting than the real thing.

Oh well, that's what's popping out of the keyboard today.

Love,
Fuzz

May 9, 1985
Hotel Santo Domingo

Dear folks,

We're having a *vacation*, yes, that's right, the nose-to-the-grindstone Vreelands finally decided it was time for a break in the Dominican Republic. We're staying at a capital 'L' luxury hotel which we can afford because of the low value of Dominican currency compared to the $.

It was hard to decide just how to spend our precious three days, while Sonjel is being looked after by Deb Currelly. We settled on a combination of shopping, eating, watching TV and going to a movie. The prices look so good to us we bought Paul three pairs of pants, three shirts and three pairs of shoes for Sonjel. We ate and ate. The coffee is good here too. People are very friendly. There is good service in the hotel, in the restaurants and stores. We went to see *Passage to India* last night. I thought it was great. Paul's assessment, 'fair'.

Mercy, I forgot to tell you. Paul was hired for that job he's been awaiting. They are paying him as a consultant for four days at Canadian rates which is equivalent to a month's wage. After that, they will assess whether they want him to continue. I know Paul has to work hard for it, but it all seems such a bonanza after our long hard times.

Love,
A.

(Undated)

Dear folks,

Alanna is in Port-au-Prince taking a UNICEF course for pre-school centre supervisors sponsored by the same people who offered the course last year.

Marianesse and Sonjel are in Port, too, so I am here alone for two weeks, cleaning up after the dogs and fighting with the computer. Cleaning up after the dogs? Yes, we got a puppy to chase away the voles or the thieves and I'm also dog-sitting for the Belgians up the road who are in Europe. With no other demands at present other than the morning dog routine and five hours or so at the computer, I've had another good read and have discovered Canadian fiction . . . The trouble is that when I finally get time to read, I quickly exhaust the literature we have, most of which was brought back from our last visits. I crave more Canadian lit, and have only two or three novels yet unread. We read *Time* or *Newsweek* from cover to cover when we get them and sometimes when Michael Bannister is passing through, he'll leave a *Miami Herald* or *New York Times* and it's all old news by the time we get it.

I'll be going into Port-au-Prince Friday for a job interview. I've just posted a long letter to the pioneering committee about our activities here. Since the computer file on it is so long, I have trouble getting any copy of it out of the printer but at least I have one hard-copy first draft. The computer is acting up. Some days I can work for hours. Other times I can't get into any of the files.

Love,
Fuzz

(Undated)

Dear Paul and Claire,

I am longing to visit you guys and remembering my very first visit with you; the walk we took over the woods road and going out in the boat. Shopping for wedding rings. You and I standing at the window at the foot of the stairs, giggling together as we watched the two Pauls pitching horse shoes. Enjoying the books and magazines and neat catalogues you have there.

We, too, are happier even though we have been without water for the past two weeks. We have to carry buckets of water upstairs for the toilet and for handwashing. We've had to bathe outside.

We have been busy producing Creole materials for the Bahá'ís and just recently published a booklet called *Kwen Se Bahá'í* (I am a Bahá'í) completely illustrated. Having that bit of accomplishment seemed to be a turning point for us. We are taking much more satisfaction in our Bahá'í work these days. That one small success seemed to break the cycle of depression, our feelings of struggling but getting nowhere. Nowadays we seem to expect more confirmations, more successes and we have been getting them. This morning Paul had a visit from a minister and they talked for a couple of hours in Creole about the Bahá'í Faith. The man seemed sincerely trying to figure it all out and left saying he was going to pray for guidance in knowing whether or not what Paulie said to him was true. Our fellow teachers at the English school have been very kind to us, visiting us often and making every effort to befriend us. That is so encouraging! Sonjel was given some toys and a tricycle and that has made her very happy.

Really, things are so very much better I wish you guys could visit us again. It's easier now there is a direct flight from Jeremie. I have a few cooking utensils now and we even have furniture! We are eating like kings! Shepherd's pie, pizza even. Really, my cooking is getting to be not so bad. Ask Paul!

All our love to you and June and Jenny too!

A.

With Alanna's second pregnancy, Paul and Alanna knew they would have to return to Canada for the birth. It was time to assess their situation and determine their next course of action. Neither wanted to leave their post in Haiti permanently. It would be difficult for Paul to support the family there. Could a way be found? Elliott Paul was born February 1, 1986.

In 1989, Paul, Alanna and the two children went to Haiti on a travel teaching trip. Seeing the well-thumbed copies of Pawol Bon Dye *and finding those they had taught continuing to teach there, gave them a great lift. Little Sonjel, only a toddler when they had left, seemed to flourish in the sun of Haiti. It was as if this was the home she had remembered.*

In the autumn of 1990 it was decided that Alanna and the two children would take on a short-term pioneering post in Guadeloupe, returning to Canada in mid-March when a relief short-term pioneer would go out to remain until June.

This second pioneering experience was very different from the first. Although the family disliked being apart and Elliott Paul, particularly, grieved over his father's absence, the experience made the family unit even stronger and had many fringe benefits.

Alanna wrote of this experience to members of the Pioneering Committee in Canada:

February 14, 1991
St Anne, Guadeloupe

Dear Members of the Committee:

At this point in this little short-term pioneering venture, I feel as though I need to touch base with you and let you know where I am at, where my family is at, where Guadeloupe is at.

I arrived here on Saturday, October 13, stayed with the Floods for a week and then Sonjel, Elliott and I moved into our new 'digs', a two-room apartment, five minutes from Jim and Sheila. It took me a few weeks to get my French back in shape. Well, that may be overstating it! It's not good, but it's as good as it ever was. Was really surprised to discover that people here understand and love my Haitian Creole. So, lazy so-and-so that I am, I revert to Creole whenever and wherever I possibly can.

Let me say at the outset that the idea of coming somewhere where I already have friends was the best move I ever made. Were it not for the Floods, I don't think I would have lasted a month.

I met with the national spiritual assembly. Told them I have a lot of experience doing children's classes (oops) so now I give a class at the National Centre every second Sunday and a class here in St Anne every second Wednesday. Three non-Bahá'í kids and five Bahá'ís in the St Anne class. Eleven Bahá'í kids at the National Centre. One family (pioneers) drive an hour to bring their two girls to the class at the centre. It is satisfying work as there is lots of support for the classes. Travel teacher June Battrick from New Zealand happened to be passing through just before the start-up of classes and she gave me a million and one ideas for the curriculum: visual aids, puzzles, etc. This whole children's class thing has been a big deal for me. I spend several hours preparing for one class. But I, and the kids, both seem to be getting a lot out of it. Especially good for me is that Sonjel, my seven-year-old, is really turned on now and asks questions and helps me prepare my materials for the class.

But, that's it, folks. I have not been successful teaching adults the Faith. It works for me (somewhat) in North America but here I feel the need to be more audacious. I feel I should be, but then the idea inhibits me so much I get paralysed and don't do anything.

There are so few active Bahá'ís in the country and the need to do teaching is so great, we are all pressured and I feel this inhibits our efforts, at least, it inhibits me. Much of the time I just sit around moping about how inadequate I am. I know that I have to stop wasting time focusing on the negatives and just get out there and mingle and let God do the rest. It now seems to me that back at home Paul and I accomplish quite a lot. I realize how much our strengths supplement one another's and how when we are together we reinforce one another or one can take over when the other is flagging. It's quite the challenge to be away from him and from telephone conversations with him, I think it's even harder for him. He is, after all, the one who is all alone. He says he's paranoid that something will happen as a result of the war and we will be separated permanently. I don't fear that, but I worry a lot about him. Paul tends to work too much and to ignore things like food, rest and health. So I am returning to Canada February 23 to assess the 'damages' and we will decide if the family can endure three more months of separation. Target date for my return here is March 15. Although having the family separated has been hard on all of us, there have been some bounties. The kids have developed close friendships with the Flood children. These are their first really close friends. Sonjel has become so much more interested in the Faith since we came here and she understands why we are here. I am becoming a better children's class teacher and for the first time, I'm getting a lot out of it myself. And one bonus was the perfect two weeks we had when Paul came to visit. It was like a honeymoon/family vacation all rolled into one. I feel it was a special gift from Bahá'u'lláh. At home we both are working regularly all the time so there have not been many family trips or vacations. The kids are finally old enough to really do stuff and we went to a lot of natural attractions here in Guadeloupe, traipsed through the rainforest, swam in the hotsprings and under waterfalls. It's a beautiful country. There are lots of places to walk. Compared to Haiti this place has a lot to offer. But the people, unfortunately, are caught up in their comfortable lives and are not as open to hear the message of Bahá'u'lláh as are the Haitians.

I decided to look up the Haitians here at the market. As a result I have made a friend right here in St Anne. She is a single parent and is very busy as she goes to her stall in the market in Pte a Pte every day from 7 a.m. to 7 p.m. She has been very kind to me, took me home for a meal and it feels good to be around her. As this has been about the only door that has opened to me, I feel I should pursue it. But she is very heavily into the evangelical movement. Oh, well. Maybe she will lead to someone else. Anyway, she has taken me under her wing and that is good.

The Floods plan to leave here the same day as I do, June 15. That means I will have been here eight months minus the three weeks I'll be in Canada. The original plan was for me and Linda McMahon to combine to fill the 12-month goal. I'm disappointed that she seems not to be coming here but I understand God does like to meddle in these plans that we make. I'm grateful that the doors opened and I was able to make it here but wish I could do more. Looking after the kids on my own takes up a lot of my time and energy. But, at least I am here and that's better than having no short-term pioneer here at all.

The country is in a delicate state. Of the twenty Bahá'ís who attend any Bahá'í functions in the country, seven are pioneers and five of us are leaving in the near future. Of the remaining thirteen, three are leaving the country. That leaves only eleven or twelve Bahá'ís. The only functioning assembly is the national spiritual assembly. We should, however, have a functioning local spiritual assembly by Riḍván as another family has moved into St Anne from guess where? Haiti. They are new Bahá'ís. She is Haitian and he is French. They are wonderful people and, I feel, a tremendous asset to this country. Their problem right now is finding work. I pray that something will work out for them as they want to settle permanently here. So it looks as if we will have a functioning local spiritual assembly from April to June at least.

To summarize, this is a wonderful, albeit tough, experience. For me, it's like getting a second chance. I keep trying to synthesize what I learned in Haiti with what I'm learning here to become more effective. The building up of experience is a cumulative process. I am doing so much better here than I did in Haiti. But still it is inadequate. Because the pioneers here are so few in number, we are unable to perform the tasks that need doing. But, we're all we've got, so we might as well not be too down on ourselves. It is easier to keep perspective when you're a short-term pioneer.

Yours respectfully,
Alanna Vreeland

3

Tundra Thunder

Galen Insteness

Alaska. A quiet land, but a restless land. And, until just before the end of the nineteenth century, inhabited in the majority by the Athabascan Indians and the Eskimo. The Russian government was interested mainly in the fur trade of the coastal regions and accomplished little of note in the interior. With the purchase of Alaska by the United States, for a pittance, a survey of the area became a primary concern. The village of Fort Yukon was discovered to be over a hundred miles west of the Canadian border, whereas before the survey, Canada claimed Fort Yukon as its territory.

Then, before the turn of the century, gold was discovered on the Klondike and the territory burst its seams. Miners poured in by the thousands. But in a brief period the gold was gone. Some became rich. Many men perished in the harsh climate of the interior and the disenchanted either left the country or found other means of livelihood there. The country became spiritually dead.

Then the call for Bahá'í pioneers to the territory of Alaska was issued from the Bahá'í World Centre. They first came singly, then two by two, until the migration of Bahá'ís to the Far North became a reality. Those hardy souls who first answered the call were ill-prepared for the harsh climate. There was no one to greet them when they arrived. There was no employment office, no food stamps, no Welcome Wagon. Immediately they had to depend upon their own faith and ingenuity and ultimately this strengthened both their faith and their confidence. They soon discovered the warm hospitality of the people.

The first pioneers to Alaska were women, among them Frances Wells and Janet Whitenack Stout. They appeared unprepared for survival in this tough land, but survive they did. Janet first came to Fairbanks and found employment in the Adler Bookstore. Frances ended up at Barrow, the top of the world, and until recent years, a most primitive community.

I remember a time, back in the 50s, when Frances came down from Barrow with an Eskimo child of about ten. I picked them up at the airport. The child seemed especially quiet, but then, I had expected her to be shy. Frances later told me this was the first time the child had ever seen an automobile, let alone ridden in one. Much about the trip impressed the child, but no doubt Frances, a very pure soul of kindly nature, left the most vivid of impressions.

Janet Stout always reminded me of the rock that kept the administration of the Faith anchored to the teachings of Bahá'u'lláh. She could not be swayed. She could not be pushed and she did not deviate one iota from that which administration prescribed. I tended to humour her at first, but she had a way of putting me back into proper perspective very quickly and always with dignity. I learned to marvel at the way Janet and her husband, Vern, complemented each other so well.

My introduction into the Faith seemed to be more a means of survival than a spiritual solution to my material attitude to life. My first wife joined me in Alaska shortly after I had obtained employment at Eilson Air Force Base south of Fairbanks. I had convinced her that this was the land of milk and honey but forgot to mention that the milk stayed frozen nine months of the year. All this was in 1954.

We froze ourselves out of several homes near the base before finally moving to the metropolis of North Pole. Bonnie was an out-going, friendly person who liked to talk, but she was left at home alone day after day with long, lonely dirt roads separating her from the base 16 miles away and from Fairbanks, 13 miles to the south. Somehow Bonnie found Rosie Yarno Perkal, who, along with her husband, Ken, were the only Bahá'ís in North Pole. Rosie was a Knight of Bahá'u'lláh. Their talks got deeper and deeper and soon the bed, chairs, couch and table in our little house were overflowing with Bahá'í literature. I ignored all of this but it was not very long before Bonnie took the plunge and Rosie had her first Bahá'í declarant at North Pole. I kept taking Bonnie over to Rosie's for firesides and feasts, and it kept getting colder and colder, too cold for me to sit in the car, waiting for feast to be over and watching them through the window enjoying a coffee chow-up after the devotional portion of the feast.

One night I cracked under the strain. I pounded on the door and when Rosie answered, I said, 'I surrender. Where's a pen? Just let me come in where it's warm and I'll sign anything.' Then the fireside began all over again as they made sure I was aware of the tenets of the Faith. I signed that night and it was the greatest decision I have ever made. It was on a cold December night in 1955, but the welcome I received from that little group of Bahá'ís has never been equalled. I was not only welcomed into the Faith, but on that very same night was also elected treasurer and named to several committees.

Mabel Amidon was our secretary. She was so upset one night when I was just one penny off. I dug a penny out of my pocket and offered it but she insisted the error had to be in the treasurer's box somewhere. I took the ammo box we used for the funds and dumped the whole thing out onto the floor and invited Mabel to help me correct the error. She was another Bahá'í I admired for her courage. She was well into middle age when she came to Alaska. She was very delicate, but she moved to Hamilton Acres, just outside the city limits of Fairbanks, and opened up the Faith in that area. She lived in a little log house during the severe winters of 1955 and 1956. Not only did she hold down that post until other Bahá'ís moved in, but she pioneered to Barrow after Frances Wells left that area. She found conditions devastating in Barrow but she stuck to her post until Tom and Dottie Baumgartner were able to move there.

Rose Yarno Perkal was a dynamic and vibrant soul. She was never still, but the worst I ever did see was when she was learning to drive Ken's Jokeswagon. She was completely out of touch with anything mechanical. Whatever gear she happened to be in when she hit downtown Fairbanks, that was the gear she drove in. If she happened to be in fourth gear she would go chugging down the street with the Jokeswagon screaming in protest, while she remained frozen at the controls shouting the Greatest Name over and over. God was certainly her co-pilot.

I remember the time she thought she was taking a side road into North Pole but was actually following the power line. She went about 300 yards before she got hung up on a stump. It took Ken and me all day to drag the poor Jokeswagon back to the road.

She finally upgraded the Jokeswagon to a '54 Ford. After she had driven it for a few months, the rear end went out. It was Leo Thornton, I believe, and I who put another rear end in the car but unfortunately it was the wrong gearing so the speedometer now reflected 15 mph less than the true speed. We turned the car over to Rosie and headed for home. The next day when we saw Rosie, we asked her how the car was running. She said, 'Oh, just great but now something is wrong with the steering. It wants to go into the ditch and it never did that before at 50 mph.' We never had the courage to tell her of the mismatched gear. I guess all the nine great Prophets continued to watch over her, for she went on to pioneer in Switzerland and in Africa.

If anyone ever needed a helping hand, or if their spirits had hit a rock-bottom low, one had only to go to the Guffey house at 401 Eleventh in Fairbanks, the real heart of the Faith in the 50s. This was the place where the door was always open and no one was ever a stranger. Elmer was the silent type whose actions spoke louder than words. Back when he was staying on the Post, before he bought the house in Fairbanks to have a home for Marie, it was necessary for each person to share a room. No one apparently wanted to share a room with the one black man but Elmer asked Jim to move in. Jim was suspicious of Elmer and it took a while for Elmer to gain his confidence. Jim's wife became ill, in Texas, I believe, and Jim had no car. Elmer simply reached for his car keys and said, 'You'd better get goin', Jim, if you're to make it to Texas.'

Marie was a beautician at the Northward building and was well-known in Fairbanks. I remember the two of them at meetings. Elmer would get a talking streak and Marie would reach out with her foot to tap his foot to halt his dissertations, but once he got going, he paid no attention to her signals.

Once I bought a car from Elmer. After we had swapped the title, we drove back to his place in his car, expecting to find the car I had just bought in front of his house where we had left it. No car. We drove all around Fairbanks looking for that car but could not find it. When we returned to his house there it was, parked out in front. Seems a wrecker had picked up the wrong car and returned it in our absence.

One time when Kathryn Alio came to Fairbanks to attend a winter workshop, she came from her home in Anchorage. I was working the graveyard shift and did not realize she had arrived the night before and that Bonnie had given her our bed. When I got home from work, I planned to hop in bed for a nap before the meeting started. When I pulled back the covers and saw a redhead where a brunette belonged, I hastily went searching for my misplaced spouse. Kathryn always allowed as she was the one who was slighted.

The Baumgartner clan made a grand entry into Fairbanks in 1958. We were all gathered at the Guffey Grand Central Station when Tom pulled up in an old Ford station-wagon, wall-to-wall kids, the top of the car bulging with cargo and a tree cut to size and fitted into the rear to hold the top of the vehicle a reasonable distance from the floor boards so the human beings in the vehicle could have some breathing space. Often the Baumgartner clan would come into town and drop in on us to share our bread. If we knew they were coming we would make a pyramid of sandwiches and when the boys, all five of them, and Tom came in, it would disappear, as if sucked up into a vacuum. Plate full, then swoosh, plate empty.

Tom was into food conservation in a big way as he struggled to keep his brood well-fed. He experimented with 500 ways of making a loaf of homemade bread feed seven mouths with enough left over for lunch next day. Ernie, the eldest son, commented, 'It usually lasted for two meals because it wasn't too good in the first place. But it did have body.'

One summer day, Bonnie, the girls and I went out to check on the Baumgartners and found only Dottie, sitting on the front step, looking depressed. When we asked her what the trouble was she invited us to look inside. There, over the stove, hung row upon row of raw meat, which Tom had decided to cure. It had deteriorated very rapidly and the stench was horrible. Just one of the little trial-by-error learning experiences that family went through learning to adjust to the rigours of Alaska. The most difficult trial for Dottie, I think, was the fact that the entire family of seven lived in a little Quonset hut with 12 by 16 foot dimensions.

There is simply no way you can tell anyone beforehand what living up here is like. Take the Reeds. Came from Nebraska in 1960 to fill in a slot in the Fairbanks community. They hauled a mobile trailer home and it was a long thing. The trailer park had limited access. Getting these people set up in that trailer became a major project. They found it rather chilly in early fall when sometimes it would get down to zero. They marvelled that I walked around with my coat unbuttoned. One day I went to visit them wearing my parka zipped up tight against the 30 below zero cold. Blaine took one look at me and said, 'No way am I going out there today!' I jokingly told him he had better install a bayonet on the front of his bus in order to cut through the fog which could get very thick in winter. Blaine looked at me as if I were some kind of endangered species. Several months later, however, during a severe cold spell, he phoned and asked me where he could get one of those bayonets.

The Reeds answered a call to pioneer to Nemana and they left just at spring breakup time when the mud was knee-deep. A Bahá'í named Smith attempted to help them get their trailer onto the muddy lot in Nemana. They all stuck at it so long that Smith, driving his pickup with the door open to guide the trailer in, fell asleep at the wheel and fell out. During the flood of '67, the Reeds had their home flooded to a depth of about six feet. All their valuable tapes and books were lost.

Let me tell you of the time Bev Kolstoe, Nancy Sloan and

I went to Fort Yukon for the funeral of Charlie Roberts, the first Indian to become a Bahá'í in Fort Yukon. It must have been in the spring because I was dressed in a suit but wearing hip boots – quite an ensemble. There was no fancy casket for Charlie, just a plywood box. Nancy played her portable piano and Bev and I gave the Bahá'í readings. Then the coffin was carried out to a pickup. I was given the honour of being asked to ride with the pallbearers to the cemetery, sitting on Charlie's box. Every so often, one of the pallbearers would say something about Charlie in the Athabascan tongue. Then they would slap the box with their fists, all would be silent for a moment, then another would think of something. It was very unusual for the Indians to invite whites to participate in one of their burials. At the cemetery, the villagers chanted in their own language. Then each was invited to throw one shovelful of dirt on the grave.

The Kolstoes brought Charlie into the Faith and it was also they who brought in Pete Simple, the second Bahá'í in Fort Yukon. It was John who helped Pete cope with the English language. Pete could not read or write until he was in his late 50s, then he started to read labels on grocery boxes. He more or less taught himself with a lot of help from John. Pete was the one who said, when giving a talk at the convention in Anchorage, that he couldn't 'do so pretty good, because he didn't carry his brains in his briefcase' like another Bahá'í. Asked by the Bahá'ís to carry their love to Fort Yukon, he said, 'I sure will, if it's not too heavy.'

I was asked by the national assembly one April to go up to Beaver to help form their assembly. This was some project as I could not tell the Bahá'ís from the rest of the people. I finally got them all rounded up in Turak Newman's cabin. The rest of the village gathered around the barrel wood stove to watch the goings-on. Each proceeded to take a fresh chew of snoose while I was getting things under way. There were only nine members so, thankfully, we did not have to have an election for the assembly. Only Turak could read and write, so he was automatically voted chairman, secretary and treasurer. Every time we voted on anything or agreed on any matter, the villagers would applaud. Then the Bahá'ís would clap their hands. I came away not quite certain just who was elected to the assembly, Bahá'í or otherwise, yet the spirit that prevailed at the election would have melted a glacier. I had brought along enough treats to feed the assembly members. Amazingly, like the story of the fishes and the loaves, there seemed to be enough to serve the whole village of Beaver. I fell in love with that place and the people.

Travelling to and from meetings was usually uncomfortable when it was not downright hazardous. Like the time I was riding shotgun with Jim Baumgartner in his little plane on the way to Fort Yukon and we hit a whiteout. We turned west and tried to follow the frozen Yukon, hoping for a place to land and wait out the storm, but there were too many drifts of snow. Suddenly we saw a flat place near the river, so we brought her in, and by golly, if we didn't land smack dab on the runway at Beaver. When we inspected the plane to see why it handled so strangely when we landed, we found we were dragging the tail wheel. Arthur Henry wanted to fly back into Fairbanks with us but he took one look at that wheel and said, 'Me walk back to town.'

I took Jim Walton with me on a teaching trip to Canada and about a hundred miles south of Fairbanks I got sleepy and asked Jim to take over the wheel. He appeared startled but agreed. I hadn't been asleep for 30 minutes when I realized the engine was labouring. I asked Jim why he didn't shift down on the hill. Jim began a stuttering explanation, revealing that it was the first time that he had driven a car and that he did not have a licence. So I took the wheel once again and did not get tired all the way to Whitehorse.

Jim stayed at Whitehorse for awhile so I had another Bahá'í ride back with me. We got into some 70 degree below zero weather. The heater had always behaved more like an air-conditioner but in this intense cold it appeared not to be coping at all. Suddenly I smelled smoke. Thinking there was a fire in the engine compartment, I began to slow down. It was then I noticed my passenger had built a fire in his snoose can to warm his hands. I was sorely tested and could barely see for the smoke. It did, however, take a little of the chill out of the car. Somehow we made it back to Fairbanks.

Once when I was on a survey crew working out of Homer and hungry for some good food, I wound up at the small farm of Art and Wilma Gregory. From then on, every Saturday I would find myself hiking in that direction, always showing up just at mealtime. They already had a big family to feed, but when it came to good food, I never let my conscience bother me. I got to be such a regular I would plumb ruin their Saturday if I didn't show up. Janice Gregory Taylor likes to remind me of this whenever I drop in on her when I am in Juneau.

During the Fairbanks flood of '67, all my winter clothes were stored at the Post in the basement at my quarters. I was stranded at the water plant for three weeks. I then left for Anchorage to check up on my things and found I had lost the clothes in the flood. The Bahá'ís of Anchorage had organized a central distribution centre for old clothing. Since I was heading back, I loaded up several boxes in my car and departed. I was so tired when I got there I asked Stu and Donna Ashton to unload the car while I took a short nap. When I awoke, I found they had unloaded the boxes and distributed the clothing, giving away my new clothes as well. I went down to Serious Sawbuck and ordered another whole set of winter clothes. I was there to keep an eagle eye on this new shipment when it came in.

In 1961 I got word that Hand of the Cause William Sears would visit Anchorage, so we got a gang of us together to make the trip in Blaine's car. There were six of us and it was very cold. Those of us in the back seat bundled together in layers of blankets. We had to drive the old highway and the hills were steep. The Jokeswagon had limited power, so we never took the throttle off the floor, just shifting gears to change speed. We made it to Anchorage just in time for the opening of the meeting. We all enjoyed Mr Sears's humour and the way he could take charge of an awkward situation. There being no podium, he began constructing one, describing it as it was being erected. Certain parts were the believers and so on. In his talk Mr Sears described an infamous character who was so unsavoury, he said, 'His morals were as loose as the lug nuts on a Model T.'

Humour is so often the saving grace in difficult circumstances. At one institute held in Joe Leaner's basement at Badger Slough, there was such a crowd, no one had any inkling as to how many were there. Only I could even hazard a guess. As chief janitor, I was responsible for supplies and reported it was already a six-roll conference.

There are so many stories to tell. How precious were those days, and these days, too, if we but knew.

4

Alaskan Adventure

Beverly and John Kolstoe

John and Beverly Kolstoe pioneered for 27 years in Alaska. Each has told aspects of their story, sometimes relating the same experience, remembering the same people and yet each version has subtle differences.

Beverly begins the story:

It seems we have always pioneered somewhere and that is the way we prefer it. I can think of nothing more boring than moving into a settled, functioning community where there is no challenge.

John and I became Bahá'ís together. We had discovered the Faith soon after we met. I lived in Waukegan and attended the National College of Education in Evanston, Illinois. The Bahá'í House of Worship, in Wilmette, an outstanding landmark, was just down the street. I was familiar with the House of Worship with its nine doors always open to those of all faiths but did not investigate Bahá'í beliefs until John and I went together. He was in the navy, stationed at Great Lakes. We attended firesides in Chicago but soon he was transferred to Norfolk, Virginia. I continued to study in the Chicago area and he pursued the Faith in Virginia and up the East coast. We married in August 1952 and became Bahá'ís in April 1953. My closest Bahá'í friends were Pat and Georgine Moul and it was their firesides I attended in Chicago. I visited the Temple on Sunday afternoons.

After I finished college, I joined John in Virginia. We were the only Bahá'ís in Portsmouth. There was one white Bahá'í and one black Bahá'í couple living in Norfolk, a Persian Bahá'í in Norfolk Beach, a black family in Suffolk and a black woman in Hampton Beach. That was the extent of our Bahá'í association. And, of course, it was at the heart of the battle of segregation, so interracial meetings were out of the question. We did the best we could, mostly meeting in the homes of the black Bahá'ís.

John was discharged from the navy. We moved to North Dakota where he finished his Bachelor's degree, and then we went on to graduate school at the University of Minnesota. There we lived in a small suburb north of Minneapolis where we were the only Bahá'ís.

In 1958, after two years of graduate school, John went to the International Conference in Chicago. We were poor graduate students and could afford only one bus ticket, so he went alone. When I picked him up at the bus station on his return, I had a feeling he had volunteered us to pioneer, but he chattered on and on about all the people he had seen. Finally I interrupted.

'All right! Where are we going?'

He swallowed and said, 'Alaska!'

I knew he had spent time with the Mouls and that they had pioneered to Alaska, so the location was not a complete surprise. But when I asked, 'When?' and he replied, 'August', I was surprised. He had just finished work on his Master's degree and was part of the way into his work for a doctorate in psychology. I had completed course work for my Master's in speech pathology but had not written my thesis.

In retrospect, although I have never regretted pioneering, I believe it would have been wiser to complete the courses we had begun and to have delayed our pioneering by a year or two. It has been a slight handicap, professionally, although it has never prevented us from getting the positions we wanted.

We had been living in a 28 by 28 foot mobile home outside Minneapolis and all we owned was the car and the mobile home. These we sold and moved our personal possessions to Anchorage. At that time, all the Bahá'ís were single or married to non-Bahá'ís so there were no Bahá'í homes. We arrived in August 1958. John got a job as counsellor in Anchorage High School and I became speech therapist at the Crippled Children's Treatment Centre. By the end of December, we had found a small but lovely two-bedroom home which we could afford and had moved in. We had many happy times there. Hand of the Cause William Sears visited us there and spoke at meetings in our home. Many travel teachers stayed with us, as well as Bahá'ís from all over.

We took our first child while there, a seven-year-old profoundly deaf Athabascan Indian boy named Alfred Kazooklik. I met him at the Treatment Centre. We were able to have him as a foster child but he was not available for adoption, in spite of the fact that no one wanted him except us. Years after he left us he became a Bahá'í. During that time, we adopted our first child, Ruth, who was also Athabascan. She later took the name Tahirih. She was five when we got her and had been raised in a Christian orphanage since birth. The next year we adopted our second child, Karl Jamal. He was just ten weeks old, born July 4, 1960, half Athabascan and half white.

During the three years we stayed in Anchorage we were continually involved in some way with Bahá'í adminis-tration. John was elected to the national spiritual assembly the first Riḍván we were there and served almost con-tinually with just a couple of breaks until we left Alaska in 1985. I served on the NSA for one year and was on that body when William Sears met with it in October 1960. At that time we reviewed the goals which Alaska had for homefront pioneers. There were a few volunteers for some of the more 'civilized' goals and for a few Eskimo villages. But no one wanted to go to Fort Yukon, which had the title of 'Cesspool of the North'. The NSA even considered deleting it as a goal because it seemed so impossible. Well, I've always been the champion of the underdog, so I raised my hand and said we would go there. Mr Sears was ecstatic and announced that I should go immediately on an investigative trip and the National Teaching Committee would pay for it. I was swept along in his enthusiasm.

But facing John was another matter. I was so worried that I called a Bahá'í ally to go home with me while I broke the news. I'm not sure what I expected John would do. He just looked grey and murmured, 'Well, all right, but that cancels my pilgrimage,' and went on to bed. Fortunately, he was still able to go on pilgrimage, which began a few weeks later, and he had an opportunity to pray about our new goal while at the shrines in Haifa.

While John was away, I went to Fort Yukon on my investigative trip. I loved it immediately. It was a picturesque settlement of tiny log cabins clustered along the Yukon River. I talked with the superintendent of the school about getting teaching positions there. He was enthusiastic. He promised to recommend us to the department of state-operated schools responsible for 'bush' schools. He also pointed out a large house directly across the street from the school and said he thought we'd be able to rent it. I cabled John all the good news and he felt as happy and content as I did with the decision.

We put our house in Anchorage up for sale and moved to Fort Yukon in August 1961. By this time, Tahirih Ruth was seven years old and in the second grade and Earl Jamal had just turned one. We got to Fort Yukon, to the big house across from the school, just two weeks before school started.

That gave us time to get the house ready to live in. It was a mess, filthy beyond description and badly in need of repairs. It took two weeks of hard labour, even a bulldozer to clear the yard of debris, and to make the house habitable.

Then came the blow. The first day of school, John and I came home for lunch and there was a knock on the door. A stranger stood there and said, 'I've just bought this house. How soon can you move out?' The world came crashing down around us.

Obviously, Bahá'u'lláh knew what He was doing but we only realized it in retrospect. We searched day after day for a house and finally found a small four-room log cabin way down by the river, far from school. But it was adequate and we moved in. The good thing about this move was that it was down in the village among the Indian people, where the poor people lived. We were village people, not white schoolteachers. The Indians were familiar with the house and comfortable with it, so they came and went and were our friends. It was there that the first Local Spiritual Assembly of Fort Yukon was formed, on August 1, 1962, before the end of the Ten Year Crusade. There were 19 Bahá'ís by that time and that assembly has never been lost, even though the teaching committee is probably still having to go in at Riḍván to help it form.

The bad part was that because it was so close to the river it flooded nearly every year and washed away the mud foundation, leaving the floor boards exposed to sub-zero temperatures. That first winter was the coldest on record, with weeks of 50 to 60 below zero temperatures. We closed off the bedrooms, which were 'add-ons' with log inside walls. All four of us lived in two rooms. Karl got pneumonia during one spell and it stayed with him for weeks. Every day a public health nurse came and gave him a penicillin shot, but he just wasn't getting any better. We had nearly reconciled ourselves that our baby boy would be a sacrifice to our pioneering post but we wrote to the Hands in the Holy Land and asked for prayers. Suddenly, miraculously, Karl got well! A few days later we received a letter from the Holy Land: 'We prayed for your son at the Shrines today.'

It had always been a puzzle to me why God had not seen fit to give us children, when we wanted them so much. I had many pregnancies, always with the very best of medical care, yet all ended prematurely. When we adopted Tahirih and Karl, both Athabascan Indians, we had no thought of pioneering to an Athabascan village. Nor had we specified race when we applied for adoption. It just worked out that way. But in Fort Yukon, those children opened doors for us and gave us a credibility that could never have been achieved in any other way.

During the time in Fort Yukon, we decided that it was time to adopt a little girl and so Lynn Jalal joined our family. She is the only one who is not an Alaskan native, although she was born in Alaska. She is mostly white, with just a hint of black blood. Yet the welfare department held up placement for months because they were afraid to tell us of the suspected racial mixture!

We loved Fort Yukon. Many of our happiest memories are of that pioneering experience. Yet it was not called the 'Cesspool of the North' for nothing. The moral decadence was easy enough for John and me to understand, but our children had to be out in the community and forming their peer relationships where drunkenness and immorality were the norm. We had several scares and finally decided that it was not a good place to raise children, especially an adolescent girl. More and more the local Bahá'ís were leaving decision-making up to us instead of assuming the responsibility themselves. We felt for these reasons it was best to leave. John was offered a position at the University of Alaska in Fairbanks and we decided that we could be close enough to be a support base for Fort Yukon without being in the midst of problems. During the summer of 1964 we moved to the Tanana Valley community, outside Fairbanks, where we spent the next five years. Our friends from Fort Yukon did come and visit and stay and develop their Bahá'í association at our home there.

After one year as department head at the University of Alaska, John decided to leave the field of education and go into business. The truth was, we were unable to support our family on the university salary, plus it did not offer the freedom to serve the Faith which he needed. I protested bitterly as I felt the field of education was losing a great teacher and administrator. Nevertheless, he signed on with a major insurance company as an agent and I have never been sorry he made that decision. Then the baby-bug bit again and we added number four to our family, a six-week-old Eskimo boy whom we named Brent Wells, the Wells being for Frances Wells, who had been our friend and who so dearly loved the Eskimo people. Brent was born in September 1965.

In 1969, during the Nine Year Plan, there was a great need for homefront pioneers in Alaska, and so we moved again, this time to Palmer in nearby Matanuska Valley. John's company had no objection to moving his office to Palmer, and so, in September, just before school started, we moved the family down. We found a large house on the main street which we purchased and lived in for 16 years. The Local Spiritual Assembly of Palmer was formed in April 1970 and the community continues to be strong and active, although never very large.

Too much has happened to sum it all up neatly in one paragraph. I think what stands out most was that so many holy day observances were held in our home. It is a large house with two living rooms, with the dining room and kitchen in between, making it functional for large gatherings. The adults used the large living room and the children the small one. For our nineteenth anniversary as Bahá'ís, our first váḥid, we had a big party which attracted scores of people. We made a bulletin board with calendars for each year, outlining major events in our lives and in the development of the Faith wherever we were for that year. A major event was the publishing by George Ronald, Publisher of John's book *Consultation*. It was the culmination of many years of work and we felt very good about it. Earlier John had been instrumental in the publication of *High Endeavors*, letters from the Guardian to Alaska. My basic Bahá'í commitment other than local activities was as secretary to the International Goals Committee for Alaska and as secretary of the national convention for a number of years.

After 27 years of service in Alaska, it was time for me to get my original wish, a chance to pioneer in a warm place. John was finishing his twentieth year with his insurance company and was eligible for a pension. The children were pretty much raised. We began looking forward to this new arena of service. Our grandchild, Terianne, had been living with us for several years. We approached her mother, Tahirih, for permission to adopt Terianne. So our first grandchild became our fifth adopted child. And we set our faces towards a goal for Alaskan pioneers, in St Lucia. At last, a warm place!

At the end of June 1985 we emptied our big house in Palmer, settled 20-year-old Brent, our only adult child still at home, with friends, and took Terianne off to the West Indies. John was elected to the NSA and was elected chairman. I was elected in a by-election in October. John spends a great deal of time writing. I am editor of *St Lucia Bahá'í News*. We are knee-deep in children's classes and consolidation projects. We attended the Caribbean Peace

Conference in Barbados in October and the joint NSA consultation following. We're back into a real pioneering role again. It feels good!

John has his own perspective on Alaska:

Fort Yukon, eight miles north of the Arctic Circle at the northernmost point of the Yukon River, is inaccessible except by awkward water travel or air. The village of about 600 Athabascan Indians and a hundred whites is in the heart of the Yukon Basin, a vast expanse of thousands of square miles in the midmost part of the interior of Alaska. At one time it had been an important trading centre, but with the decline of fur prices, little of its economy was left intact.

We were soon to find out that the whites and natives did not mingle. We were accepted because we lived about a half mile from the school and had to walk; we attended and enjoyed the local dances, and two of our adopted children are Athabascan Indians.

Living in a remote area in a cabin without plumbing, cooking on a wood stove and having heat furnished by a converted 55-gallon oil drum which burned spruce logs was a new experience for us. Our first winter was one of the coldest on record. Liquids spilled on the floor would freeze unless wiped up quickly. At 40 degrees below zero we had to sleep next to the stove. At 60 below, we had to fill the stove every few hours. Still the cold would encroach. The walls would frost and the cold seemed to stalk inward, relentlessly nearing the stove. The cold that winter was long and oppressive. When it warmed up to 40 below zero, it was wonderful.

The spiritual climate seemed more oppressive. While many had heard of the Faith, there were few questions. Quietly living the life is not nearly as thrilling as 'seeing the hosts of success following one another' (*Tablets of 'Abdu'l-Bahá*, p. 331). Merely staying alive called for our best efforts.

It was during that long, cold winter that lasting relations with people of the community were cemented. I was asked to serve as clerk for the city council. This required keeping records, writing letters and recording the minutes of the council meetings. It made me aware of everything going on in town but kept me removed from controversies. Many future Bahá'ís were met through this position.

Early in April Fort Yukon holds a spring carnival, complete with dog sled races, snow shoe races and snow shoe softball. That was when Marie Guffey arrived for a visit. As a beautician, she was immediately pressed into service. Our kitchen became a makeshift beauty parlour as Marie gave each of the carnival queen contestants her first professional hairdo. She is still remembered for this action. A bright spot in the frozen Arctic!

During the carnival tug-o-war contest, I tugged away on the rope next to Charley Roberts. This started a friendship that brought Charley into the Faith as the first Athabascan Indian from north of the Arctic Circle. Charley is illiterate but by no means simple. He is a man of courage and fierce independence.

The first time I went to visit Charley, about a week after the carnival, I decided to say nothing at all about the Faith. Soon after entering the cabin, Charley asked me, 'What church do you belong to, John?' What had been intended as indirect teaching with a social call turned into a lesson in progressive revelation and the fulfilment of all prophecy by Bahá'u'lláh.

Two weeks later I made another visit. Charley chided me for staying away so long.

'Tell me again what you were saying about how God speaks to man.'

Before much was said, Charley put a big stick in the ground and said, 'There's Christ.' He placed many smaller sticks around and said, 'There's all the people.' Then he took a small twig which he placed at the periphery and said, 'There's Dninjinju.' This is the Athabascan name for themselves which translates as 'the little people'. This is not a reference to physical stature. He picked up the twig and moved it further away and said, 'Dninjinju can't see Christ, too many white people get in way. Christ can't get to Dninjinju.'

Then I picked up sticks about the size of the one representing Christ and said that this kind of thing had happened all over the world. Others, like Christ, had come, but the little people couldn't always see them because of those who got in the way. Then, with a big stick placed in the middle, I said, 'Now, Bahá'u'lláh has come and everyone can see Him.' I then placed my eye by the smallest twig and said, 'Even Dninjinju – everybody.'

Charley looked at the whole thing for a long time. Then he said, 'Yeah, John! Yeah, John, good! That's good!'

We were busy with end of school activities and there was the usual confusion associated with the annual break-up of the Yukon River and the threat of flooding. Charley and I saw little of each other until the middle of May, when we went hunting. Charley said, 'Tell me again all about it.' After some explanations, I asked, 'Do you believe this, Charley?' and he replied that he did. After further specific questions, I told Charley, 'You are Bahá'í.'

'I hope so, John, I hope so.' Charley later signed a declaration card in the presence of Tom and myself.

And afterwards? During his first year in the Faith, Charley was responsible for 25 declarations and assisted in the formation of two assemblies, Fort Yukon and Nanana, and for planting the seed that blossomed into a third assembly at Beaver.

The Feast of Light was on June 5, attended by the Bahá'ís of Fort Yukon including Charley Roberts, Pete Simple, Drury McGundy and me. Before Feast started, Pete and Charley excused themselves and retired to the kitchen for a long talk in their own language. When they had finished, Pete apologized and explained how he and Charley had been close friends years ago. They now began a new life together as Bahá'í brothers.

Charley could neither read nor write. When he got his letter of welcome and other material from the national spiritual assembly, he took it to his friend and neighbour, Charles Biederman. Charlie Biederman read the material to Charley Roberts and, halfway through reading *Your Experience as a Bahá'í*, Charlie Biederman decided that he, too, wanted to become a Bahá'í.

By the middle of June Fort Yukon was abuzz with talk about the Bahá'í Faith. It was vigorously denounced from one of the pulpits in town. This caused at least one person to become a Bahá'í. The rest of the month was the most active as six more declared their faith in Bahá'u'lláh. In July three of the new believers made a trip with our family to the annual Yukon Conference held near Whitehorse, Yukon Territory, Canada.

By August 1 there were 13 new Bahá'ís and the first assembly north of the Arctic Circle was formed. It soon became apparent that the problem of deepening was greater than that of conversion. We were overwhelmed. The sincerity of the new believers was not questioned but habit patterns built up over the years were not easily broken.

Pete Simple brought three non-Bahá'ís to feast one time saying he couldn't find any Bahá'ís to notify. Despite the unusual attendance, it was a wonderful feast. One declaration resulted. About this time, the Episcopalians started to sit up and take notice. They ordained a native lay-priest. On that day, October 6, the first white man from Fort Yukon became a Bahá'í. By year's end, there were five more declarations. At Naw-Rúz, an event celebrated by the serving of mooseburgers, about 35 people attended. This was the first time we became aware of just how much of an impact the Faith had made.

Just prior to Riḍván, Pete Simple and Tom Russon took a teaching trip to Beaver. This resulted in the first indigenous assembly in Alaska, representing Athabascan Indian, Eskimo, white and Lap races. From a village of 80 people, including children, this was a good representation. It was during this time that our baby-sitter, Josephine Herbert, not a declared Bahá'í, made a beaded replica of the Greatest Name for my birthday. It remains my most prized possession. Auxiliary Board Member Florence Mayberry arrived in Fort Yukon in September 1963. She held the first two public meetings for proclaiming the Faith. Both were well attended and sparked with enthusiastic discussions.

During the 1964 Intercalary Days, the Bahá'ís of Fort Yukon hosted a dance for the whole community and over 300 persons attended. One problem was how to advertise the dance in such a way that it could remain free of the drinking that is a normal part of other dances. It was suggested that no mention be made of the dance until it was too late for people to send to Fairbanks for their liquor supply. It worked!

It was during this time that it became apparent that the presence of the Bahá'í Faith here was the fulfilment of many old Athabascan legends and prophecies. It was only the old timers who remembered these legends. If these prophecies are valid, it appears that more trials are expected for the Faith but the trials will be overcome and the Indians will again be a fine and noble people.

I have learned much from being a pioneer. For those

thinking of pioneering, know that there will be tests,
enormous tests. Rely on prayer. Read the creative word.
Daily reading is oxygen for the soul and pioneers need it
most urgently. Follow your own heart. Allow for private
time, space and adequate R & R. Warning! Once a
pioneer, always a pioneer. When the condition reaches
advanced stages, it's incurable and there is no graceful
return to 'normal' life.

*Beverly Kolstoe lived her dream of pioneering in a warmer place for
only a short time before the Kolstoes were called back to Alaska. Here
are John's impressions of St Lucia:*

Vieux Fort, St Lucia, W.I.
December 2, 1985

Dear Friends,

A hazard in this age of computers is that the people who
were never capable of taking up pen are suddenly overcome
with the desire to communicate. That, of course, is a ruse.
The reality is that communicating becomes a noble-sounding
excuse for the little child who likes to tinker with fancy
gadgets.

I intended for this letter to go out by late August, but all
our stuff sent from Alaska and expected by mid-July got
here October 9. This was all our household stuff and the
computer.

We live on the south of the island, halfway between the
brewery and St Jude's Hospital on the way to Augier
(O-zhay.) That's two-and-a-half miles from Vieux Fort
(View Fort) and about three miles from endless expanses of
gorgeous sand beaches on both the Atlantic and Caribbean.
We choose our swimming beach by what size waves we
desire that day.

As newcomers to St Lucia, we have found a few items
which seem worthy of note. Something that struck me as

odd was that it did not seem incongruous to dodge a chicken while eyeing a goat contemplating passage from the other side of the street amidst the hordes of pedestrians and street vendors in front of Barclay's Bank in the business district of Vieux Fort. With 4,100 souls in town and 17,500 in the area, this is the second most heavily populated region on the island.

Much goes on in this tiny mountain top in the southeastern part of the Caribbean. There are some things which take getting used to. According to the map, it is only 27 miles long and 14 miles wide at the widest, shaped like a teardrop. It is hard to find a mile of straight level road. There is always something in bloom in addition to bananas and coconut palms. There are cactus in the semi-desert areas and pine trees on the cool ridge of the central mountain which is like a spine traversing much of the length of the island. The rain forest of the centre and west enjoy about 160 inches of rain a year with most of the rest getting less than 60.

But the term 'rain' is misleading for one used to the prolonged drizzles of south central Alaska. It is a rare day here that is without sunshine. Likewise it is a rare day with no rain. Generally, it only takes a few minutes for the rain to do its work, then the sun gets on with it.

Shopping: Beverly wanted ten simple items available at any Safeway store. It took visits to five supermarkets, two street vendors and a bakery, where they also sell ice cream and the weekly newspaper, to complete the task. Frozen meat is purchased at the Tru-Value Hardware Store which sells neither plumbing supplies nor pork. Plain yogurt is available through one of the book stores in Castries. You rarely find all you need in just one shop, although there are a lot of general stores. The photographer has a general store in which the laundry detergent is right next to the gin, above the boxes of galvanized nails, across from the bolts of yard goods. I found 30 metres of garden hose by looking behind the shirts.

Customs: Getting a parcel post item from the post office can often be accomplished within half a day but involves the following: three trips to the post office, two trips to customs and one intermediary stop at a stationery store to buy the proper form, of which I now keep a supply. Signatures are required from two different people at the post office and two or three people at customs. That is, unless the value exceeds $250 (95 US dollars) in which case a trip to the airport is required to have a 'broker' fill out a long form in triplicate. It is then returned to customs where the errors are pointed out for you to correct, initial the changes and pay 37% duty on the total value plus postage.

Economics: Prices vary greatly. Bananas, mangoes, limes and other fruits and vegetables are low cost, purchased from the ever-present street vendors, selling their produce by the heap or small pile from which a banana or an orange will cost 3.7 cents US. Meat is about the same as it costs in Alaska. Durable goods are high in price and low in quality. While the people are poor, starvation is unheard of. There is some malnutrition but not much. Wages are pathetic. In spite of that, there is an eagerness to work. We are frequently asked if we need an extra pair of hands.

Business on the island is as low-key as one can imagine. The pace may be slow, but oh! the paper work! I got one dozen cup hooks from one clerk and a second made out a bill in triplicate. This was taken to the cashier who took my money while someone else wrapped them, as the manager looked on. All in what would be a one-, or at most, a two-person store in Alaska.

Welfare and jobs are both limited. The only way people

get money or things is by working, selling something or stealing, although there is less stealing than in Alaska. Most people subsist with little cash, but the land gives plentifully of fruits and vegetables. Most people have a garden and a 'little piece of ground' which they call an estate.

In theory, bananas and coconuts are the basis of the St Lucia economy. In reality, much of the national budget comes from the United States, Canadian and other foreign aid. They are eager for foreign investments and many firms, including some Korean garment industries, are investing here to take advantage of a good quality and low-cost labour force.

So it goes in the business world of St Lucia. It's easy to be critical of local inefficiency. However, it was a reputable American firm that delayed my shipping for two-and-a-half months. Another one, a prominent airline, is taking two weeks for an overnight delivery. So, while the nature of inefficiency may be different here, St Lucia has no corner on the market.

Driving: We were undecided between buying a nine-passenger van or a sedan. The advantage of the van is that it will hold more people. The disadvantage of the van is that it will hold more people. There is an acute shortage of wheels among the Bahá'ís. Before the ink was dry on our entry visa, I was pressed into service as a taxi driver. Never mind that the steering wheel is on the wrong side and so is the traffic; the streets are narrow, winding and potholed. A retired geologist friend says he is working on another PhD – pothole dodger. As a retired life insurance agent, I have a new view of apps (applications). Apps now means avoiding people and potholes.

One-lane roads have two-way traffic plus parking, plus pedestrians milling about, plus vendors, plus children, plus chickens, goats and dogs. If one looks at the purpose of a journey as going from one point to another, frustration is guaranteed. However, if one has the attitude of embarking on an adventurous and leisurely obstacle course, the trip will go better. The hairpin turns and switch backs of the Rocky Mountains have found their match. Beverly maintains these roads were designed for cars which are hinged in the middle. From our house near Vieux Fort to downtown Castries is about 14 miles as the crow flies but about 35 automobile miles. It takes about an hour and 15 minutes if you take the good road on the east (Atlantic) side and cross over the mountain. The scenic route on the west (Caribbean) side is about the same distance (read three hours). The road looks as if it was designed by a pretzel maker riding on a roller coaster.

People: Predominantly of African descent, particularly from the central west coast of Africa, there is also a heavy contingent of East Indians. St Lucia seems as free of the taint of prejudice as any place I have seen in the world. It is most refreshing. The primary identity is that they are from St Lucia and not from some other part of the world. There is an open, ingenuous gentility which is touching. Most people are friendly and helpful in a charming, soft-spoken manner. Telling the neighbour that I'd be in Castries for the day goes something like this:

'Ah, good morning, Mr Brice, and how are you today?'
'Oh, not so bad, thank you, brother John, and yourself?'
'Oh, just fine, thank you.'
'Oh, that's good, and how is the Mrs.?'
'Oh, she is just fine, too. Those were lovely to MAH toes you sent over and we thank you very much.'
'Well, not at all, not at all. Did you get the coo come bah seeds yet?'
'Well, yes, I did.'

'Good, we will plant cucumber on Friday.'

'Oh, by the way, we will be going to Castries for the day and won't be back until late.'

'Oh, that's good you told me, because you never can tell what some people will do. Just leave the porch light on and I will have a look. There are some people here, not many, but a few, and you can't be too careful. They will see that you are gone and you never can tell. Now, I will keep an eye on your place.'

'Thank you so much.'

'That's quite all right. I am glad to do it.'

'Well, good-bye.'

'Good-bye.'

Creatures: This is no place for people who get disturbed by bugs. It is marvellous for those who are awed by the number and variety of creatures sharing this terrestrial home. Our flypaper is an entomological showcase. Never knew there were so many lovely moths of every colour and size. Thumb-sized tree frogs could win the Calavaris County contest hands down. With a sudden leap, he's halfway up the walls; a plink and he's on the ceiling; then, kerplunk, and he's on the floor, all the while substantially decreasing the mosquito population. They serenade all night. They use the same score and arrangement as does the cricket, but with different instrumentation. Instead of a crick-creek-crick, it is sort of a rich-reech-rich, like the rhythmic and unending swing of a rusty gate.

Sanitation: Below North American standards, it is way above much of the world. Treated water is piped within the reach of most people. There are standpipes with faucets where people come to get water. An increasing number of homes have running water. A Bahá'í traveller from India remarked on the cleanliness of the place. She went on to say, 'You can always tell where there have been Christian missionaries because its cleaner than other places.'

Home: Our home is large by St Lucian standards, about 1,600 square feet with three bedrooms. The largest is the study/computer room. The house is on a heavily travelled road and we are a curiosity. Necks crane as people walk by. Enjoying the porch, chatting with a stream of visitors and passers-by during the gorgeous sunset and dusk is a major daily activity.

Family: Slowly, we are getting settled in. Terianne, who is 13, has a horse and is in form 2 of junior secondary school. That is roughly equivalent to the eighth grade. She wears a uniform consisting of a green blouse and black skirt which is very attractive. The school bus picks her up in front of the house at 7:40 a.m. for classes which start at 8:00. She is home by 1:40 p.m. She is enjoying school and is doing well.

Beverly is busy with all manner of things. She has volunteered to be the editor of the *St Lucia Bahá'í News*, a bi-monthly newsletter with about a thousand on the mailing list. She recently attended a drama group meeting and has been asked to join a 'charity' group which seems to be a community service women's group. All in all, she loves it here and exclaims over the weather nearly every day. She has had enough of northern winters.

I am busy around the house, getting things built and fixed. I try to spend as much time as possible at the computer, but other things keep interfering. For the past week, Louis Gregory Robinson, a Bahá'í from Guadaloupe who is a computer programmer, has been setting up the programs used at the Bahá'í World Centre to work on the IBM PC. I have been gratified to learn that *Consultation*, judging from readers' comments, both verbal and written, has been well-received. It is now in its second printing and

an agreement has been made for an edition for the visually
impaired in braille, large print or tape.

The challenges here are many but the problems are those
of growth and vigour. There are always certain difficulties
when living in a land where the life-style, language and
customs are unfamiliar and one is supremely conscious of
being a 'guest' in the country. Staying is a privilege not a
right.

Bahá'í status: St Lucia is a brimming, potential paradise.
The more than 1,400 enrolled Bahá'ís represent more than
one per cent of the population. There are varying degrees of
understanding. Most members of the national spiritual
assembly live in the Castries area which has the only
functioning local spiritual assembly. We have started to
hold feast in the south of the island, alternating among
several communities. It is the first time that many of the
Bahá'ís have ever been to a feast. The biggest problem is
having the time and energy to get to all the places which
show potential. There is an openness and eagerness to talk
about God. Given enough people to travel about, there is
little doubt that the Bahá'ís would soon be a significant
minority and could even make St Lucia the first place in the
world in which the majority of the population are Bahá'ís.

5

Wolf Mother and K'eech Gow

Joan and Ted Anderson

John Kolstoe suggested that the story of the Andersons of Red Deer, Alberta, Canada be included.

Although Bahá'ís had visited the Yukon as early as 1905 (Agnes Alexander, who became a Hand of the Cause of God), we were greatly privileged to be the first Bahá'ís to make our home there. We arrived at the new little capital city of Whitehorse on September 23, 1953 on the narrow gauge White and Yukon Railroad, a relic of the famous Yukon gold rush.

Back in December 1948, about nine months after Ted had first learned of the word 'Bahá'í' while browsing through a Spiritualist book, A.D. Watson's *The Twentieth Plane*, he made a decision.

Ted takes up the story:

I considered myself a believer in Bahá'u'lláh. I felt that one day I might become a 'missionary' for His Cause. I had a strong urge to tell my father, a Lutheran clergyman in Mt Horeb, Wisconsin, but decided first to investigate the tremendous claims of the Bahá'í Faith further.

I promptly transferred from the post-graduate study of philosophy at the University of Chicago to a study of the history of religion at the Federated Theological Schools (Baptist, Congregational, Disciples of Christ and Unitarian churches). My plan was to prepare to teach the world's religions at college.

Shortly after receiving a prompt reply to a letter I had written to Shoghi Effendi, I formally enrolled as a Bahá'í. This precious letter, written on behalf of the Guardian, was dated April 16, 1950 and included this very interesting sentence:

> In principle it is good if the young Bahá'ís seek a career which would enable them to find employment abroad, as then they can render valuable pioneer services.

The full meaning of this reference to pioneer services did not become apparent to me until three years later when Shoghi Effendi's wife, Rúḥíyyih Rabbani, a special representative to the historic All-America International Teaching Conference held in Chicago in May 1953, raised on his behalf the call to pioneering to a hundred remote goal areas of the world where no Bahá'ís as yet resided. I nudged Joanie, whom I had married in June 1952, and said, 'Let's go!' She promptly agreed, so it became our very great bounty to be among the 150 who responded to this exciting call to service.

The following month, while at Bahá'í summer school in Ontario, members of Canada's New Territories Committee invited us to move to the Yukon Territory. We took a short walk in the woods, consulted and prayed and returned then and there to tell them we would go.

After surviving several tests and obstacles, including my chronic strep throat and our failure to find jobs in the Yukon before leaving, we eagerly boarded the train in Chicago on September 12, 1953, stopping for a warm visit of several days with my parents in Wisconsin. On September 19 we sailed from Vancouver on the S.S. *Princess*

Louise, the last passenger ship of the year to Skagway, Alaska. Flocks of geese were flying south and we wondered if we should not be doing the same, especially when we glimpsed briefly the dilapidated buildings of the old 1898 gold rush port of Skagway.

Early in the morning of September 23, the old steam locomotive started chugging slowly along an old gold rush trail up to White Pass summit and beyond, arriving about noon at Lake Bennett's little station for roast moose lunch. After a short stop at the village of Carcross (Caribou Crossing), a future strong centre of Bahá'í activity, the little train finished its 110-mile journey at Whitehorse about 4 p.m. After a long day of rigorous travelling we had finally arrived at our new home, a bit shocked to see the unpaved streets, tar-paper shacks and leafless scrawny trees. A fellow passenger from the train, who was aware of our plans to settle in the Yukon, exclaimed, 'If I were you-all, I'd get right back on board this train and head south.'

It seemed then we were hit by a series of shocks, tests and interesting situations, which Counsellor Angus Cowan was later to term simply the difficulties and troubles that come to Bahá'ís when they arise to do service. Our prayers increased. Within five days of our arrival at this tiny city with a population of about 5,500, we were amazed to find our little home inside the railroad turnaround and a job for me at the US Army pipelines office.

Our first winter was cold and lonely but by spring my health was restored. Our first close friends had been found. We came at last to feel at home. We were surprised to receive a wonderful letter written on behalf of Shoghi Effendi on June 4, 1954, which said, in part:

He urges you to concentrate on the native population, as it is for that reason that we have opened new countries to the Faith. We have entered new fields all over the world, to bring the light of Divine Guidance to the native populations, who have thus far been deprived of the spiritual teachings of Bahá'u'lláh.

As the process of crises and victories unfolded, more and more golden Yukon hearts were discovered. As the Ten Year Crusade came to a triumphant close in 1963, we were astonished to witness the formation of three local spiritual assemblies – Whitehorse, Whitehorse Peaks (both with all-native membership) and Carcross (with a native majority) – the incorporation of the Whitehorse Spiritual Assembly on March 14, 1961; recognition of Bahá'í marriages by the Yukon Territorial government; government approval for Bahá'í children to be absent from school on Bahá'í holy days; Yukon's first endowment (a big log cabin) at Jackson Lake, site of five large conferences; and, best of all, having 110 Bahá'ís living in the Yukon. There were 68 Yukon Indians, 29 Tlingets, one Cree and 12 others, including two Hungarians and one of African ancestry. We also learned that 28 others who had become Bahá'ís in the Yukon had moved on to such widely scattered places as Alaska, Alberta, British Columbia, California, Germany, Nova Scotia, Ontario, Oregon, Quebec and Washington DC.

In 1964 the House of Justice launched the Nine Year Plan. We Yukoners were initially dismayed to learn that it was expected that by 1973 Yukon would have at least ten local spiritual assemblies. We realized that meant that every Yukon community of 300 or more should have an assembly if we were to reach that goal. This clearly reinforced the importance of the native population of the Yukon.

A number of Bahá'í institutions, including Hands of the Cause of God, counsellors, auxiliary board members, national and local spiritual assemblies and their committees, collaborated to plan and execute a unique and exciting proclamation campaign during October 1970. It resulted in finding 231 new believers throughout the Yukon, making it possible to establish 11 local spiritual assemblies by the following April, two years ahead of schedule!

We now felt it was time for us to go and for the Yukon Bahá'í institutions to grow on their own. In August 1972 we and our two Yukon-born sons moved from Whitehorse to Red Deer, Alberta, Canada. So . . . from Whitehorse to Red Deer!

We have returned a number of times. In 1984 we were delighted to be able to attend the dedication ceremonies of the Yukon Bahá'í Institute at Lake Laberge. We were adopted by the Tlingets. Joan was given the name 'Wolf Mother' and I 'K'eech Gow', which means the whoosh-whoosh sound made by the wings of the crow as it flies. We were presented with an original painting of a wolf and a crow in the mountains. I was given a lovely moosehide beaded vest. This adoption ceremony and the realization of its meaning was a highlight of our years in the Yukon.

6

Climbing Peak 8100

Sharon O'Toole and Earl Redman

Among John Kolstoe's first bundle of scripts from Alaska, received when I was wintering in Florida, was this one. Reading it in the warmth and sunshine, I felt vicariously the cold winds described by Earl Redman.

I stood on a narrow snow-covered ridge in the Alaska Range. It was dark but the moon had painted the jagged crags and icy crevasses with pale silvery-gold accents. Behind me were the tents in which my companions had settled snugly, surrounded by their thick down sleeping bags, and from which the grumbling purr of small mountaineering stoves crawled out into the night. We were there to climb a mountain, one without a name, known simply as 'Peak 8100' for its altitude.

As I stood there alone in the night, facing the long, ragged, mysteriously dark shrouded ribbon of ridge we proposed to climb the next day, it wasn't the unknown, unclimbed ridge, the tortured silvery glaciers ravaged by great crevasses or the face of the black cliff that made me gaze transfixed. It was because this seemed to be the House of God. This magnificence of creation was the sign of His work. I was full of awe, here in this most magnificent House of Worship, the one that God Himself had built.

Supposedly, I was a Christian, a Methodist, for that was what my parents had been and their parents before them. But I had become disenchanted because I felt something was missing. The people were friendly, the pastor open-minded and helpful, the sermons occasionally interesting. But my soul hungered for something else. I hadn't a clue as to what it was.

New Mexico State University was the centre of my universe in those days. I was studying to become a geologist and life was full of rocks, minerals, faults, ore deposits. In spite of weekdays spent in classes studying and weekends out mapping rock units or searching for a sample of some mineral called hemimorphite, I also had a quest to find the 'right church'. As yet, no 'right church' had spoken to my soul. Many were peopled by kindly souls, yet still something was missing. My background was Christian and, unfortunately, it did not even enter my mind to examine the other major faiths of the world.

At that time I had a friend who had been an all-A student in his first year-and-a-half of college. Suddenly he dropped out of school, grew his hair to shoulder-length and vaguely hinted that he had experimented with pot. So when he returned to the university a year or more later saying he was a Bahá'í, it provoked no queries, alarms or interest. To me it was just another in the multitude of eastern cults. He took me to the local student Bahá'í Centre and I sat with other Bahá'ís drinking coffee, but never once did any of them offer me any words of spiritual wisdom or give me an explanation of the new religion called the Bahá'í Faith. Because of thick, unseen veils surrounding me, I had no questions to ask. Even when my friend told me he was pioneering to Samoa, it raised no interest in me to know why. It was my first encounter with the Bahá'í Faith and it left no conscious impression.

I was a hiker, backpacker and mountain climber. Those paths did not lead to God. Alone in some mountain vastness or forest, I could feel God, and He and Christ were real. My religion became very personal and completely divorced from the normal divisions of Christianity. Nature was my church. It was all I needed to be close to God. A building, a preacher, or a ritualistic worship service were unnecessary.

My college career ended with graduation and with it passed my search for Truth. With the years, my path led me to Alaska where the University of Alaska in Fairbanks became home. There was an active Bahá'í group at the university at the time. They proclaimed their religion, put up posters and generally made themselves conspicuous to the academic community. But not to me. My veils were so thick that I saw absolutely nothing about that 'little cult' that was first introduced to me in New Mexico.

I became seriously involved with mountaineering in its grandest sense. The mountains remained my most inspirational place of worship and meditation. A month-long climbing expedition provided abundant time for the reflection and meditation that were part of my personal religion. Denali (Mount McKinley) kept me for 32 days in my church and left me with a deeper faith in God.

Then I went to climb Denali's wife, Mount Foraker. Foraker's massive summit loomed up in the clear, blue sky, while a jumble of arrogant lesser peaks strutted about its base. Flat, green lowlands laced by tributaries of the Tanana and Kushokwim rivers lapped up against the lumpy toes of the great mountain range. A biting wind alternately whipped the lifeless slopes with 30 miles per hour blasts that faded to a zephyr, barely noticeable in the 20-below-zero air.

Two of us were descending from our three-week attempt to reach Foraker's winter-bound peak. The attempt had been stymied at 14,000 feet by boisterous winds and engulfing clouds. To get home, however, we had to journey across 30 miles of Alaskan wilderness, descending 10,000 feet while doing so.

Mike led the way down through the battering wind and the frigid air. Our appreciation of the realm through which we travelled was limited to brief glimpses from behind drawn parka hoods as we tried to thwart the ever-persistent frostbite.

Then Mike fell. A marauding gust slapped onto his face, instantly changing him from a heavily burdened, bipedal creature to a human toboggan on a polished glacial surface. I saw him fall and instinct threw me to the icy surface, ice axe plunged deeply into the crusty snow to stop his slide. Suddenly, I was floating, drifting down the mountain like a feather, calm, rational, unworried. In the background, a vibration drummed lightly against my consciousness, a persistent feeling, but one of little importance. I knew I was falling, my body being dribbled down the steep flank of Mount Foraker, but my soul was unconcerned. Without worry, I asked myself what was below on the slope and noted there was a 5,000-foot drop, then casually observed, 'I think I've bought the farm.' I wondered calmly what others would think when they found out I'd died in a fall on Mount Foraker.

While my consciousness floated serenely down the frozen slopes, concerned but little with the body's rapid descent to disaster, the body was frantically fighting to retain the life it had. When Mike had fallen, the body instinctively tried to stop his fall. Mike, unfortunately, was going too fast and the snow was too poor for an ice axe to arrest, so his momentum yanked my body down the slope. We cart-wheeled down, switching positions on the way. Instinct made my ice axe claw desperately at the rapidly passing slope. My body was racing towards doom when it hit a snow-filled crevasse. One leg poked into a hole and my body went over backwards. My consciousness, still totally divorced from the battered body, calmly noted that had I flipped over forward, I would have shattered my knee.

For an instant I hung immobile, head down on a 60-degree slope. Then Mike flailed by and the rope came tight with a tremendous jolt that brought Mike to an abrupt stop but jerked my leg from the crevasse. Despite being bashed and battered after a thousand feet of steep slope, the body still scrambled wildly, clinging to its life. As the rope jerked my leg from the crevasse, the body did some stupendous contortions and managed to get an arm into the crevasse where the leg had just been. Those contortions retained its life.

The body had saved itself, so the soul returned to make it whole. The soul's reaction after recombination was one of intense disappointment that it was forced to return from a better world. The second reaction, from the body, was one of intense relief to be alive. The fall had been stopped but I still clung to a 60-degree ice face with one arm over the top, two crampon points embedded in the steep ice, one crampon dangling from an ankle and the ice axe stuck feebly in the hard surface by an arm dislocated at the shoulder. But getting out of a precarious position is easy when both body and soul are together.

Abruptly, my unconscious doubts about the soul and the world after death were gone. I had been there, or at least to the edge of the next world. My own experience told me that it was so much better than this one. I now had proof that this world of earth and air was simply transitory. I had been allowed a glimpse of what life would be in the next world. There were no doubts about God.

So I was prepared when in the next year I began using the small Alaskan village of Tenakee Springs as a base for geological operations and met Sharon Pegue O'Toole. She sent my mail, sold me supplies and dialled my phone calls from the village's only phone. This intriguing woman kept me returning to visit her in Juneau after the summer's project was completed. And she reintroduced me to the Bahá'í Faith.

This time, however, the veils were parting and what she told me found its way through to my more highly-aware soul. It took only a few brief discussions to realize that the Faith revealed by Bahá'u'lláh was close to my heart. But it took a year of logical mental arguing in my head about the reality of a new Manifestation sent by God before I could act. Ultimately, it wasn't the logical arguments of a left-brained male that stripped away my final veils. It was the decision to let the heart make the final verdict. Sharon's patient teaching had its effect and my heart accepted Bahá'u'lláh. I became a Bahá'í on the day we married.

This was the beginning of a long apprenticeship. Though I had declared myself a Bahá'í, attended feasts and other activities and practised the outward forms of my new Faith, I was not able to submerge myself in the love of Bahá'u'lláh. When I attended my first national convention, I was deeply impressed at the evident lack of discrimination by the Bahá'ís, but for the first six years the Bahá'í Faith was a mystery as well as a comfort, and a perplexing, although welcome, addition to my life. I said the noonday prayer and read the holy Writings morning and evening, if I remembered. Often I did not. I fasted, unless I could find an excuse, and I tried to read a few Bahá'í books, but never could manage to finish them. It was a struggle to accept everything that this new Faith included and during much of those early years I exerted only a minimal effort to live the Faith.

Although I was not a particularly energetic Bahá'í during my first six years, I was given an amazing amount of success in all that I did. I had been given an exceptional wife and a bright son. My mountaineering adventures were astoundingly successful, partly because of the companions who joined me. Professionally, I found myself working in just those areas which so excited my interest. And the signs of my acceptance as a professional geologist were manifest with numerous publications, requests for public appearances, and even the acceptance of a paper at an international symposium. I completed a book which others appeared to enjoy. Those years became the happiest and most comfortable of my life.

Then came India and the dedication of the Bahá'í House of Worship in New Delhi.

It was mid-afternoon on Christmas Eve when I first saw the Lotus Temple. The soaring white marble petals suddenly appeared from behind a cluster of trees. My feet continued to carry me towards the main gate but I kept stumbling because it was almost impossible to take my eyes from this newest Bahá'í House of Worship. The pictures I had seen of it did nothing to prepare me for the majesty and other-worldliness I saw before me.

The experience of the dedication of the House of Worship in New Delhi is beyond my ability to describe. I was allowed the bounty of worshipping God in a building that was not just a stone edifice but a spiritual bond with other, spiritual worlds. No physical building had ever affected me as did the marble lotus filled with the prayers of all the great religions of the world and all the diverse flowers of the one human garden. I saw the Bahá'í Faith in action among nine thousand people from a hundred countries. I saw the hope for the future. This was God's invitation for me to work for His Faith.

It was past midnight as I sat thinking in the big Thai Airlines plane. Ahead were Ireland, England and Denmark, as yet unknown to me, but I could not think of them. My mind was filled with the Lotus Temple. I had been changed by the short time I had spent there. Now, as I sat in the darkened plane, a long-ago talk with Marion Johnson kept running through my mind. She had once told me that, after a number of years of being a Bahá'í, she had startlingly realized that all of the things she had really wanted to do had been done. She felt as if Bahá'u'lláh had given her all her heart-felt desires and that now it was His turn to get from her what He wanted. So she offered herself to Bahá'u'lláh and soon found herself visiting far-flung corners of the world with His work.

Still overwhelmed by the deeply spiritual experience of being in the Lotus Temple, I began to examine my list of goals and hoped-for achievements. With little surprise, I realized the great majority had been accomplished. It was with a sense of trepidation that I looked to the future and saw nothing of significance planned for my life. Marion's story paralleled mine. It took some bit of courage, but I then did as she had done. I thanked Bahá'u'lláh for the bounties I had received and offered my future for His use.

A few months passed after we returned from India before Sharon suggested that we pioneer. She had been hinting about pioneering for years, but I had always just sloughed the idea off as impracticable. This time, however, a small corner of my mind perked up and began to examine this idea further, though the greater part still figured that pioneering was for exceptional people and not for me. More time skittered by and I found that the little corner of my mind that was thinking about pioneering had been busily expanding its area of influence and I actually began to consider the possibility. Sharon quietly picked up information on Alaska's pioneering goals and soon I was reading statistics about Argentina.

Sharon went to work in the post office to save enough money so that we could pioneer. For over a year we slowly worked towards the goal of pioneering to Argentina. It was, however, a period characterized by a remarkable lack of highlights. Our progress seemed to halt.

Then, in May 1988, I went to Melbourne, Australia, to a

geologic conference. While I was away, Sharon was invited
to a slide show about Chile. In spite of having too many
things to do, she went. While there, she suddenly felt that
Chile was the place we should go. Half a world away, I'd
startlingly come to the same view after meeting people who
had worked in geology in Chile!

Our goal was abruptly switched to Chile and the whole
process of pioneering became transformed. A brisk wind
terminated the doldrums we had been languishing in and
put us in the centre of a storm of information on Chile:
magazine articles, newspaper stories, friends who had been
there. Even a piece of mail which passed through the post
office and was referred unknowingly to Sharon came from
Temuco, Chile. Our pace accelerated.

Committed to going, but still uncertain about the whole
adventure, I tried to prepare myself for pioneering while
retaining a desperate grasp on the security of my life in
Juneau. My boss suggested a year's leave without pay
could be arranged. I quickly accepted that as a security
blanket. I could always change my mind and quit my job
after we had been in Chile for a few months.

I found it difficult to accept that pioneering is a lifetime,
or at least a long term effort. Slicing the bonds that held me
to the old way of life was a formidable challenge. While
Sharon talked of spending a year or two in Chile for the
sake of the peace of mind of our relatives, I was really
expecting that pioneering would consume only a small part
of my life. The total commitment needed truly to pioneer
continued to keep just beyond my intellectual grasp.

During this time I found that I had an insatiable urge to
read the Writings of Bahá'u'lláh, 'Abdu'l-Bahá and Shoghi
Effendi. My plunge into Bahá'í literature included the
Kitáb-i-Íqán, Epistle to the Son of the Wolf, The Dawn-Breakers,
compilations of the Universal House of Justice, books by
William Sears and many others. With all of my reading

there came a need to pray continually for steadfastness and for the wisdom which would be needed in a new country and culture.

Then, with a startling suddenness, my acute need for security vanished. I abruptly told my boss that taking a leave of absence would not work and that I would give up my job permanently. The concept of pioneering expanded within my mind and I began to talk of a long-term, indefinite stay in Chile. Doubts dissipated. I was ready to pioneer for as long as I was needed.

Throwing myself completely into the great undertaking, though, brought an overwhelming cascade of problems to solve and difficulties with which to deal. Our house had to be rented to provide us with an income in Chile; visa problems had to be worked out; all of our personal possessions had to be divided into those which went into storage, those which could be given away, and those which would accompany us to Chile. Housing had to be secured in Chile; cars had to be sold; money transfer had to be worked out between our Juneau bank and Chile. It all seemed just too much. I felt buried under the avalanche of the responsibilities of relocation.

Again, my life took a radical turn. This time, when I prayed to Bahá'u'lláh for help with some of the details, the response was almost immediate. Problems suddenly were solved or solutions made apparent. When I put my faith in God, our whole pioneering effort began moving much more smoothly. We made progress. During the final three weeks before departure, the magnitude of this act suddenly struck home. It was no longer just a grand and noble goal, to be discussed with great excitement. I was assailed by doubts, fears and anxieties. The mountains surrounding Juneau were abruptly transformed from the everyday to the unique and beautiful. Friends suddenly revealed their most endearing qualities and it was difficult to see my world without them in it. Juneau and our friends began to glow with an irresistible allure. Their siren's call nearly did to my pioneering hopes what the original sirens did to Odysseus and his crew. Odysseus tied himself to the mast of his ship. I tied myself to the security of prayers to Bahá'u'lláh for steadfastness.

Sharon seemed to face none of the temptations with which I was afflicted. She was preoccupied with packing and sorting to the exclusion of all else. It was only at the very end that the sirens began to call to her.

Sharon now takes up the narrative:

My sirens were the friends I had not yet said a 'proper' good-bye to, my grandchildren and a handful of intimate friends who were part of my life. For the two years we had been planning this move, I had been slowly, subconsciously, cutting many of the ties. Whenever one of those ties seemed to have too firm a grasp, I remembered a long-ago summer school and something Stanwood Cobb had said about sacrifice, that it was simply having to make a choice and giving up what you did not choose. So this was not the negative choice of giving up a friend, a home and garden, a country but the positive choice of pioneering in a goal area, an area I would never have chosen on my own, but yet will look back on and realize it is one for which I'd been preparing all of my life.

My Bahá'í parents, Pat and Georgine Moul, had instilled in me, by example, the importance of pioneering goals, of moving on when the community gets sufficiently large. Having had a small sweet taste of pioneering to a homefront goal long ago in Hoonah, that importance remained in my blood like a spiritual virus, just patiently waiting for the right opportunity.

Whenever I feel a little bit scared or overwhelmed or

unworthy, I remember that this is a goal of the Universal House of Justice. It has to be right; somebody has to do it and the promises of help from Bahá'u'lláh if you 'heed not your weakness' and 'arise to aid our Cause' point me back in the right direction.

Earl continues the story:

The final days were a chaos of decisions, packing and trying to see friends one last time. To see friends required sacrificing precious packing time. The final night was a nightmare of last-minute panic. With the aid of understanding and patient Bahá'ís, we arrived at the ferry ten minutes before departure.

With the departure of the ferry from Juneau, it became Regan's turn suddenly to discover just what he was a part of. Sharon and I slumped into our stateroom exhausted. Regan went to the stern of the slowly moving ship and watched the lights of Juneau retreat from his life. It was traumatic for a ten-year-old who had lived his whole life amidst these lights and tears fell. We soon joined him and we suffered together the pangs of separation from our old lives. To alleviate the pain, we talked of our future and what a great chance we had been given by Bahá'u'lláh.

With the passing of the night, the pain eased and our lives again began to fill with the excitement of pioneering. The next three weeks were spent enjoying friends in Seattle and parents in New Mexico, but it was an up-and-down time of alternating eagerness and anxiety. The travelling and visiting placed us back into the easy times before departure, when pioneering was just a fascinating topic of endless discussion with many people.

Then came Miami. When the big Pan American 747 came into view from the terminal window, a rush of anxiety crashed down on me and a sense of panic returned. But now I was committed and there was no turning back. The tide of panic waned though it continued to ebb and flow for most of the flight to Santiago. As we approached the Andes, standing bright with their mantle of snow, the adventure began, again.

The great nebulous anxiety of early times was replaced in Santiago by the everyday trouble of dealing with the down-to-earth problems of Chilean customs. There we stood with nine large pieces of luggage and my computer. In the luggage were my printer, a stereo, a tape deck, a set of new dishes and bright shining new cookware in addition to the usual items. With a great deal of trepidation but a faith that God wanted us in Chile, I led our little procession towards the declaration side of customs. There I showed them my computer and told them that we had been invited to the country by the National Spiritual Assembly of the Bahá'ís of Chile and hoped to stay. Fears of high duties orbited in me but we were suddenly waved through and found ourselves outside without a bag having been opened.

During the next two weeks we waited anxiously as our 19 boxes, air-freighted, worked their way through the byzantine mist of Chilean customs. Bahá'í friends in Santiago helped us find an agent to fight our battles in Spanish but we spent a worried week waiting for the customs bill. I planned to leave money for the bill with a Bahá'í friend to pass on to the agent. Upon arrival at his office, I found only a secretary present. I was late for a meeting so left a large amount of cash with this unknown woman. I said some prayers about it and appealed to the Concourse on High, to Betty Becker, the first Alaskan pioneer to Chile, and to Don Anderson, who knows all about money, to keep everyone honest. The next day all of our boxes were released for half the estimated bill. Customs had opened boxes to ascertain their contents but nothing was missing and there was little damage.

Then we climbed aboard the overnight bus which drove down the Pan American Highway to Valdivia, our initial pioneering goal. The night we left our old home in Juneau it was raining. The morning we arrived in our new home in Valdivia it was raining. It felt as if we were coming home.

The Alaskan goal was to send two pioneers to the Mapuche region of Chile. We spent a year outside of that region, in Valdivia, at the request of the Chilean National Pioneering Committee. This temporary location was to ease us into Chilean culture and give us time to learn the Chilean form of Spanish before being thrust into the main teaching effort among the Mapuches. It enabled us to move from the material-rich urban North American culture into the simpler urban culture of Chile before requiring us to adapt to an unfamiliar rural setting and the Mapuche culture.

In front of us stood a Mapuche woman. She was ancient. Her brown face was wrinkled like the convoluted mountains around us. She had no teeth but her smile was broad. She babbled happily on, giving us a handful of Mapuche words to remember. Her great-grandson said she was about a hundred years old. They lived in a small wooden house around which swarmed chickens, pigs and dogs. There was no electricity. There was no car in the driveway, just a wooden yoke for oxen. Other oxen were being used to work the nearby fields.

A short while later we sat inside another wooden home with an elderly Bahá'í Mapuche woman. Her house had a living room and a minuscule bedroom. As she served us milk, fresh squeezed from the cow, the woman told us of her pacemaker for her heart. She chased the chickens back outside. A huge pig peered in through the open door over its wriggling snout.

It was our first trip to the Campo, the rural part of Chile. In the area surrounding the city of Temuco live about

14,000 Mapuche Indian Bahá'ís. Most of them live in small wooden houses or grass rukas. Windows are of clear plastic or sport a wood panel over an empty window frame.

Rich Mapuches plough their fields with oxen. Heat is provided by the wood-fired cooking stove. In the rukas, smoke from the stove usually swirls about inside the houses because its only exit is through the grass roofs. Each house has its fields and its rose bushes, its chickens and pigs. A few have a horse. Most people listen to Radio Bahá'í, which broadcasts in both Spanish and Mapuche. It is common for a teaching project among the Mapuche to find over a hundred new Bahá'ís during a weekend.

In addition to the Mapuches, there are about three thousand non-Mapuche Bahá'ís among the 13 million people in Chile. Within the Bahá'í community are approximately 30 pioneers, mostly from Persian and North American backgrounds. The Mapuche Indians are the main focus of teaching work. About a half million Mapuches live in the region centred in Temuco. For the last several years Radio Bahá'í has broadcast its message from a small town of Labrunza, near Temuco, reaching the isolated family groups in the Campo for a radius of 50 miles. The radio provides a message service that people can use in place of the telephones that none can afford, enabling them to keep in contact with each other. It also teaches them the principles of the Faith.

Now, after a year, we are moving to Labrunza to be neighbours with Radio Bahá'í and to live even closer to the Mapuches. We have struggled to acquire a working vocabulary in Spanish and a few basic Mapuche words. How can I write about the seeming coincidences that have occurred, such as finding, on the very last day of their stay, the Baptist missionary family who were leaving Chile and selling all of their furniture and who, out of desperation, cut their price in half? Or the times at firesides when our ability to understand and speak Spanish would suddenly and dramatically improve? And about the thrill when a class of third graders spontaneously broke out into applause when I showed a slide taken at night of the illuminated Bahá'í House of Worship in India?

Before moving to Chile, I read many of the Writings of Bahá'u'lláh, 'Abdu'l-Bahá, Shoghi Effendi and the Universal House of Justice about pioneering. They all spoke of the indescribable bounties that come to those who sacrifice home and country to spread the teachings of Bahá'u'lláh. I wondered if these bounties were something we would receive in the next world.

But then we became pioneers. After a year in Chile, the meaning of the Writings is clear. Our spiritual gifts have been overwhelming! How can I describe the extraordinary gifts that have been bestowed upon us? Words are not enough. It is easy to describe most of what we sacrificed in Alaska – a high-paying job, beautiful home, the abundance of things available in stores, comfort, the spectacular country – because all of these are material. I can also write of the sacrifice of leaving close friends. Virtually everyone has, at some time or another, been separated from someone for whom they care. But how to describe the tremendous aura of nearness of Bahá'u'lláh that we have developed while pioneering in Chile? Or the vast potentialities that we have uncovered within prayer? The spiritual feelings, the language of the heart, is impossible to translate. I can tell the tangible results of our prayers, such as the time we wanted to help elect assemblies during Riḍván in the isolated villages in the Campo but our car kept breaking down. How we began then to wonder whether we were supposed to go into the Campo or whether Bahá'u'lláh wanted us to concentrate on teaching in Valdivia. We prayed to Bahá'u'lláh to tell us what He wanted. Our mechanic then told us it would take at least ten days to

repair our car. Yet it seemed that Bahá'u'lláh sent enough
seekers to our home during Riḍván to keep our evenings
full. Bahá'u'lláh has very distinctly answered our prayers
many times.

Sharon, our son, Regan, and I, are pioneers in Chile. We
often felt we could not do it, but we did. We are here and
we have gained so much more than we have lost. Our house
is smaller, our finances tenuous, many friends and relatives
are distant. But all that we have left behind has been
overshadowed by the treasures we have been given – the
spiritual education we have received which simply cannot
be put into words. It is all impossible to convey with such a
simple medium as words. You will have to become a
pioneer to find out.

Until a being setteth his foot in the plane of sacrifice, he is
bereft of every favour and grace; and this plane of sacrifice is
the realm of dying to the self, that the radiance of the living
God may shine forth. The martyr's field is the place of
detachment from self, that the anthems of eternity may be
upraised. Do all ye can to become wholly weary of self, and
bind yourselves to that Countenance of Splendours; and once
ye have reached such heights of servitude, ye will find,
gathered within your shadow, all created things. This is
boundless grace; this is the highest sovereignty; this is the life
that dieth not. All else save this is at the last but manifest
perdition and great loss.

'Abdu'l-Bahá

7

From Apollo II to DC-3s

Joyce and Bob Chalmer

It was 1969. Our family was living in Slidell, Louisiana. We had six years of homefront pioneering under our belt and wanted to become 'homeless in the Name of God', part of the exodus of Bahá'ís to other parts of the world. Bob was working as an aerospace engineer with the Boeing Company in Louisiana. Joyce, a registered nurse, was taking care of their children at home – Karen, 10, Rob, 9 and Valerie, 4.

In those days if one wished to pioneer abroad it was necessary to contact the Foreign Goals Committee, choose a country, make your own arrangements and leave. We had a friend who was a pioneer in Ecuador at the time. In letters we exchanged with Jerry Bagley he had emphasized the needs in that country. Jerry needed a jeep to provide transportation for the local people, and it seemed he may have been more interested in our vehicles than in us. We could have simply sent the money for the jeep but we wanted to go there ourselves. We began to make plans.

We felt a vacation in Ecuador would give us a chance to see something of the country we might make our future home. Bob had been assigned by Boeing to monitor the Apollo II launch at Cape Canaveral in Florida in July, so Florida seemed the place to embark on our flight to Ecuador. We sent our itinerary to Jerry.

Following the launch, we boarded Ecuadorian Airlines in Miami. It was midnight and the family was excited if bleary-eyed from a nerve-wracking day watching the launch of the first manned flight to the moon. We felt the success of the mission boded well for our own journey. This thought was dispelled in about two hours when our Electra airliner encountered a thunder storm over the Pacific. For 45 minutes we felt certain that we and all aboard were going to join the fish below. Bob knew the propensity of the Electras for breaking up in heavy turbulence, and Joyce, afraid to fly in anything, wondered if the Supreme Concourse really did hover, and prayed. The plane finally emerged from the maelstrom and descended into Quito, capital of Ecuador.

We were met at the airport by members of the National Spiritual Assembly of Ecuador and the local spiritual assembly. We stumbled from the plane, bone weary, into the thin air of the ten-thousand-foot-high Andean capital and stared unbelievingly at the group of smiling Bahá'ís holding flowers in their arms and singing 'Alláh-u-Abhá'. Surely this was a bit of heaven on earth!

The friends whisked us away to a hotel and allowed us to sleep most of the day, without telling us they had arranged a press interview for that afternoon. Bob was to be given VIP treatment because of his involvement with the Apollo II launch, a fact that the national spiritual assembly seized upon as a vehicle for publicizing the Faith. In addition to the initial press interview, arrangements had been made for a TV interview in Quito and a lecture circuit to an outlying town.

The next few days passed in a whirl. We were guided by local believers on a tour of a hundred miles of countryside surrounding Quito. Magical vistas flashed by our bus window and we listened enchanted to the names of the towns as they rolled off the tongue of our driver:

Latacunga, Ambato, Riobamba. The latter was of great interest, as we had been advised that should we decide to return to pioneer, Riobamba would be our post. It was an arid town in desert country, sheltering beneath active Chimbarazo volcano and desolate to our eyes. We stayed in a local hotel and had our first taste of 'living native'. Beds on straw mattresses, piglets in the kitchen, fleas in our soup. It was a grand adventure for the children.

Our decision to return as pioneers was made before we were halfway through our vacation. Quite simply, we had fallen in love with the people, the country and our need to serve Bahá'u'lláh. Our children were interested in everything they saw. Not a single complaint issued from any of them. It was a collective decision to return.

Arriving back in Louisiana, we immediately put our house on the market, hoping for a quick sale. Bob handed in his resignation at Boeing. He was considered a madman by his supervisors and co-workers. 'Giving up a good job to go *where*? What will you do? There's no work in Ecuador. How can you subject your children to such hardship?' All the questions that pioneers hear over and over. Our families were equally distressed.

Waiting for our home to sell was the first intimation that the road to joining 'the homeless in the path of God' is not always a smooth one, for in a couple of weeks we were visited, as was the whole of the Louisiana and Mississippi coast, by Hurricane Camille. Our house and property were damaged and we despaired of ever being able to leave. But as miracles do occur in such circumstances, a buyer appeared on the scene even before we had removed the nine trees from over our house and were still mopping mud from the floors. Our house was sold in one day. The buyers even took our two cats into the bargain! We had a moving sale in the week that followed and in a matter of a few days our household furniture was gone.

One month later we again boarded Ecuadorian Airlines in Miami and were bound for Ecuador.

Arriving as a pioneer was decidedly different from arriving as a tourist. We had the loving support of friends in Quito but we no longer had the North American version of success, money and prestige. We were now ex-patriates, without the language of the country, in need of work and with three children, cast adrift in a strange land.

Our first priority was to find a place to live. Bahá'í friends helped. We found a house in a neighbourhood near the school the children would attend. Much repair was needed on this dwelling and we spent two weeks painting, de-mousing and getting accustomed to cold water baths. We shopped in the local mercado for basic items. We had no furnishings or appliances, none of the things we so depended upon back in the States. We purchased beds and they were our sole furnishings for a few weeks until we could orient ourselves to the city and find furniture that was made on the local market. Already we were worried about money. This is the concern of every pioneer, especially those with children.

We enrolled the children in an English-speaking school, Cotopaxi Academy. Bob and I began a six-week course in Spanish at the local university, a crash programme that would enable us to handle the necessities of conversation. With the children in school and us already well along in the language course, we all began to feel a bit smug. But then things began to happen that quickly reminded us that we shouldn't get too comfortable. Karen fell onto a spike topping the iron fence around our house and impaled her underarm, missing a major artery by millimetres. Fortunately, an American pioneer was visiting us at the time and was able to arrange for us to get to a hospital immediately. Multiple stitches and the placement of a dram in the arm were required along with massive dosages of antibiotics.

Dorothy Campbell, the veteran American pioneer, held our panic at bay.

Thieves broke into our house. Our strict budget for food was decimated as we were robbed in the local markets twice. A lady we hired to help with the laundry turned out to be the neighbourhood prostitute who invited local swains to frequent our home. I am certain the neighbours speculated about the crazy Norteamericanos thrust into their midst, who hadn't a clue how to do anything correctly.

Our four-year-old, Valerie, got lost on the bus that was supposed to bring her home from school. She boarded the wrong bus and was not found for hours. To say we were overwhelmed with anxiety is an understatement.

Quito was the centre of political foment at the time. Coups were threatened daily. Bob kept getting caught in demonstrations whenever he went into the city to buy household items. Curfews imposed by the government often found us in restricted areas at hours that were wrong.

We struggled with the language, culture, customs and with each other. We cried a lot, laughed a lot and prayed not a little. We made many mistakes and probably offended every Ecuadorian we met. One serious mistake that still haunts me is the night we heard moans outside our gate. We went out and found a man lying on a sidewalk in a semi-coma in the rain. Fearing injury or imminent pneumonia for the man, we notified the police who came and took him away. Then we learned that our good samaritan act had probably imprisoned a man who had merely been drunk. Once in an Ecuadorian prison it is very difficult to get out, especially if one is poor. This man was decidedly poor.

Like most pioneers in those years, untrained and ignorant, we survived only with the support, humour and company of other pioneers. Each had learned the hard way and their visits sustained us.

Our first four months were over. It was time to move now to our new post in Riobamba. I remember the town as being very poor, without hospitals. We were willing to go there of course, but I was afraid we were not really ready for such a big move. As luck would have it, we were informed by the national spiritual assembly that another family had arrived from the United States and had already filled that post. We were now needed in Cuenca. Cuenca, we learned, was one of the three major cities in Ecuador, the cultural centre of the country, replete with writers, poets and painters and was the ancient seat of the Incan Empire. In other words, it was provincial, colonial and traditional. We flew to Cuenca immediately and were hosted by the Congers, long-time pioneers to the Bahá'í community. We looked for housing and found an apartment in town. Bob arranged for a truck to transport our furniture from Quito and travelled with the load, over twelve hours along a washboard and mud road, a trip our family would make several times by bus in the year ahead.

Getting used to our apartment was another hurdle. Two families and various animals, including a turkey, lived below us. The upstairs tenants were equally decorous, a widow with six children who was alone most of the time. Sandwiched in between these three families were the five of us. We could watch the activities of everyone from the open well which descended from the roof of the building to the courtyard at its base. The families below, we learned, were renting for the holiday. They were from Quagaquil, a city on the western coast, and had come for carnival in Cuenca. Carnival is the annual pre-Lenten festival and it was very much in progress. We became constant victims of celebratory water barrages, being pelted with water balloons and doused everywhere we went during the next two weeks.

We enrolled the children in a bi-lingual school twelve

blocks from our apartment. The school building would have been boarded up and condemned anywhere in the United States. The stench from the open restrooms permeated the foyer of the school. The system of education was strictly non-progressive: one textbook for all subjects, copy and repetition the models for learning; corporal punishment was common. Few people spoke English in the school so we felt that the children could audit the classes to learn the language, as there were but four months remaining in the school year.

I would teach the children at home in English, using the International Calvert system and texts we had brought with us. The children hated going to school, where Karen became the 'gringita' victim of the other children. She was teased and ostracized.

Each morning found us depressed. I walked the children to school and ruminated on the poverty etched in every block and punctuated by the piles of human faeces that littered the streets. My heart broke over and over as I saw countless infants with running ears and eyes in little faces bobbing from serape carriers on mothers' backs. So much pain. So few resources. Stunted lives. Would we ever become accustomed to our new home?

I worried about the children, about their safety. The road fronting our apartment was a maze of culverts nine feet deep awaiting the installation of sewer lines. One evening a man fell into one of the ditches and broke his back. There was no safe place for the children to play in the barrio. Soon they began to react to being homebound. Again, help came.

Karen, our eldest, found a vacant house while out walking with some of the Cuenca Bahá'í youth. It was on top of a hill overlooking the city. She hurried home to tell us about it. That a vacant house even existed was a miracle, for every rental in town was occupied. We hurriedly found the landlord, rented and moved in, all within two or three days. Now life settled into more pleasant patterns.

We decided not to submit the children to the school experience for another term. Instead we enrolled them in the Catholic school across town, even though all the courses were entirely in Spanish. The school vacation gave us time and opportunity to explore the countryside and to get to know our Bahá'í community. Bob, meanwhile, purchased a jeep which would be used to take local Indian believers into the 'campo' on teaching trips.

The teaching excursions were high adventure for Bob, but less satisfying because finding new souls for the Faith in that traditional area of Ecuador was difficult. The team would usually go out in the early morning after choosing a village or settlement that looked promising. Native Ecuadorians did the teaching, quite often in Quechua, the ancient language, and in Spanish, while Bob acted as driver and observer and a representative of another nationality. Frequently pioneers from North America simply serve in this manner, an important role, for the diversity seen in action gives credence to Bahá'u'lláh's message of the oneness of humankind and of one world.

Getting to the areas to teach was difficult, driving up rutted one-lane paths in a jeep laden with people, stopping to pick up one or two Indians walking home from market, crossing mountain streams, learning to use the pulley chairs across the river, eating the typical energy diet of the Indians, parched corn, and becoming accustomed to the sweet, humble, wonderful hospitality of the villagers. On occasion the team would be met with hostility or suspicion, especially if the cura (priest) warned his flock that strangers might come who wanted to capture their souls for communism. Just before we arrived in Cuenca, a team of agrarian reformers for the Ecuadorian government had been killed by villagers under such circumstances.

Teaching was usually verbal as few Indians could read. There were prayers, of course, and pictures to accompany the message. Again, pioneers provide an invaluable service by merely purchasing and giving local teachers such items as books or pictures. It has always been a puzzle to me why the local spiritual assemblies of North America and Europe do not adopt the national assemblies of the third world and contribute funds or supplies.

The summer passed quickly. Bob's nephew from Oregon visited. Kris was eighteen and had opted to complete high school credits in the United States with a trip to Ecuador and a promise to return home prepared to lecture and show films of his experiences of life in the Andes. Kris fell in love with the country, the people, the Faith and a girl, in that order. The girl he met was some years older and he courted her persistently. He did not understand that such courtship in Ecuador is serious and means a wedding is imminent. When he began to get this message from his girlfriend's parents, he decided it was time to return to the States.

Another guest arrived, my niece from Connecticut. Michelle was young, only eighteen. She had been reared in a protective and protected environment, so she experienced some very real culture shock initially. I was not conscious of how much she had been conditioned by the fear engendered in American cities until I noticed her nervously looking all around one night as we walked through Cuenca's dark, narrow streets. She confessed that she was afraid of being mugged and raped. These crimes were in those days virtually unknown in Ecuador.

Michelle became a Bahá'í during an overland trip with Bahá'í pioneers Ed Jones and Ralph Dexter. They persuaded her to accompany them to Bolivia for an International Bahá'í Conference. She set out with great trepidation for she knew the trip would be harsh. The trio had little money. They rode buses, camped out and ate native fare. When Michelle returned she was dirty, smelly and aglow. She had made her decision on the road. Later she and her husband pioneered to Indonesia.

School started once again. This time we were happy with the arrangement. The Catholic school in Cuenca proved to be an excellent choice. The nuns who taught and administered the school were from Spain. They ran a tight ship but were kind to the children, accommodating them whenever they could. Classes were entirely in Spanish. The children knew their adjustment to school was strictly a sink or swim proposition. How nervous they must have been but they had apparently decided they would give it their best try. They did not complain. Perhaps they were spurred on by the fact that at last they could escape their mother's home teaching. I believe the children were so successful because, in the purest sense, they believed in the assistance of Bahá'u'lláh. Soon their Spanish proficiency raced miles ahead of ours and they were reading in their textbook. Rob was elected president of his fifth grade class and scored high marks academically. Karen, in the sixth grade, took the third place prize the first semester and the second place in the following term. Their teachers expressed to Bob and me most favourable impressions of the children and attributed it to their family. We said nothing about the Concourse which we felt certain was with them every single day.

Valerie, our smallest child of five, entered first grade bravely. She did well, but was often ill with childhood maladies such as bronchitis and colds. One of these illnesses gave me quite a fright. She developed huge, grossly enlarged nymph nodes in her neck. It wasn't the mumps. She did not get better with my ministrations. I took her to a local doctor. He felt certain she had a form of tuberculosis and ordered blood tests at the local TB sanatorium. I was frantic. Hospitals in Ecuador bore no similarity to those in the States. I was a nurse so I have a very critical eye. Imagine my fear when we entered that sanatorium with my child, awaiting diagnosis.

The hospital was old, no, more than old, it was ancient, mediaeval. Once a monastery, the corridors were dark and ominous. The equipment was minimal. Patients peered at us over white cotton masks. Blood drawn, we escaped feeling certain we would be on the first plane out once we got results. We would go back to the States and the better facilities there.

The results finally came. They were negative. Val's symptoms subsided as mysteriously and quickly as they had appeared. We never learned what her illness was.

Val resumed school. School in Ecuador was very different from in the United States. Here children wore uniforms. This reduced the cost of clothing and eliminated jealousy. Classrooms were structured in grade levels with one teacher for each room. All skills were taught, including sewing for the girls and woodworking for the boys. The arts – drawing, painting and music – were part of the curriculum and of school festivals and pageants. Field trips, sometimes lasting for several days, were part of classroom work. Discipline was firmly maintained. Our oldest daughter, Karen, now a teacher for some years in Guatemala, observed recently that in Latin countries, children are allowed to 'act out' at home in early childhood, but once they enter school for formal education, they learn the sterner societal values and obedience to authority. In the States, she commented, children get little societal training, either at home or in the classroom.

Subjects were taught from a single textbook which contained all lessons for the grade level. Homework was a 'given' in all subjects. Valerie learned to write in script and to use maths-solving skills in first grade – addition, subtraction and multiplication. Religion classes were mandatory and a source of some bewilderment to our children and of amusement to ourselves. Val was frightened on Ash Wednesday when the priest put 'dirt' on her forehead. She understood the ritual was connected with the death of Jesus and thought the priest had marked her for death too. The nuns knew the children were Bahá'ís and there was mutual respect between them and the children.

By this time our bank account had nearly slipped into the red. Bob learned that a job as a co-pilot was available with SAN Airlines, a local carrier transport into the jungle areas. He applied and was promised the job if he could pass the civil aeronautics exam in Spanish. He laboured over the rules and regulations, went to Quito, took the exam and passed with an 80 percent mark. The job paid $200 a month. We could live on $450 a month, so the salary meant that we did not have to dip so heavily into our rapidly diminishing savings. However, we hadn't counted on the other costs of flying.

The airline fleet comprised three ancient DC-3s. Each morning when the weather was good the planes ferried people, gasoline drums, building materials, truck parts, cows, food and sundry other needs to the jungle settlements of Sucua and Macas. In those days, travel to the jungle towns was by mule pack or plane. There were no roads. Weather is extremely erratic in the Andes. Flying that route was hazardous. Navigating the DC-3s through the perilous mountain passes, normally obscured by clouds, was accomplished by dead reckoning using a compass and a stopwatch. No radio beacons or radar were available in that region. We never got accustomed to Bob's absences. He would leave in the mornings, flying out in clear weather, but by afternoon the jungle would be socked in, cancelling the return flight to Cuenca for that day. I was always aware that he might crash, a grim reality in that region.

One evening Bob came home highly nervous. They had had to 'May-day' he said. On the return flight, they were flying in the clouds near 14,000 feet altitude and according to their calculated position were just approaching the crest of the mountain range. One of the two engines failed and the overloaded plane started down towards the rocky ridges hidden by the clouds. Fortunately, they broke out of the cloud directly over and parallel to a river valley. While the pilot was desperately searching for a flat area close to the river, Bob was radioing the base to give them their approximate location and trying to determine the trouble with the engine. He found the problem and was able to restart the engine just before impact. The plane gained altitude again and wove its way out and above the mountain range. Despite Bob's long flying career and his term as a naval carrier pilot during the Korean war, this was perhaps his most harrowing flying experience. It was also my most harrowing experience, or almost.

In 1971 a dear lady whose name was Rosario asked for a job helping me at home. She was 26 years old and pregnant. She was the mother of two children and her husband was often out of work. She became my dearest friend. Rosario was 'mestizo', a blend of Indian and Spanish, as are many Ecuadorian people. She was literate and had gone to school through the elementary grades. This was unusual for the poor of Ecuador. In those years most had little schooling and the Indians had none. Schools were for the privileged. Rosario's dream was for her children. Perhaps they would be able to attend high school if she could afford the tuition. Public schools offered only an education up to the fourth grade at the time.

Rosario was wonderful with the children and kind and patient with me. My Spanish improved under her tutelage. But having a maid proved difficult for me in another way. I suspect this is true for all North American pioneers. I found myself cleaning before Rosario arrived. I spelled her with the ironing, helped her cook and in general did as much work as I always had, except for the afternoons when I could enjoy the luxury of writing in quiet.

The national teaching committee had asked me to develop Bahá'í children's class materials to be used for the Ecuadorian community at large. I wrote a series of stories illustrating the kingdoms of God and a play which was enacted by our local youth. I wrote radio scripts about campo teaching. These were my happiest moments in Ecuador. At last I was serving the Faith.

One morning while Rosario and I were sitting at the dining room table, I suddenly felt dizzy. My chair began to wobble. I looked at Rosario who was watching the curtains swaying over the windows. 'Terromoto!' she said. An earthquake. The room righted itself after a few seconds and Rosario regaled me with stories about other earthquakes. Little did I know that we were soon to experience a big one.

It happened at night when Bob and the children were at home. We awakened on a dancing bed. Window panes rattled and pictures dropped from the walls. Through the din we could hear an ominous rumble and children crying out. I jumped out of bed and lurched into the children's rooms. We escaped the house and ran for the cornfield at the back. Bob remained inside. Sleepy still, he watched from the living room window and could see power lines arc in a colourful explosion of light then fade into darkness. We could hear the cries of people in the city below and prayed the movement would stop. The quake lasted almost three minutes. The aftershocks continued for two days. There was a minimal loss of human life but property damage was extensive. The adobe walls around our property were down. Other than that, we were okay. I worried about our friend, Marina, and her son, Andres. They were living as

pioneers in Loja, at the epicentre of the quake. Word finally
came that they were fine.

Now it was spring. The household was busy and happy.
The children had made friends and often had visitors. My
family came for a visit. My mother was approaching 70,
and my brother was fascinated with Cuenca and life there.
But they were concerned about my health. I had been
feeling very tired and had lost some weight. I, in turn, had
my own worries about my mother's health. She was
beginning to look frail and she was planning to retire the
following year. She was a widow with no family at home.
We had a wonderful visit and it was hard to see them
return to the States. Another guest arrived, this time a
Bahá'í we had known in Alabama. His visit was brief. I had
not been a very energetic host. I just did not feel well. I
became nauseous even contemplating food. We put Marty
on the plane and I went to the doctor. 'You have hepatitis,
Señora,' he said, after I explained my symptoms. Blood
tests confirmed the diagnosis and I was sent home to bed
for a month. I don't remember much about those weeks. I
slept most of the time. Valerie later confessed she had
feared I was going to die. My colour was green. Rosario
went to the local herbalist and got remedies to brew in tea.
She fed me every two hours. Bob gave me injections of
vitamins. Slowly I began to recover. I had lost fifteen
pounds.

Soon we were facing another problem. The Ecuadorian
government had impounded and fined American tuna
boats inside their protected waters. The United States cut
all foreign aid in reprisal. Bob's job with SAN was in
jeopardy. We waited the situation out, hoping for some
reasonable solution. Meanwhile, Rosario invited us to the
confirmation of her oldest daughter, Gloria. We were
thrilled. Seldom does an Andean Indian invite foreigners to
her home for such an occasion.

The ceremony was lovely. Gloria looked the picture of purity and innocence in her white dress and veil. Rosario had prepared typical foods. The table was laden with native dishes. She must have been saving money for this occasion for a long time. In the middle of the table was a bottle of Four Roses. Rosario does not drink so I wondered what this was for. I hadn't long to find out. As each guest arrived, the bottle was produced with a shot glass and each was expected to drink. It was part of the ceremony. What were we to do? The Bahá'í writings prohibit the use of alcohol. We didn't want to offend. We drank. We did not realize that each time a new guest arrived our glass was to be refilled and we were expected to drink again. It wasn't long at that altitude, and after years of total abstinence from such beverages, that I was drunk. We were expected at home directly after the ceremony to meet with a member of the continental board of counsellors. And here I was, about to come face to face with a counsellor, giggling and sloppy. We were simply reeking! After the meeting, I explained the situation. The counsellor was kind. In such situations it is best to find out beforehand what the ceremony includes and in that way to avoid the occasion or to explain to the host.

News of Bob's employment situation came. It was bad. The airlines would no longer employ 'gringo' pilots. Our savings were gone. We had enough money for tickets home and to live for a couple of months if we stayed with my mother. This might tide us over until Bob found work in the States. I weighed the possibility of staying 'on faith' and then remembered my mother's situation at home. I was her only daughter. Our hearts were twisted. What should we do? The children were quiet. Years later they confided they had gone out to the cornfield and discussed chaining themselves to a tree so they wouldn't have to return.

We made a trip to Quito. Bob looked for work. Nothing.

We returned and prepared to leave. Hearts breaking, we opened our house to sell our furniture. We found homes for our two dogs. We purchased our tickets.

We left Cuenca in August, quietly. A few friends gathered at the airport. Rosario was there, clutching a newspaper-wrapped parcel. She presented it to me with tears and a hug. It was a beautiful handwoven cape, embroidered with exquisite coloured flowers. My last memento of Ecuador. We had found the spiritual sun in Ecuador. It is a bounty that lasts forever.

8

They Took to the Seas

Gina and Russell Garcia

Russell and Gina Garcia were everything most young people aspire to be. Russell was a successful Hollywood composer, arranger, conductor, at the peak of his career, and Gina was enjoying great popularity as a singer. They lived in a beautiful Hollywood Hills home, the site of frequent firesides, workshops and deepenings. Russ conducted the California Bahá'í Victory Chorus. They were gloriously happy and fulfilled. Well, almost. In November 1964, Russell got the idea of building a 41-foot sailing trimaran and sailing around the world, stopping at otherwise inaccessible places to teach the Bahá'í Faith. Gina has written the complete story in Adventures of Dawn-Breaker, *published by Naturegraph. She generously wrote a few pages for this book:*

When we first started out in our trimaran called *Dawn-Breaker* we thought we were going travel teaching for three years. That was in 1966. In the years since we've returned to Los Angeles, our last home community, only for brief visits.

To say that something happened to us during those first few years is an understatement. Whether it was meeting an expanded and wonderful Bahá'í family, or finding waiting souls, or learning how to measure everything we did with Bahá'í standards, or our pilgrimage to the World Centre at Haifa, or all of these combined, we certainly underwent some degree of transformation and changed our goals in life.

We seemed to stay longer than planned at all ports of call

and sailed to islands in the South Pacific that weren't part of our original itinerary. We were really hooked on sailing to unusual ports and making friends for the Faith wherever we stopped.

Once we received a cablegram from New Zealand: 'Phone immediately.' The cable was three months old. It had gone to Fiji, Samoa, back to Fiji and finally reached us in Tonga. It was the New Zealand Broadcasting Commission wanting Russ to work with New Zealand musicians on concerts and radio and television shows.

Several months before, we had met a few New Zealand musicians in Fiji who had spoken to Russ about this. Having lived so many years in Hollywood, we thought it was just the old 'we must do lunch' routine. We were surprised! The tour through New Zealand went very well, both musically and for the Bahá'í Faith.

When Russ was finished with his music tour, a friend suggested, 'Why don't you and Gina borrow my car and go up to the Bay of Islands? It's a yachter's paradise.' How right he was. We loved the area at first sight.

There sparkling in the warm winter sunshine were a myriad islands nestled on the blue, blue sea. Auckland is about 200 miles south of the Bay of Islands and has cooler weather. Here, down under, the further south one goes, the colder the weather.

To my surprise, Russ said, 'Why don't we find a real estate agent to show us around? Maybe we can find something for our future.' The agent showed us several properties but none captured our hearts. Then, standing on a hill, Russ looked across the bay and said, 'There! That's the kind of place we'd like,' and pointed to a little farm house down on the beach. There was an old jetty and a boat tied out on a mooring.

'Forget that!' said the agent. 'That's Bob Harnish's holiday house. He'd never sell.'

Soon it was our last evening in Auckland and we were with a dear friend, Beryl Van der Vaardt. When we told her that we had looked around the Bay of Islands but had not found anything, she said, 'My brother Bob has a beautiful place up there. He's going to put it on the market because he's just bought a business in the Cook Islands.' When she got him on the phone, we learned that he was Bob Harnish. Then Beryl told us that the house was in a goal area.

Russ immediately called the Aero Club of Auckland and chartered a little plane to fly us to Kerikeri. On his first pass over the strip the pilot scattered the cattle. When all was clear, he landed where only moments before the cattle had been feeding. Today Kerikeri has a tar-sealed runway.

The very surprised real estate agent met us and drove us the 19 miles over dirt roads to the homestead. It was an old kauri wood house on 13 acres of land, with four running streams, its own spring for drinking water, and a small secluded beach. We felt we were meant to have it. Although it took several months of telephone calls, cables and letters, we eventually paid a deposit and applied for residence visas. All this took about a year. One wonderful thing that resulted was that Ruth and Bob Harnish became Bahá'ís and went as pioneers to the Cook Islands.

We knew very few people in Kerikeri when we first came, but after an article appeared in the local paper about our sailing adventures and our immigration to New Zealand, it seemed everyone knew who we were. A Bahá'í family with four children lived but 50 miles away from us. Through the newspaper article we learned we were in the same community.

We knew from Shoghi Effendi's writings that we should make friends and then tell them about the Faith, so we got involved in community service activities. Russ started the

Kerikeri Singers, a group of 25 adults. We put on shows and raised money for hospitals, schools, women's refuge groups, homes for the aged. The group is still going strong after 18 years. Four of the singers became Bahá'ís. Russ and I speak at Rotary clubs, schools, convalescent homes, hospitals, homes for children with learning difficulties and disabled civilian groups. We have a little programme that we do with singing and sing-alongs.

As we meet people, we invite them to come to dinner or for coffee and cake. We find the larger the crowd, the more trivial the conversation, so we keep it small, limited to four guests. Our home has lots of Bahá'í books on the shelves, calligraphy of the Greatest Name, pictures of 'Abdu'l-Bahá and Shoghi Effendi on display. Often visitors will ask about the Faith. When they show sufficient true interest, we offer to lend them a book.

When about 30 people have shown interest, we hold a fireside for them. At our first-ever fireside in Kerikeri we prayed that at least a few people would come. Not only did they all come but one person phoned ahead to see if she could bring a friend. Russ and I gave a brief talk and there were excellent questions and a lively discussion.

During the tea break, I spoke to a gentleman we had met at the Rotary club. Both he and his wife had shown great interest in the Faith when they came to dinner. He said to us, 'This has been a stimulating evening. When are we going to have the next one?' Before I could answer, he suggested that the next one be at his house.

An interesting pattern began. At the next fireside, another couple asked to host one. It continued on like that, with firesides at the homes of numerous inquirers.

The Bay of Islands community grew and we held an election for our first local spiritual assembly. The assembly became incorporated, a believer donated a piece of land for a Bahá'í centre, and through extension teaching new areas have been opened. The community has sent out many travelling teachers and pioneers.

When I was a new Bahá'í often I prayed that one day Russ and I could go travel teaching. More than 35 years later we are still travelling. *Dawn-Breaker* is moored outside our door, though we mostly use her in New Zealand these days. Now we fly, drive and take trains and buses on our travels around the world. With Russell's musical work, we travel for five or six months of the year. Wherever we go, once the music programme is finished, we assist with firesides, deepenings and summer and winter schools. We help organize choirs, shows and conferences. We've had exciting and interesting journeys in eastern Europe and have found the receptivity to the Faith in both East Germany and Poland absolutely wonderful.

Every morning and evening we read from the Writings and say prayers. We never let a day go by without thanking God for the beautiful Faith. We also pray every day for firmness in the Covenant.

When we look back, we realize how important it was that we did not limit ourselves. I never dreamed as a new Bahá'í that I would go off around the world in a sailboat, yet I did. Neither of us were sailors. I couldn't even swim and had to take swimming lessons. We both had to learn to navigate. We set the goal, then took the steps, one by one, to fulfil it. As the Writings say, when you arise to serve, something mystical and wonderful happens. You become transformed. You achieve things you never dreamed of. There are as many ways to serve this wondrous Cause as there are Bahá'ís and God will use each of us as His instruments when we make our services available to Him.

9

Mama Came with Me to Martinique

Ludi Stritt

Ludi Stritt's health and vitality belie her 69 years. She has pioneered in Martinique for the last 13 years and enjoys swimming, windsurfing, catamarans and sailing. She loves the tropical fruits which are in such abundance: mangoes, papayas, fresh pineapples, lychees from France and an array of vegetables with strange-sounding names such as christophine, dasheen, breadfruit. A papaya tree grows on her terrace and the sound of the ocean is always near. Sounds like a paradise, right? But let Ludi tell her story:

In 1966 I went from Urbana, Illinois to Gainesville, Florida as a homefront pioneer, accompanied by my four children. I taught library science at the University of Florida. I was determined to become an international pioneer as soon as an opportunity presented itself.

There were only two other Bahá'ís in Gainesville when we arrived. We found a house in a black neighbourhood and the children went to black schools. Karla and Kent were the only white children ever to attend A. Quim Jones Elementary School. Michelle and later Kent went to Lincoln High School, where, again, they were the only white pupils. Everyone knew us and I think many thought of us as 'that crazy white family that lives on Northwest 7th Avenue', yet we felt their opinion of us was predominantly positive. The woman who gave us Welcome Wagon gifts as newcomers to the community could not believe we had deliberately chosen to live in the area. We stayed for seven years.

We had many wonderful, and some scary, experiences. The house was always full of young people. I bought oranges by the bushel and everyone was welcome to eat as many as they wished. I think we were popular partly because we were such a novelty. On one or two occasions runaway teenagers even tried to stay with us.

We had enough youth, had they been of age, to form a local spiritual assembly long before we had a sufficient number of adults. Our Bahá'í youth singing group sang at conferences all over the South and at the Bahá'í centre in Wilmette several times.

We transported the youth in our green van, known as 'the jolly green watermelon'. Once we were stopped by members of the Ku Klux Klan, which was frightening. On another occasion, while returning from Miami with eight youths asleep inside, the van skidded on an oil slick, rolled over and slid on its roof for several yards. Everyone walked away unscathed and the van escaped with only minimal damage. We travelled thousands of miles without major problems and even went to conferences in Jamaica and Panama, though occasionally we had trouble finding a restaurant that would serve mixed groups. My university colleagues could not understand me, but we were respected.

When the assemblies of Gainesville City, Alachia County and several outlying towns were firmly established, I heard of a need in Greenville, North Carolina. I applied for a library science job at East Carolina University. We were homefront pioneers in Greenville for five years and established local spiritual assemblies in several communities.

I itched to go pioneering to a foreign goal, so when my youngest daughter graduated from high school, I attended a pioneer training institute in Wilmette. In 1978 I was ready to fill a foreign post. My mother, nearly 80 years old, lived with me and I intended to take her with me. I had studied Swahili at the University of Florida and hoped to go to Africa. My second choice was Haiti. However, the pioneering committee recommended that I not take mother to these countries because of her precarious health.

My mother and I were ready to go and were waiting for an assignment when Mary Lou Suhm phoned and asked if I would be willing to fill a Canadian goal in the French Antilles. I said yes immediately and we were off. We flew first to Haiti where we spent one day and one night and visited the Bahá'ís. Next stop was Guadeloupe at 11 o'clock at night.

There was no one at the airport to meet us – the telegram sent to notify the Bahá'ís of our arrival had not been received. The French I had learned 40 years earlier in high school was inadequate. A taxi driver at the airport, however, had heard of the Bahá'í Faith and he took us to his home for the night. The next morning his wife gave us breakfast while he went to the Bahá'í centre and brought back Cameron Dodds, a Canadian pioneer. As it happened, the Local Spiritual Assembly of Guadeloupe, Martinique and St Martin was meeting at that precise time and decided to send us to Martinique.

We stayed for two weeks at the Bahá'í centre in Fort-de-France, Martinique and then found temporary housing for one month with a Bahá'í woman. My mother was a valiant trooper. She seemed to be content wherever we were and never complained. You can imagine our early days in Martinique with Mama never speaking a word to anyone and me struggling to communicate with the neighbours.

Whenever I was away, Mama had no idea where I might

be. Usually I was scouting for an apartment and for students to whom to teach English. We had virtually no resources, only Mama's social security cheque and the little bit that was left from selling the house after settling the children in schools back in the States.

Thanks to the American consulate, we found an apartment in a commune several miles from the capital. It was owned by an American and his Martinique wife. We lived in the basement where the servants and animals wandered in and out at will.

Mama was fascinated with the activity, and as I was out a lot, she looked forward to my return so she could give her report of the day. She'd say, 'There are two eggs that two hens laid, one over there and the other there,' pointing, or 'They killed the huge pig that came into my bedroom last night.' Once at 4 a.m. we were awakened by strange sounds and flashing lights outside, and we were frightened. Later in the morning we found it was just a man hunting for land crabs who had permission to be out there in our front yard.

The landlord's family celebrated Christmas by cutting just one branch from their evergreen tree and decorating it. The children received one or two small gifts. It was nothing like the Christmases of some American families who habitually go into debt in order to provide an array of gifts.

Mama and I watched from the double bed when the water came up nearly to mattress level during Hurricane Alain and again the next year during Hurricane David.

My happiest experience in Martinique was when my mother became a Bahá'í. Angela Szepeau, a Canadian pioneer, said to her one day, 'Mama, how come you haven't yet become a Bahá'í?'

'What good would I be as a Bahá'í with my health? I couldn't do what all of you do.'

'Do you believe in Bahá'u'lláh?'

'Of course I do!'

'Then you are a Bahá'í. Why don't you sign a card and surprise your daughter?'

Mama did and I was ecstatic.

Mama was anorexic most of her life. She became so thin that I feared for her and took her back to the States. My sisters put her in a nursing home and two weeks later she died of a flu too strong for her 70-pound frame.

Martinique is an overseas department of France. It is wealthy and there is no poverty among the people. It is very different from the pioneer post I had dreamed of, in Africa, for instance. In Africa, I believed, there were 'waiting souls' ripe to be told about the Faith. Here, while people are kind and friendly and totally accepting of others having a religion, the feeling is that they, as individuals, do not need it. They are Catholics for christenings and funerals but few go to church regularly.

After living here for 13 years, I have many friends but the teaching is very slow. There is no visible sign of the 'entry by troops' reported elsewhere in the world. There is only one pioneer who has been here longer than I. Many beautiful pioneers have become discouraged and returned to the United States or Canada. More Canadians come to pioneer than do Americans because of their advantage in having the French language, yet few stay. Here, Bahá'ís enjoy a good relationship with the Prefecture and little problems with visas are soon taken care of. There is freedom to teach but firesides and conferences are poorly attended.

The first few years a 'Bahá'í car' was available but it succumbed to old age. Many distinguished travel teachers have visited over the years, including Hands of the Cause Dr Muhajir and Rúḥíyyih Khánum. There are about 250 Bahá'ís altogether but the active believers are few.

Here we wear many hats. I, for instance, am adjunct secretary of the national spiritual assembly, secretary of the national youth committee, assistant to the auxiliary board for protection, secretary of the local spiritual assembly. It is always a case of too few people having too much to do.

I long for the opportunity to speak to people who really want to hear that the whole world is but one country, who want to hear about unity in diversity. I do feel I am needed here, and as the Guardian requested that pioneers remain at their posts, I expect I will do that. But the pioneering experience has not been at all as I had expected. The basic thing for all pioneers anywhere, I believe, is to be flexible and accepting of whatever the situation is. But it is difficult when there is so little receptivity. The people here seem very passive and content. Most are very well paid in their employment. The 'functionaires' (civil servants) get a 40 percent cost of living adjustment because it is considered a hardship post. Still they strike. The dock workers hire Haitians, Dominicans and illegal immigrants to do their work for a pittance while they go to the beach. Yet they strike. There are frequent strikes of taxi-drivers, utility workers, etc. The cars seen here are mostly Mercedes or BMWs. Most families have two automobiles. There is racism among different strata of the native black populations and among the descendants of the former slave owners, who are called Behes. It is they who own much of the land and most successful businesses.

I feel fortunate that I can visit the United States each summer to see my four children, nine grandchildren and two-great grandchildren and to renew friendships with an extended Bahá'í family. Here I teach English as a second language but my students are rarely motivated to continue for long. They get discouraged when they don't become fluent in six weeks, with their two-hours-per-week classes!

My income is most unpredictable. As I have an apartment very near the beach, I sub-rent my bedroom and live on the terrace much of the time. This is how I afford the rental. The climate is marvellous. As I am a vegetarian, I spend little on food, yet eat very well. I take aerobics, gymnastics and yoga classes and work out on machines four times a week. I am healthy and would say I have a very good life. I carry my prayer book everywhere, wear my Bahá'í ring and necklace, and am frequently asked questions which enable me to talk about the Faith nearly every day. Rarely, though, are people here really ready seriously to discuss religion or to study. Many French here say religion is just a crutch and they don't need it. Of course there are wonderful exceptions. I pray every day to recognize opportunities.

I believe there are too few pioneers here. Assemblies are 'paper' because there are no 'self-starters'. At times things seem to stagnate. Yet I know that when Bahá'u'lláh wills, the way will be made ready and there will be entry by troops. I intend to take part in it!

10

Lettuce Seeds for Belize

Violet Clark

Violet Clark of Highland Park, Michigan, drove a station wagon pulling a house trailer the 3,600 miles from Michigan to Belize:

One of the reasons I chose to pioneer in Belize was because Belize is in partnership with Michigan, my home state. Just how are these two places connected? Through the Partners of the Americas, a private, non-profit organization which links the citizens of each of the American states with a sister in Latin America or the Caribbean. For example, Alabama is linked with Guatemala, Arizona with Mexico, California with Mexico City, Kansas with Paraguay, and so on. The goal of the partnership is to mobilize resources at the community level for technical and cultural projects which are based on the principles of self-help and benefit to both parties.

I was interested in the Michigan State University programme, Bootstrap International. They needed someone to transport fifteen boxes of seeds to Belize – enough to grow food to feed a village for an entire year. Since I was retired and wanted to pioneer, I offered my services to the Partners programme and to the Bahá'í pioneering committee.

Things worked out well and fairly quickly. I bought a Chevrolet station wagon and a house trailer from a younger brother who became my companion as we travelled the

3,600 miles from Michigan to Belize. One of the members of the pioneering committee took me to an auto supply store and we bought all of the auto parts we could think of, just in case these would not be available in Belize. In time, every spare part was used, especially tyres! During the rainy season, the main paved road in Belize becomes a rock-strewn battlefield which splits even the steel bands of steel-belted tyres. You can see the bright golden bands of steel sticking out through the sides of your flat tyre as you are mired in the mud in the middle of the road. Copper tyres became the answer.

The trip down through the United States was fine. It was when we came to the border at Brownsville, Texas, that we ran into trouble. Immigration refused to allow us to take the seeds through Mexico. The inspector said we would have to go to Mexico City to get permission from the Health Department to take the seeds through to Belize. Mexico City is some 8,000 feet above sea level and I was not about to drive the wagon and trailer up there, wherever it was, to ask someone for permission to take those fifteen boxes of seeds across Mexico when they were destined for Belize.

The inspector said we could leave the seeds with him and pick them up after we came back from Mexico City with the necessary papers. This did not set well with us. So we sat in the parking lot over the weekend trying to figure out what to do. I wandered around the office building and came to a door which was labelled 'Salud' something.

On Monday morning we went to see the inspector again and asked if that department was not the same as the one he had asked us to contact in Mexico City. Reluctantly he admitted that it was. We asked whether this local department could give us the necessary papers to take the seeds through Mexico. The official hesitated.

At this point I produced the map provided by the

Partners of the Americas and showed him that Mexico City was in partnership with California, and Mexico with Arizona, New Mexico and Texas. I also showed him that Michigan was in partnership with Belize. He still hesitated. There was no way I could know what he was thinking. So then I went a little far and told him that if he held us up and would not allow us to take the seeds through Mexico, I would have to inform the State Department of the United States that Mexico would not cooperate with the Partnership.

Quickly he agreed to issue the required papers and asked if he might have some of the seeds for his own experimental planting, just to see how they would grow.

By this time we all understood one another and everyone was smiling. We gave him the seeds and received the permits. My brother and I were soon happily on our way to Belize with the station wagon, the trailer and the seeds.

In Belize, my brother, who is not a Bahá'í, boarded the plane back to his home in Roscommon, Michigan. I shall always be grateful to him.

It was now my job to contact the National Assembly of Belize and the Partners of the Alliance of Belize. Everyone knew I was coming but no one seemed to know just when.

I went to the main hotel in Belize City and asked the porter where I could find the Bahá'ís. He answered, 'Oh, they are all over the place.' This was not exactly true, but it boded well for the future.

Travel in Belize in those days was from the main road which runs north and south through the country and then down a secondary road to the villages which are inland along the river. The only way to travel from one village to another was by boat along the river or by coming back to the main road and then from the main road to the river.

Each Sunday a group of Bahá'ís would travel to some remote village and meet with the people. I remember one

Sunday when Dr Hedayatoullah Ahmadiyeh was with us. He was a veteran traveller-pioneer, a popular teacher of the Faith and chairman of the national spiritual assembly for many years. He received a warm reception from the villagers, spoke with them about Bahá'u'lláh and the new revelation, and 32 people declared their wish to become Bahá'ís. One young lady frankly asked, 'Now that I have become a Bahá'í, what are you going to give me?'

On our way back to Belize City, we realized we had to offer more than words to the people who wanted to become Bahá'ís. Out of this discussion, we developed the teaching book. I still have a copy. It is a compilation of pamphlets explaining progressive revelation and the Bahá'í principles, with pictures of Bahá'ís around the world and some of the Bahá'í Houses of Worship. Later, the teaching book was published in a glossy edition entitled *The Bahá'í Faith* and is used all over the world.

I lived in Boom. The story goes that the village was named this because it was one of the places where the British cut down the mahogany trees. When they fell there was a great BOOM!

I wasn't able to adjust to the weather in Belize. Sun in the sky. Temperature a constant 70 degrees. Warm ocean breezes. Perfect weather, day after day. You might imagine this to be ideal. But three months of perfect weather can get on your nerves. One day I emerged from my trailer to greet yet another perfect day and heard myself exclaim, 'Doesn't the weather *ever* change?' I was to rue my comment. After three months of perfect weather come three months of continuous rain. You live in boots and walk in watery, slushy mud. Driving becomes even more hazardous. The car slips and slides and often gets mired in the mud.

I did learn there is a right time to plant. The time came when we had to go to the land and plant the seeds. Eddie Hulse prepared the ground and Bertha Hulse and I planted. When it came time to cultivate the rows of lettuce, which grew beautifully, I used a hoe and went along the rows, quickly taking out the weeds. Bertha told me that the right way to cultivate was to pull the weeds out by hand. I suggested that we each cultivate certain rows in our own particular way and watch to see how the lettuce grew. The day came to harvest. There was no apparent difference in the size or shape of the various rows. We harvested our lettuce and took it to the market in Belize City.

We went to the farmer's market, spread our crops on the ground and sold them. I think we made about $7.50 that day. It was worth about $3.75 in American money. Money exchanges between countries create problems. A universal coinage, one standard for all countries would stop the game of buying money of one country and exchanging it for the money of another for a gain, a practice that means someone, somewhere has to be the loser.

I hated to leave Belize and my new family of friends there but felt I had to when I learned that my sister was dying. I was heartbroken when Bertha Hulse suffered a heart attack and I was unable to get back to Belize in time to attend her funeral.

I did return to Belize on a travel teaching trip in 1980. I went to Bertha's grave with members of her family. We said the Bahá'í prayers for the departed and my soul was relieved.

Recently I met a Belizean who works for the county. It is such a pleasure to get the latest news from Belize from him, to learn how the country is growing, to know that the world community becomes ever more united.

11

The Banana Dancers

Edmond Wilke

Edmond Wilke writes from Columbia:

It started out as a trip to Brazil to help build a rural school. My carpentry skills were needed for one to three months. Pioneering just happened after that.

I had left my job as a therapist in a counselling centre and had turned down a teaching contract for the next semester at the community college in order to move out of state. Then suddenly nothing was going to plan. Everything I'd lined up fell through. I had to fall back on my carpentry skills to get by until I could find something else.

One day while flipping through a two-month-old *American Bahá'í*, a classified ad jumped out at me: 'Carpenter wanted for 1 to 3 months for school project in Amazonas, Brazil.' Well, that sounded perfect. Why not be a carpenter in Brazil and have an adventure? I dialled the phone number in the ad and was surprised to be talking to an old friend in California who had recently visited Brazil. She screamed, 'Great! You're perfect! Go! You're just what they need.'

Well, one thing led to the next and in a few months I was leaving for Brazil, having arranged all of my affairs so as to allow me to be away for at least two years. Wow! I'd just been swept off pioneering! The idea of pioneering was not new to me. I'd contacted the office of pioneering about two years earlier. Now, almost overnight it seemed, I was going. My house was rented and I could live on the income. Nothing else was keeping me. The time had come to pioneer.

I arrived in Brazil on November 19, 1987 with two suitcases and a bent for adventure. I'd had a vague idea of what it would be like from *National Geographic* magazines and from the Portuguese language tape I'd been listening to in my car. I had learned to say things such as 'Is room service available?' and 'Do you have a fixed price menu?'

I spent two months helping with the construction of the rural school in Iranduba which is part of a Bahá'í development project. Then I was off travelling for a month-and-a-half as the only non-Brazilian member of a teaching team. Because my communication skills in Portuguese were so poor, I really felt out in left field. For me to be useful to this teaching project the hosts of divine inspiration had to descend.

Every day I went to the plaza in the centre of town where people stopped to rest under shady trees. I gave everyone a pamphlet, saying that it contained a beautiful message and that they should call me if they had any questions. I'd practised these sentences beforehand with friends. Then I sat and watched the various people reading the pamphlets. People did call me! I showed them a teaching album and asked them to read aloud. While they learned about the Faith, I learned Portuguese. On several occasions, others stopped to listen to what was being read so the people I was teaching were teaching others too. The hosts of divine inspiration had indeed descended!

After only a few months I was off on other teaching trips, talking about Bahá'u'lláh to groups of 30 or more people in schools, plazas and in the streets. Talk about confirmations! After being in South America for almost a year the National Spiritual Assembly of Brazil and the continental counsellor asked me to go to Leticia, Columbia, to build an institute on land that Hand of the Cause Rúḥíyyih Khánum had bought during her Green Light Expedition. What a privilege!

I got on a boat headed up river with plans for Instituto Rabbani and all the building materials bought in Manaus; eight days later I got off at the border of Columbia. It took a full nine months to build the institute. During that time I learned Spanish well enough to stay on in Leticia and work with the friends using the new institute to teach and deepen the folks in the frontier communities of Brazil, Columbia and Peru.

A random sampling from my journal, while only fragmentary, gives some indication of what I saw, heard and felt:

As I ride my bicycle to and from work, a young boy calls out, 'Good morning, mister,' in English. I respond, 'Good morning. How are you?' He soon knows how to say 'Good afternoon', 'Good evening', 'How are you?' and 'Fine' as well as ask 'What is your name?' Now two other boys are calling out greetings in English. Sometimes I hear an adult calling, 'Mister, good morning.' I am the object of much curiosity here.

On December 8 in Leticia, there was a luminaria. Each house had lighted candles in front of the door. I took a picture of one house and of the girl who lived there along with her two playmates. Every day until I developed the pictures they asked me for the picture. I finally gave it to them. That day, when I was eating supper, a young boy came in (the front of my house is a store) and asked me for his picture! I had to explain to him that in order to get a picture, I had first to take one with my camera. He was satisfied with the explanation.

The young people like to play soccer and volleyball when it's raining. They get covered with mud.

The thieves are like persistent mosquitoes.

Our neighbours cook over a fire on the floor of their kitchen. I often wake up to the smell of burning paper.

Tabatinga, Brazil

The bank has one window and a door, three walls are solid. There are four floor fans but often the electricity in the town is off. There are only two tellers. Everyone must use the bank to pay water bills, electric bills, taxes for the town, loans, etc. The lines are always long and transactions take a long time. Tellers have to search for documents and lists. Counting money takes a long time. The paper money isn't worth much. People come to the bank with their money in bags or wrapped in paper.

Today I was the sixth person in line at 9 a.m. and got to the teller at 9:35. The electricity was off. There were still eighteen people in line. Because two months' money was sent to me at once, I put half of it in a savings account. To gain interest it had to remain in the bank for 30 days. After 30 days my money earned 22 percent interest. Inflation last month was 40 percent, so I lost 18 percent by saving!

Taxes were collected in Tabatinga in October, about 5,000 cruzados for each house. Elections for the mayor were held on December 15. A new mayor was elected and he took office on January 1 only to find that the previous mayor had left a thousand cruzados (one dollar in American money) in the accounts and had run away to Peru with the rest. The new mayor is collecting taxes again. They are due February 15. This time they want 30,000 cruzados for each house. A friend told me that if you don't pay, they board up your house.

In some areas, they effectively control mosquitoes by spraying a fine oil on standing water. This kills the larvae. In Tabatinga, the prefictura (mayor's office) employed this method of mosquito control. Town workers are walking around and throwing cans of oil in every puddle, even in mud puddles in the road. Now the roads are greasy mud. My friend Asaner says that now Tabatinga is well lubricated!

Leticia

Rats enter the house from the area outside my room. They go under my door and up the wall to a space in the wooden ceiling. There was a block of wood on the door-jam nailed through the middle which could be used to lock the door from inside. The rats, running up the wall, turned the block and locked me out of my room!

It's not uncommon to see people, mostly men, outside in front of their houses, wearing towels. They like to lounge in these towels for hours.

Leticia is not as muddy as Tabatinga; it has more paved roads. The women dress more elegantly. It still seems funny to me to see an elegantly dressed woman carrying a chicken by its wings as part of her morning purchases.

A joke in Leticia is to call Tabatinga 'Lamatinga'. 'Lama' means mud in Portuguese. Another mud joke is 'Onde nao esta lama, esta barro' – Where there is no lama there is barro (mud in Spanish).

People don't talk about the weather much. They talk about the mud.

My friend Artidaro warned me that when it rains very hard

we have to be especially watchful of thieves. The houses here have corrugated metal roofs and heavy rain on them is very noisy. The thieves know this is a good time to break in.

When I first came here I rented a room in a house near the centre of town. The windows of the neighbouring house looked into our dining area and a few of the windows in our house looked into the kitchen of the next house. It's still possible in Leticia to find a small lot between houses and build your house by putting up a front wall, a back wall and a roof.

I ride my bicycle up the road only a short distance and I'm in Brazil, another language, another country, another culture. Peru is across the river.

A handful of local youths and four adults went visiting homes in small teams as part of a teaching campaign. In a week we had 135 new believers in Leticia. The next week they went to Tabatinga, Brazil, where 85 people declared.

An old woman I met at the junta communal meeting stopped by the construction site today. She told me that she'd had a message to go to battalion headquarters to see the colonel. He had told her that her grandson had been killed by guerrillas while he was serving in the military. She had to go home to tell the boy's mother who was sick in bed. While she was here, a Bahá'í woman came by. We read some prayers together and talked for a while; then the old woman went home to take care of her daughter. (Dona Maria became a Bahá'í and is now an active member of the community, introducing the Faith to her friends and relatives. She is always bringing people to the institute to learn about the Faith.)

Uses for Safety Pins:
Pin clothes to dry
Hang mosquito net

Pin pictures to the wall
Mend clothing
Mend strap on knapsack
Pin sheet to mattress
Mend mosquito net
Remove slivers
Fix earpiece on glasses
Fasten papers together
Hang wristwatch inside mosquito net
Pair socks
Mark clothing for laundry
Hang flashlight inside mosquito net
Use as key ring
Pin key inside pocket
Hem cuff on trousers
Rethread string in swim suit
Open tubes of ointment
Clean brushes
Pin pillow to hammock

Our sand was delivered out on the road. It was too muddy for the truck to enter the construction site. While one worker was filling a wheelbarrow and hauling the sand to the construction, the shovel was stolen.

There is a back way between the two cities. It's a foot path that goes up a steep hill. Many people use it when the police are checking documents on the main road. It's also a shortcut for many. There is a footbridge on this path that for three metres crosses above open sewage about one-and-a-half metres below. It is constructed and maintained by the people themselves. It had been 18 inches wide until a thief took many of the boards. Now it's only six inches wide.

Yesterday was Claudio's birthday. He guards the construc-tion site until midnight seven days a week. We planned to get together for a little 'festa' to celebrate and he said he would bring the Nescal and 'balaskas' (crackers). Two days ago he said we would not have Nescal. He'd run out of money. I inquired to find out what Nescal is, thinking it must be something rare and special. It's hot chocolate mix. Well, we had the Nescal last night and Claudio had the rest of the tin to take home with him.

I was riding my bicycle in town today when a group of young boys (8 to 13) stopped me, asking if I am a Bahá'í. They wanted to know where our church was. I explained that we have no church but they were welcome to visit the institute. One boy said he had heard about the Faith when we were visiting his neighbourhood on a teaching campaign and he had told these others about it.

When we visit houses to teach the Faith, often neighbours or passersby come to the doors and windows to listen. Often the listeners outside the house become Bahá'ís before those we came to visit.

I started studying Tae Kwon Do in Leticia. It is good exercise and it really helped me integrate into the community. There's something about physical contact with people that helps to bring down a lot of barriers right away. I see other members of my class around town all the time. Often they ask me to stop and have coffee or coke with them and their friends.

As I go through the streets or down to the market, there are always children who call, 'Buenas dias, Bahá'í.' These are often the children who attend classes at the institute.

The woman living in the Bahá'í centre in Leticia is very poor. She has eight kids. Only two are hers. The others belong to sisters or cousins who for one reason or another can't take care of them. They cook on a fire outside the back door. There is a gas stove but the gas tank was stolen while they were taking a nap. The cooking fire is always going. When it rains they cover it with tin. They have a good supply of scrap wood from the building project. Dona Cedalia is especially glad when we have wood shavings for her.

I made a pair of stilts for a little boy who lives in the Bahá'í centre. He was very happy to receive such a gift. In the evening we all played with them. Many neighbourhood children and their older brothers and sisters were interested. The next day, the other children living at the centre played with the stilts. They were something new, fun, different. The little boy I gave them to sold them to a neighbourhood boy for 20 pesos, about 5½ cents.

Impressions sure do change. When I first arrived in Brazil, I thought Manaus was a dirty hole in the jungle. Two-and-a-half years later my visit there felt like really 'going to town'! Before, it seemed to me to be very difficult to find what I needed there. Stores are very specialized. You buy screws in the screw store, tools in a tool store. There are lots of house-front stores which sell a smattering of specific items.

Now, on my visit from Leticia, Manaus seems like a shopper's Mecca. My shopping list included a radio with short wave bands and a tape player, bicycle parts, blender parts and band-aids. The band-aids available in Leticia are made from masking tape. Finding shoes in my size is another matter altogether.

Usually I cook my own breakfast – coffee and oatmeal with banana and nuts – but Dona Ena, a local Bahá'í, cooks lunch and dinner for me at her house. She likes to give me extra portions to 'engordar' me (fatten me up).

There's no granola in the Amazon. From time to time friends visiting from Cali, a city in the south of Colombia, remember us with gifts of granola when they come to visit. But we don't get visitors often.

On a trip through Bogota I found a health food store and bought eight kilos of granola. What a treat! We ate it by the bowlful. Then, as the supply began to diminish, by the cupful, then by the spoonful, then a little in the palm of the hand. Finally, we were down to one plastic bag.

It was time to break open that last bag when we discovered something terrible. There had been a tiny hole in the bag and a colony of ants had discovered how delicious granola is. Our last bag of granola was full of ants.

We could not give up such precious fare to the ants. How could we get the ants to give up the granola? All the ideas we had about separating the intruders from their feast would ruin the granola, except one. Fry it. We did.

Later we told a friend about this solution. He told us that when people first come to the Amazon, if they find a bug in their food they throw the food away. As time goes on, they become more accustomed to the environment and simply remove the bug and go on eating. But when they've stayed too long, they leave the bugs in the food and eat it all.

My friend sends me books in English. Books in any language are scarce but books in English are a treasure. They find their way to us through the grapevine. Various Bahá'í travellers carry them to the next probable traveller and so on until they reach their destination. The books are a lot like the granola. When there are many, you gobble them up. As the supply dwindles, you have to be satisfied with smaller and smaller portions at a time to make them last.

People call me various names here. Some call me 'gringo', some 'mono' for my fair colouring; others call me 'Edmondo,' but lots call me 'Bahá'í'. This means I always have to keep on my toes to behave as 'Abdu'l-Bahá would have. Sometimes this is a real test, especially when dealing with bureaucratic red tape. I remind myself daily that 'Abdu'l-Bahá said that if we can't reflect a certain spiritual quality, we should assume it.

One evening before a friend was to travel we had a little festa. 'Festa' means 'party' in Portuguese. Most festas include eating something and visiting. Just to be silly, I drew a woman's face on one banana and a man's face on another and made them dance together to music from the radio. It was such a hit that we have banana-dancers at every festa. When we plan to get together, someone always says, 'I'll bring the banana dancers.' Other things that dance are pens, cups, spoons and flashlights. When flashlights dance the samba, the bulbs break!

I'm taking guitar lessons in Leticia. During a class the instructor asked me about my trip to Benjamin Constant, a town one-and-a-half hours down the river. I told him that it was fine but there was no river bus-boat. We had to return on the 'despertador'. He looked as if he did not understand so I asked one of the students who spoke Portuguese what despertador is in Spanish. She said, 'It's the same,' and began to laugh. I meant to say 'dislizador' (small boat) but instead I had said 'alarm clock'.

The neighbours kept a pregnant pig in their kitchen all night because it was raining. Their kitchen shares the outside wall of my bedroom. The pig didn't sleep at all well.

One day there was a lot of commotion on the road, more accurately, the foot path, in front of the institute. Any activity brings all the neighbours out and one has only to look in the direction they are all looking to immediately become part of the scene.

This day a house had been robbed at lunch time. A woman and her two young boys were robbed of their lunch, the pot it was in, some spoons and a can of powdered milk. The milk was a special treat that the mother had felt especially good about being able to provide.

As is often the case, the thief was a drug addict who would eat the lunch, then sell the pot, spoons and milk for the equivalent of 20 cents in order to buy drugs.

The police were following a trail down the middle of the road, helped by neighbours pointing in the direction of the thief's escape, which led them eventually to a swampy area. The chase ended there.

The children whose lunch was robbed came to watch the goings-on with us from the verandah of the institute, eagerly supplying us with details of the incident. It was the older of the boys, Eduardo, who was eight, who had discovered the robbery in progress and had run for the police.

The next morning Eduardo arrived early for the children's class. He asked if we could do the play about 'Tres Pescados', which is part of a Bahá'í children's song that teaches that we should not rob and should always tell the truth. To prepare for this presentation, we made the required three paper fish and numbered them. The class began with prayers the children had memorized. Since the play has only two roles, it had to be performed several times to include all the thespians. Then Eduardo related the event of the robbery and how he felt about it. Although he could do nothing about the robbery that had occurred he knew that teaching the Bahá'í Faith was one way he could help to make a difference in the future.

Señor Lauro lives near the riverbank. His house, like his neighbours', stands on tall stilts about eight feet off the ground. For several weeks every year during the flood season, the road disappears into the river and the way to these houses is by way of a series of 10-inch wide planks which sit on a series of posts. Whenever I go to visit him, I meet someone else on the plank path coming from the opposite direction.

One day I went to advise Señor Lauro about an assembly meeting. Since he's hard of hearing and on this particular day my shouting efforts failed, I wrote a note and handed it to him. He looked at it and said, 'Good idea. I can read Portuguese.' I wrote, 'But I wrote this in Spanish.' He said, 'Sure you did, but you spelled all the words in Portuguese!'

The buses in Manaus are never full. If you can get on, you can ride. One day I was trying to get across town to a children's class I teach with a friend. I'd been waiting for the bus for nearly an hour when it finally came. When it stopped everyone else seemed to be better at finding a place on it than I. You have to be very aggressive getting on buses in Manaus. I got on, but just barely. I stood on the step to the back door. This isn't uncommon in Manaus at all, but this time a policeman stopped the bus and told me that I could not ride that way. I told him that there was no room inside but that I would get in after a few people got off. He insisted that I get on or off. I asked the people inside to make room. I knew that it was impossible, but I asked anyway. They did! I don't know how – I think they all held their breath. I got in far enough to get the door closed. When we got to the next stop, they all had to hold their breath again to let the door open.

Segagelio is 15 years old. He's never been to school but his mother taught him to read. One day he came by the institute proudly wearing a watch he'd bought from the neighbour across the road. After I admired it sufficiently he confided that he didn't know how to tell time and asked me to teach him. It took a few hours before he finally caught on. For the next two days Segagelio told everyone what time it was, including the rightful owner of the watch!

Apparently, the watch had been stolen and the neighbour had bought it unwittingly and sold it to Segagelio. Well, Segagelio got his money back but he got a lot more from the transaction. He learned to tell time.

I wanted to replace my worn hiking shorts so I bought some fabric to take to the seamstress. She only needs to see the old shorts to copy them exactly. Friends were interested in the fabric I'd bought and in what I was going to have made from it.

New clothes are a big deal here; people just don't get them that often. There's a verb in Spanish which means to wear something for the first time: 'estrenar'. Friends asked me to be sure to visit them when I 'estrenar' my new shorts.

The first day I wore my shorts many people asked, 'Estrenando?' (Are you wearing them for the first time?) When I answered affirmatively they said, 'Felicitaciones!' (Congratulations) If I had not stopped to see the friends who invited me to visit when I was 'estrenando', they would have been offended.

12

Love Song

Suzanne Schuurman

It was noon at the University of Saskatchewan. Students rushed to the cafeteria or sought an empty classroom to eat their sandwiches and study for a test. I was rushing too, glancing with satisfaction at the hand-printed posters advertising a Bahá'í talk this noon hour.

Our guest speaker was standing in the hall smiling and talking to another member of our small community who had taken time off from work to meet her at the bus terminal. I had arranged for a medium-sized lecture room. As we went in I was gratified to see several students in the middle row munching sandwiches, but where were all the kids I had especially invited? After waiting a bit, the speaker was introduced and launched into her talk on the Bahá'í Faith.

Halfway through, the students finished their sandwiches and walked out. Waves of mortification swept over me. What had gone wrong? I'd put an article in the student newspaper where I worked. I had made dozens of posters and hung them all over the campus. All my friends knew about it. Was no one interested in world peace? What had gone wrong?

The speaker, a Bahá'í from the United States, bravely carried on. She finished her talk and smiled at us. 'It is a beginning,' she said with equanimity.

A beginning! It is hard to accept this when you are eighteen and you see the Bahá'í Faith as a glorious solution to world problems.

For me it was also a beginning of the slow dawning of understanding. That day I was overwhelmed by guilt. I had come as a pioneer and I had failed. Several months before, an ad had appeared in the *Bahá'í News* stating that the Bahá'ís of Saskatoon offered a scholarship to any youth who would come to study at the University of Saskatchewan. I applied. The scholarship was for $200. I was the only applicant. The year was 1972.

It was years before I realized that teaching the Faith is all about planting seeds. Gardening is an avocation with me now, both the spiritual kind and the flower and vegetable variety. And it no longer surprises me that the seeds planted in the autumn and half forgotten turn up as vivid blooms in my August garden. When I heard of the great surge of Bahá'í youth declarations in Saskatoon a number of years ago, I smiled and remembered that empty meeting. It had, indeed, been only a beginning.

The trouble is that we don't really understand the spiritual principles. In my youth as a Bahá'í – and since I became a Bahá'í at the age of fourteen, youth is both literal and figurative – I used to feel that the spiritual world was full of laws that we only barely perceived, but which if we neglected caused us psychological pain. In the material world if we touch something hot we get burned. Our parents try to warn us but most small children get burned before they really understand this principle. The spiritual world seemed much like this but the causal relationships were much more difficult to understand because they were not as immediate. I knew that it was all in the Writings. But the Writings were like a jungle – there was so much there that I felt lost. There were treasures and sustenance and basic rules of living in the Bahá'í Faith but how to go about finding them?

It was the example of another person's life that helped me here. My mother responded to the Guardian's call to open remote areas of the globe in the Ten Year Crusade by going to the French islands of St Pierre and Miquelon lying in the Atlantic Ocean south of Newfoundland. She was transformed by her eagerness to serve the Cause.

In this transformation seemed to lie the key to the spiritual puzzle. My mother and I have been very close. My father died when I was four and we had been family and friend to each other in our travels through war-torn Europe and then settling in a new land, Canada. So I watched as my spirited, opinionated mother began to shed ingrained habits of speech and behaviour to conform her life to the standards set out by Bahá'u'lláh and 'Abdu'l-Bahá. But there was more to it than that. She had a glow, like the glow I felt when I fell in love.

When I completed university, I also terminated a long engagement and felt at loose ends, so I went to visit my mother in St Pierre. She radiated the love of God. I felt nothing. I began to pray that I might be given the grace of loving God. Slowly, while reading *The Dawn-Breakers*, something hard and cold began to melt. 'Love Me, that I may love thee. If thou lovest Me not, My love can in no wise reach thee' became a reality for me.

I spent a year with my mother in St Pierre, but I was not a pioneer because that was not my intent. But after that year I had learned enough and come to love enough that I did want to pioneer.

In Newfoundland there were only two Bahá'ís. I went up to St Anthony on the northern peninsula to teach at the Sir Wilfred Grenfell School. My love song had begun.

When you step into the valley of the love of God, all burns with that fire. Let me do something harder. Let me go to a more isolated place to prove my love, my devotion. I went to Nain Labrador, a small community of Inuits and settlers. The bay freezes over in the autumn. All through the winter the only contact with the outside world is by a small mail plane that lands on skis.

Most of my students spoke Inuktitut at home so they were not fluent in English. Unexpected problems arose. How do you explain the difference between scientific fact and superstition in a community that believes in ghosts? I got into trouble teaching evolution. 'Don't confuse them,' the missionary's wife told me.

All the time we think that we are giving of ourselves we are being showered by God's bounties and given precious lessons. I learned that the love of God is nothing if not translated into love of man, that prayer must become service.

I love Labrador. Even now, when I write about it, I can see the wooded bays, the rocky outcroppings, the lakes nestled in the hills. I remember going off on snowshoes in April when the sun poured down from the sky and the snow was crusty and firm, setting off for the day with the knapsack on my back, following the frozen brooks, crossing the lakes, making a noonday fire and watching the smoke declare the presence of a human being to the silently watching wilderness, taking off snowshoes and sliding in my sealskin boots on the smooth sea of ice and crossing over the hills to stand looking at the faint lights off Nain.

Beauty was everywhere and my heart ran to overflowing with it. It was in the old lady who served us blueberries and whipped cream. Wait a bit . . . whipped cream? How could it be fresh whipped cream when there were no cows, no fresh milk. It was pre-chewed seal blubber! Beauty was in the other teacher with whom I had so many problems. I saw it in her when I prayed for her, when I made a list of her good qualities and got to number 36, determined to see the good and not the irksome.

Floating up as bubbles surfacing in a sea of loneliness came lines from the Writings. At last, instead of a jungle growth through which I could not find my way, the pearls of wisdom were surfacing to my conscious mind, one at a time, perfectly suited to fit the occasion.

The greatest gift was that I met my husband in Labrador. I was introduced to him by the Moravian missionary. 'I heard that there was another Bahá'í here and felt you might want to get together, so I gave him your phone number.'

Hubert and I were married in St John's, Newfoundland, where we were both planning to study. It was the first Bahá'í wedding there. Peggy Ross came as a travel teacher and officiated at the ceremony. The two other Bahá'ís, Bruce Mathews and Bill Howe – the first Newfoundlander to become a Bahá'í – were our two witnesses.

Through a mistake made on both television and radio, it was announced that a fireside was to be held at our apartment on our wedding night. It was the only time I was delighted that no one showed up.

It was different having a home and being able to have real firesides. Hubert is outgoing and our weekly firesides were well attended by students and friends. Yet there were no declarations till the very evening of our departure. Millicent Penney, a painter, who had been attending firesides faithfully, timidly asked if it would be all right if she became a Bahá'í. What rejoicing!

By now we had a family of two little girls. During the year that Hubert was doing graduate work at the University of Minneapolis, we saw an ad in the *Bahá'í News* asking for pioneers to the Canadian north. Since we could find no work in Labrador, which had been our first choice, we set about preparing for this goal. Of this period, I have written extensively in my book *Tristan*.

To serve the Beloved of all worlds is so great an honour, is it any wonder that we are tested in that service? The greatest tests are our most important lessons. How little I knew when Tristan was born in the Frobisher Bay Hospital, when he was evacuated by snowmobile in the bitter February cold, when he was pronounced brain-damaged at the St Justine Hospital in Montreal, that these prodigious tests were the outpourings of God's munificence. That little infant, retarded, a vegetable, as one doctor pronounced him, would become the cause of the blossoming of a heroic love in our lives that transformed us all, beyond our undeserving.

Thinking that there would be help for our son in the cities in the south of Canada, I pushed to leave the North. It took long visits to doctors, painful hospitalizations for Tristan and endless tests before I accepted that the wonders of modern medicine had nothing to offer our son.

While pioneering you feel that you are held in the hollow of God's hand. The isolation and winter bleakness of the arctic landscape strengthens your reliance on God.

When I first went to Labrador, Jamie Bond, Knight of Bahá'u'lláh for Keewatin, had sent me a copy of the *Tablets of the Divine Plan*. They were well-thumbed when we next had our opportunity to pioneer in Greenland. This concave island, filled with the world's largest glacier several miles thick, 'Abdu'l-Bahá promises will become a lordly orchard. During the year that we were there I had the sense of immense privilege in participating, in however small a way, in the unfolding of the Divine Plan for the world.

Lotus and John Nielson and their family were a great inspiration to us. They had come to pioneer in Greenland and had lived through great difficulties. Steadfastness attracts confirmations, I learned. Bill Carr, pioneer to Thule, was another such example of steadfastness.

No longer were the Writings the jungle they were to me in my youth. They were beacons of light, a firm support and a constant source of guidance and solace in every situation.

When the children were older we had the opportunity to go for a year to the northern part of Norway and to travel extensively in Finland and Sweden in the area called Lapland. Tristan and Lisa, our youngest daughter, had to make great sacrifices in leaving their friends and comforts of home for the difficult life that this pioneer post required. Pain and illness were constantly with Tristan during that year, yet the children were our best Bahá'í teachers.

Several years went by before we were once more able to pioneer, this time back in my beloved Labrador. There were joyous times when we were seven adult Bahá'ís and nearly had an assembly. Tristan taught by his example. The years of his life were numbered, yet even in the hospital during his final illness his spirit glowed with his love of Bahá'u'lláh. The chaplains, the nurses, all those who met him spoke with wonder of his great courtesy and consideration. His last words, after naming all those he loved, were, 'I am so glad that I'm a Bahá'í because . . .' I didn't hear his reason.

As I write, it is nine years since Tristan's death. The Bahá'ís of Happy Valley sent me a wonderful photograph of a posy of Bahá'í children around Tristan's grave. There is a local spiritual assembly there now. Seeds, seeds, pioneering is all about planting seeds. Oh yes, and don't forget the love song!

13

This Day is Rain

Frank Jordan

Frank Jordan writes of four years spent in Surinam:

My pioneering experience began at the St Louis Conference in 1974. A slide show on pioneering aroused such a spirit of enthusiasm that I decided on the spot to go overseas as soon as possible. There were several obstacles in the way. My wife, Norma, and I had no money and I had no qualifications for meaningful employment. I had recently received a B.A. in anthropology, which was about as useful as a loose frog in a bed. Norma did not want to go pioneering just yet, as she was enrolled in a nursing course and wanted to finish.

But I thought the world was ready to explode and wanted to be at a pioneering post when it did, so I insisted we go immediately. In my judgement today, it was a serious error not to wait another year or two.

Norma, realizing I was adamant, resigned herself. We set about raising money to go. We worked at a Chinese restaurant for three months, saving every possible penny until we had $3,000. The Chinese owner of the restaurant paid us more than the usual salary to help us.

Meanwhile we had to choose a post. We looked at a list of countries needing pioneers and our attention was caught by Surinam because neither of us had ever heard of it. After a little research we decided it was the place for us and in early April 1975 said farewell to our families. My wife was three months pregnant.

Our first day in Surinam was a rainy one. I was moved to write this poem:

A day on earth is
still for rain to fall
this day is rain, for all
has been made silent but that
which, like liquid night
or slow-descending comfort comes
to make the waiters silent
and some to sleep . . .

Our hosts were Jamshid Ardjomandi and his lovely wife, Soekie, a Surinese of Indonesian descent. As I sat on their porch looking at the rain, I saw an apparition appear, headed straight at me. Was it a spirit? I kept looking at it and soon it became apparent that the 'ghost' was Tjon Veira, a member of the national spiritual assembly. He came onto the porch and doffed his raincoat, dripping water from his ears, nose and elbows.

'Do you want to go pick up Rúḥíyyih Khánum?' he asked.

'Huh?' was the most intelligent response I could muster.

'She has been filming in the interior and we need to go get her. I have a bus.'

'When do we leave?' I asked.

'Tomorrow at five a.m.'

The next morning we were bouncing along a hard washboard road of red laterite in a little bus that seemed ready to fall apart. The driver was an Indian. Tjon and I were the only passengers.

On both sides of the road were 50-foot high walls of thick vegetation. We drove an hour before we passed another vehicle, a Land Rover going the other way. As it flashed by,

I caught a glimpse of a veil. 'She's on that Land Rover!' I shouted.

'No, she doesn't have transportation.'

'She's on that Land Rover. I saw her.'

Our driver turned around and we fairly jumped from bump to bump as we caught up with the other vehicle. It was a miracle that the little bus did not totally fly to pieces. Rúḥíyyih Khánum generously left her seat in the Land Rover and got into our bus to ride the rest of the way back to Paramaribo with us. She told us about the Green Light Expedition film and teaching work around the world.

I'll never forget the way she described the spread of the Faith. 'It's spreading like wildfire; it's taking hold everywhere and spreading like wildfire,' she said. She said a lot of other things too but those words had seminal meaning for me at that time. Those words of amazement thrilled me to the bone.

A few days later, Amatu'l-Bahá was gone and we were faced with the reality of everyday living. We found a house. I built us some furniture and bought a bicycle to use for transportation, one of those big 28-inch jobs that one sees throughout the ex-colonies of the world. As for employment, I found a part-time job restoring artifacts for the Surinam museum. Our financial condition was very difficult and a constant source of stress.

In 1976 I had the good fortune to go with Counsellor Peter McLaren to Nieuw Nickerie, a rice-growing area in western Surinam. Among the 35,000 people living there, there were as yet no Bahá'ís. Peter and I and a little girl named Wati, who translated for us from English into Hindi, spent one weekend in Nickerie and found 46 new Bahá'ís.

One house we visited was blue and white and stood high on stilts. Underneath the house was a cool shaded area with hammocks hung between the house pillars. There we found about five people under the house, so we taught them about Bahá'u'lláh. They all declared, including Mrs Azadkhan, the house owner, a dignified woman of about 50.

We asked if we might use her home that evening for a slide show.

'Of course!' Mrs Azadkhan said. 'In a few minutes my husband will be going to the mosque and he will stop and ask the neighbours to come.'

'Mosque?' I thought. 'Wait a minute. Mosque? How?'

Just then down the steps came a man with a long white beard, dressed in a flowing abá and white cap, looking for all the world like the grand mufti of some important Middle Eastern city. It was Mr Azadkhan, the undisputed patriarch of the house and of the neighbourhood too. That evening we had a crowd of at least 50 at the slide show and more than a few declarations.

Several weeks later we returned to Nickerie and taught for another weekend, resulting in another 46 declarations. At one house we were telling the family about Bahá'u'lláh when a stranger came up. He listened for a few moments and then burst into the group brusquely, pushing right into the middle, saying, 'Yes, yes, of course this is all true! Of course it is! How can I join this religion?' After half an hour he became a Bahá'í. His name was Mohabir Dubar.

That night, Peter and I were at the little hotel, sitting on the floor of the balcony, the equatorial trade wind blowing through. Across the road was the wharf, with several boats tied up. One of them was *The Lempa*, a banana ship that plied constantly between Nickerie and Liverpool. Men were busy loading bananas onto the ship.

Peter said he hoped and prayed that we would come to Nickerie to pioneer. There had never been pioneers there. Now there were 92 believers and in future there would be many more, he said. Pioneers must come.

This was a tall order. In my mind I tried to picture pioneering in a remote place like this, a whole day's travel from the nearest city. What kinds of jobs were there? What could we do? I told Peter I would try. That was another moment that is burned into my memory.

Several months later I was offered a teaching job, instructing the children of the American and Dutch engineers who were building a railroad in the interior. I was sent to Camp 52, a place deep in the triple-canopy rainforest which is most of Surinam. There, I set up a small school and had about a dozen students. I wondered whether we would ever get to Nickerie. I prayed about it.

One night I took a copy of *God Passes By* and sat in the cab of one of the company trucks. My edition had 499 pages and I figured I would say a 'Remover of Difficulties' for each page. Someone had told me that Bahá'ís sometimes say this prayer 500 times.

Sitting in the darkness, I began to pray. Every time I said the prayer, I flipped a page. It became a session of deep prayer, the kind of prayer which consumes one's whole consciousness and focuses one's being. Gradually, however, I became tired. When I neared the end of the book, I was glad that soon I would be able to go to bed and sleep.

Finally I came to the last page and said one extra prayer to make it an even 500. Then I left the cab and began to walk towards the workers' barracks, where I was housed. Only then did I realize that, by flipping a page with each prayer, I had only said 250 prayers instead of 500. I was so tired I went to bed anyway. But still I wondered how we would ever get to Nickerie, because there were no jobs available there, none at all. None.

On one of my bi-weekly trips into Paramaribo to visit my family, I went to Transimex, a supply store, to buy a wrench. While there, I asked the manager if he had considered opening a branch in Nickerie. To make a long story short, six months later I had been hired by Transimex to open a branch in Nieuw Nickerie. The company gave me two cars, one for my family and one for sales. Every few weekends they flew me in a small plane to Paramaribo for consultations. The job involved more responsibility than I had ever had.

We were in Nickerie for two years. Our second child, a boy, was born there with the assistance of a local midwife. Norma cried every day with homesickness, wishing that her mother could help her with the kids. Norma made the greatest sacrifices and it was her sacrifice that drew the confirmations to our efforts together.

It was not easy for me, however. The heat was terrible. And difficulties with my job kept me awake many nights.

One evening a wonderful teaching opportunity fell into my lap. I was manning a booth at a small fair, giving out pamphlets and telling people about Bahá'u'lláh. A lady came and carefully examined the materials in the booth. She turned to me purposefully, without the least bit of shyness. She told me her daughter was getting married in a few weeks and she wanted me to come and speak at her wedding. I was speechless for a moment, then quickly agreed.

On the appointed day I went to the house out in the polders. Another pioneer was with me. There were three hundred people present. I showed slides about the Faith and for almost an hour the entire group was silent and listened with great attentiveness, including the two Hindu priests who were there to officiate.

After two years, Norma and I decided to return to the United States so that I could earn a Master's degree in education. Nickerie had been visited regularly by teaching teams from Paramaribo. There were six spiritual assemblies when we left. The local radio station, Radio

Rani, carried weekly Bahá'í programmes. Several big conferences had been held, one attended by two hundred Nickerie Bahá'ís.

In reviewing this pioneering experience, I see it exposes human errors but also shows many evidences of the mercy of our Lord. What would I say to those who want to pioneer?

Be sure that your decision is the result of a balanced process of consultation. Consider the wishes and needs of each individual in your family.

If you do not have specific employment qualifications for a job that is in demand in the chosen country, seriously consider getting such qualifications first.

Obey the institutions of the Faith unquestioningly. Follow their advice when it is offered. Be patient, because Bahá'u'lláh will open a door for you at just the right time.

Be aware that pioneering will change your life forever. You will never be the same.

14

With the Peace Corps in the Philippines

Neil Chase

Neil Chase of Bridgeport, Connecticut writes:

During my last year at Clark University in 1969 I was very much on fire with the Bahá'í Faith, but was still undecided about my career path. I was majoring in psychology but all I had to do was to observe the behaviour of the children of the psychology professors to see that this field's theories were unable to answer life's challenges. As I had enough credits in education for certification as a mathematics teacher and wanted to work with children and to breathe the atmosphere of another culture, I joined the Peace Corps. The Corps sent me to the Philippines. I knew nothing about the place but it turned out to be the best choice for me.

My Peace Corps training took place in Hilo, Hawaii. It really was a paradise, the place I would like to spend the rest of my life. The people, the climate, food, scenery, everything was perfect and everyone knew about the Bahá'í Faith. While at a Nineteen Day Feast, I asked a returned Peace Corps worker who had been in Tonga if he had been able to teach the Faith openly there. He replied, 'Are you kidding? My whole village joined the Faith.'

Our last night in Hawaii, one of our instructors was

directed to address us about proselytizing. He stood up and said, 'I have nothing to say about this subject – we are all adults here,' and sat down.

Gusan, Marinduque, Philippines

This delightful small town was surrounded by over a dozen barrios. My job was to implement a modern maths programme in the municipal public schools. The teachers did not have adequate materials and the children had nothing, but the enthusiasm was high. No matter how challenging I thought my questions were, every single hand in the classroom would shoot up and the correct answer would be given. I never saw these children argue, let alone fight. Their eagerness to learn was astonishing.

I stayed in the poblacion, or centre of town, with a family headed by a wonderful old woman, Pinay Rodriques. She had many relatives and was a pillar of the community. I gave her a copy of *Bahá'í World Faith* to read and she often told me, 'This is a very good constitution.'

One Sunday afternoon, Eric, her 13-year-old grandson, came to me and said, 'Our priest spoke about you today.'

Delighted, I asked him, 'What did he say?'

He answered, 'We shouldn't believe what you tell us about Bahá'u'lláh.'

'How many were in church today?'

'About 500.'

Overjoyed, I said, 'I could not have told so many myself.'

The next day, at Central School, several teachers asked for Bahá'í literature which, fortunately, I had printed in Tagalog. One of these teachers joined the Faith.

Bachao, Gasan

During my first summer in Marinduque, I taught a maths course at a barrio high school. One of the students, Nestor

Salcedo, at first seemed somewhat shy. Little did I suspect his leadership abilities. I learned that he was president of his class, captain of his Philippine Military Training group and leader of his Boy Scout troop. He was destined to start a 'Bahá'í snowball'. I offered him a copy of 'Abdu'l-Bahá's *Paris Talks* in Tagalog, which he accepted. A few weeks later I asked Nestor if he was ready to return it and he said he couldn't. He said his father had it. Cautiously I asked, 'Does he like the book?'

'Yes, he reads a chapter to us every night after supper.'

Since more than half the book had been completed, I took the plunge and asked Nestor if he was interested in becoming a Bahá'í. He asked all the right questions concerning his relationship with the Catholic Church, Bahá'í laws, the central figures of the Bahá'í Faith and so on. He then asked if he could teach his friends. By the end of the week, to the very great pleasure of the National Spiritual Assembly of the Philippines, there were 50 new Bahá'ís.

Although the family with which I stayed did not join the Faith while I was there, they graciously allowed me to use their home for deepening the barrio youth. During these sessions there was so much laughing and joking, and since my Tagalog was not all that good, I really could not tell if these kids were sincere. At our Naw-Rúz party I found out.

At the end of the party Nestor approached me. 'The girls were very brave,' he said with pride. It seems they had told their teachers they would not march in the Good Friday parade as they were now Bahá'ís. It was unheard of that students should refuse their teachers. I was astonished. By this time, more than half the students at the school had become Bahá'ís. Bachao elected its first local spiritual assembly at Riḍván.

Ifugao Province

School vacation coincided with Riḍván and the national spiritual assembly asked me if I would help with the first local spiritual assembly elections in Ifugao, a remote mountain province. We visited Balinawnaw and several others that were so remote that if you missed your truck you were stuck on the mountain for at least three more days. I was touched by the hospitality of these extremely poor people who fed and lodged us while they slept outside and probably went hungry.

An almost unbelievable incident occurred on the way there. While I was at the Manila Airport waiting for a plane to Nueva Vizcaya, Josie Lava, a member of the national teaching committee, found out from her friends at Philippine Airlines which flight I was taking and booked herself on a connecting flight. This was a pleasant surprise. When I asked her about her return trip she said that the central bank, where she was an economist, expected her back on Monday morning. I told her that the place was so far that she wouldn't even have time to get there, let alone do anything. She saw the sense in this, postponed her flight and cabled her office. It transpired that a bomb on the plane she would have taken exploded during flight. The mayor of the town, political figures and 35 other people were killed. Many said they believed that this was Bahá'u'lláh's protection (bagong bubay – meaning 'new life') for Josie. My reaction was that it was a lesson for me too. Often I hope for something which does not seem to be the right thing for me. Since that episode, I believe that I am exactly where Bahá'u'lláh wants me to be spiritually and geographically.

When we reached our destination, the people in the sitio stared at me. Grateful for my language training, I smiled and said, 'Nagandang umaga po sa inyong lahat!' (Good morning, everybody!) Everyone kept on staring. I thought my pronunciation was wrong and tried again. 'Kamusta po kayo?' (How are you?) Everyone just looked at me. I turned to my companion and asked, 'Are they shy or do they dislike me?' I was told, 'They like you but Ilocano is spoken here, not Tagalog.' Then I said, 'Hi. Good morning!' Everyone greeted me in perfect English.

Boac, Marinduque

After my two years in Gasan were completed, I was asked to stay for another year and work with the schools in the next town, Buenavista, and its barrios. I accepted and am particularly grateful for the help I received from the Olmedo family, which provided hospitality. One of the teachers, Tik Soleta, guided me to every barrio captain of the municipality to deliver the Message of Bahá'u'lláh.

Auxiliary board member Freddie Ramirez asked me about teaching the Faith directly in the public schools. I told him I thought that was pushing it and that it might prove to be impossible but that I would see what I could do. I decided the wisest course would be to approach the principal of the largest high school in the province's capital, Boac. I told him about my friends in Manila who were speakers for the Bahá'í International Community and about the Faith's principles and founders. Somehow I never got around to mentioning religion. I requested a meeting in the auditorium, but he told me there was no auditorium and that he wanted discussions in each class of senior year students.

It was all so incredible. First I broke the ice by attempting to give an introduction to the Faith in Tagalog. The students saw quickly that the Faith was greater than my command of their language. One of the new Bahá'ís, Chris Salamanca, a college student, quietly said a few words. Then Freddie got going, speaking of the elimination of extremes of poverty and wealth and of the need to establish a new administrative order. There were plenty of questions from both teachers and students. At the end Freddie asked, 'Who would like to be a Bahá'í?' and 300 enrolled by the end of the day.

15

We Saw a Tarzan Movie

Susan and Shidan Kouchek-zadeh

The beautiful stamps on the envelope received in October 1990 told me this was a script from Africa. The return address of Conakry, Guinea confirmed this was the awaited material from Susan Kouchek-zadeh, one of the many Bahá'í pioneers solicited for scripts for this book. The provision of the following account was typical of the generosity of pioneers in a globe-encircling chain. I began avidly reading about Sierra Leone:

In 1958, when he was 18 and I was 16, we knew that we would marry; but we had to go through university first. It seems to me that we had always known that we would serve as Bahá'í pioneers. We both assumed, I think, that it was the logical outcome of being a Bahá'í. Shidan came from a Persian Bahá'í background, third generation on his mother's side of the family. We married the week after our final exams in 1963. Shidan started to work a few days later to begin paying off a debt to a local firm that had helped him finish his course of studies. So we set up our home in Gatley, just south of Manchester.

It was fun building a new life, a married life in a pleasant little house, buying bits of furniture, entertaining friends, holding Nineteen Day Feasts and youth committee meetings in our home. Before long, Shidan's debt was paid, but still we did not move.

It took the appearance of Marion Hofman, speaking at a teaching conference in Manchester in February 1966, to nudge us in the right direction. We offered to pioneer. After consultation with the committee, we wrote to the University of Sierra Leone, trying to get Shidan a job teaching and doing research. The engineering department was fairly enthusiastic, but money was short. Our correspondence languished. Then Betty Reed, secretary of the national spiritual assembly, rang us up in April. The Universal House of Justice wanted someone in Sierra Leone, so what were we waiting for? What, indeed? Although we had no commitment from the university there, we packed up and went about putting our house up for sale.

We took a roundabout route to our destination, visiting Shidan's uncle in Italy on the way. The last stage of our flight was Dakar to Freetown in a Ghana Airways prop-jet. It wasn't long after that all prop-jets disappeared. We took a paper from the pocket in front of us and learned for the first time about the dangers of contracting malaria. The paper was an advertisement for the prophylactic Daraprim. 'Ask the hostess for some now,' the ad read. We did. We have flown hundreds of times around West Africa and between West Africa and Europe but have never again seen such an advertisement. Of course, much later we learned that Sierra Leone had been called 'the white man's grave' because of malaria.

Landing at Freetown's airport, we saw the red earth and palm trees of Africa for the first time. It wasn't jungle, nothing as I had at first imagined it would be. It was wonderful! From the airport the bus drove along a red dirt road to board a ferry which took 30 minutes to cross the estuary of the Sierra Leone River. We were fascinated by the scenery. Green mountains. And Freetown itself was colourful, alive, like nothing I'd ever known.

As was our first meal. That first night, exhausted, we immediately took a room in the hotel where the bus stopped. It proved to be the most expensive, so the following morning we looked about for less expensive restaurants and somewhere else to stay. By chance we turned left instead of right which took us away from the more western centre of town and into Kroo Town Road, a more African quarter. We entered the first restaurant we came to. They offered us a stew of meat and fish cooked together in the hottest pepper sauce.

We returned to the more familiar western side of town and looked for a bank to deposit our meagre supply of travellers' cheques. The bank manager was English and curious as to why we'd come to this 'God forsaken part of the earth'. We decided to be prudent and murmured something about looking for somewhere to invest. In that case, he said, we should definitely go to the R nightclub that very night, 'as everyone who was anyone would be there'. It was a Saturday. We thanked him for his advice, inwardly scoffing at the idea of beginning our pioneering at a nightclub. Neither of us had ever been to one.

That evening, sitting forlornly in the lounge of the hotel, we wondered if perhaps we should take his advice. So, when he turned up, we went off quite happily with him. The club was dark, noisy and stuffy and we were startled when he offered to introduce us to a compatriot of Shidan's. We had felt certain there would be no Persians in Sierra Leone. Papasian, when we were introduced, was equally startled. Extremely suspicious of us, he toyed with us for weeks before finally offering my husband a job.

You see, when we went to the university on Monday morning, the head of the engineering department was extremely kind but he could not give Shidan a job. Sierra Leone was financially in trouble and the United Nations had cancelled all its various funds to the university. There was no money for us. Other people at the university were also sympathetic and kind and we were allowed to stay in the guest house there for several weeks. Such care and loving attention did we receive from the bursar, the manager of the guest house, the university doctor and others that we formed a favourable impression of Sierra Leoneans that will last forever.

I was offered a job teaching at the Technical Institute and took it without real enthusiasm because I had so hated my own secondary school experience I had sworn never to have anything to do with teaching. But we needed the money. Soon I realized teaching was the one thing I actually enjoyed and could do to earn money.

The engineering department gave Shidan a part-time teaching assignment which helped until Papasian gave him a job. It was only temporary and required Shidan to go out into the country. I disliked having to stay alone in Freetown in the flat we had rented. I used to dream that a thief had entered the house and I would open my mouth to scream but not a sound would come out. I would awake drenched with sweat. That doesn't mean much, of course. Most of our time in West Africa has been passed in a terrible sweat. The climate is something to contend with. Fortunately, when thieves did enter our house it was at a time when Shidan was at home so I didn't have to cope all by myself.

We gradually became used to various aspects of life in Africa. I had been determined not to have servants. It went against my left-wing upbringing. But the first time I washed our double sheets, tying myself in knots bending over the bathtub, trying to wring all the water out, staggering downstairs to hang them on the line with the dog belonging to the people downstairs rushing over trying to bite me on the bottom, I returned to bed in a state of exhaustion. I quickly realized I could not do the work all by myself. We compromised by hiring a schoolboy who couldn't pay his school fees. He did our washing on Saturday morning and we paid the fees.

The first Saturday he brought along a shirt that needed a button sewn on it and asked that I do it for him. My little jobs increased until on the fourth Saturday he brought along a book-size handwritten manuscript that he wanted typed.

And then came the flood! Shidan had noticed that the tank on our roof was fixed on the slant with the overflow on the higher side. One day while I was at school the stopcock ceased to function. When I got home, most of our flat was under four inches of water. None of the floors were level and they all sloped inward. Our precious Persian carpet was afloat!

The little formica table we had bought to eat our meals on was hideously warped. From then on, we had to eat with one hand, using the other hand to keep our plate from sliding off the table. Our neighbours, the Beckleys, all came to help sweep the water out. It took six men to carry out the sodden carpet. That incident convinced us it would be a good idea to have someone in the house all day. So we finally did what everyone else did and hired someone to clean and wash on a regular basis.

I only vaguely remember Mr Sesay, the first man we hired. I think he was quite pleasant. But what I remember with great clarity was coming home from school one day and finding him in a very strange condition doing the ironing. He didn't seem to be able to focus his eyes on me. I nervously suggested that he forget all about the ironing and go home for a rest. He put out his hand to switch the iron off. The switch was on the wall in front of him, but his hand could not seem to make the connection. I took out the plug for him and repeated my suggestion. 'Madam, he said, 'I beg you to forgive me and not to tell the master.' He made a deep bow from the waist and could not get up again. He remained in front of me, doubled in two, swaying slightly. I had no idea what to do. I think it was the neighbours who helped me out of that one. When Shidan came home that weekend we asked Mr Sesay to leave. You see, I was, and still am, frightened of drunks.

Papasian solved our problem by telling us that as Shidan had been with Deg for some time now, they would supply a servant who could, if we chose, remain with me in Freetown. I went to collect Mr Camara at the Deg office. He was a dapper, cheerful little man who embarrassed me by insisting on walking a few paces behind me. And by rushing into the centre of the road clicking his fingers and shouting, 'Taxi for Madam!' However, he was a marvel, and could cook wonderfully with the minimum of equipment and ingredients. He was also a very interesting personality. I remember asking him if he could cook curry. He drew himself up and said, 'Madam, I can cook three kinds of curry, Indian curry, Scotch curry and West African curry.' I was impressed. His curry is excellent although I never noticed that he made three different varieties.

At this point I decided to impress my left-wing beliefs on everyone by insisting one Saturday when Shidan came down to Freetown that his driver, also named Camara, and 'our' Mr Camara sit down to eat with us. They were both very reluctant and were altogether embarrassed, although little Mr Camara's ebullience soon overcame this. He became quite exhilarated and gradually began to talk and talk, giggle and talk. It was fun but it certainly was not something I was going to insist upon doing again. I could see it simply was not fair to them. This experience shattered my belief in what human dignity depended upon.

Another aspect of life we became accustomed to was the thieving. The first thief fished out our clothes that hung, for want of a wardrobe, on a string between two windows. Poor Shidan lost the only custom-made suit and blazer that he ever owned. I think he mourns them still. The next thief actually inserted himself through the guard bars 10 by 6 inches. Kept awake by the first of a multitude of ear infections, I saw this head bobbing about in the living room. We both began to yell in voices turned strangely hoarse and squeaky, got ourselves tangled in the mosquito net and went racing out the door after the thief who had miraculously squeezed himself through those narrow bars. Suddenly we remembered we were stark naked and returned for our dressing gowns. We were able to get only a last glimpse of the thief legging it up the road. After that, we got ourselves organized. We kept belongings away from open windows and closed those windows through which thieves could enter. We moved from the flat down to a little house behind it belonging to another of the Beckley clan. This house had much narrower guard bars. We also hired a watchman. I continued to have nightmarish dreams but no thief ever got into our new house.

In retrospect, it seemed many of my 24 years in Sierra Leone were spent waiting for Shidan to come home. All week I taught at the technical institute and greatly enjoyed it. Every day I stayed in Sierra Leone I grew to like the people even more. In the evenings a group of children formed the habit of visiting me. I gave them paper and pencils and taught those who wanted to learn. I gave them biscuits and squash. They were good company and gradually more and more children came to these sessions. I made friends with a dog I spotted in the bushes. I left food for her and while she would not come near to me to get the food, I watched her after I got indoors and saw that she came to get it. Gradually she grew tame enough to accept food from my hand. Later she had two puppies, scrawny little things. I grew attached to the three of them and missed them when we left.

The weekends were like honeymoons; no, better than

honeymoons, except for those occasional times when he didn't come home or couldn't make it until late on Sunday. At the end of the school year we knew that Shidan's job was permanent. I gave up teaching at the institute and was free to travel with Shidan. Every Monday we drove up to where we were stationed. The rest of the week Shidan toured the various water stations he was supervising. He travelled hundreds of miles a week, long, hot, dusty miles. He learned how to deal with contractors who by nature seem always to try to take short cuts and to hide their mistakes. I pottered around our home wherever it was and explored the local village. I read books and sewed and cooked and chatted with anyone there was to chat with.

Our first home was on the newly-built Mattru Jong water station about a mile from the village on the banks of the Mattru Jong River. The big open compound went right down to the river and was surrounded by tall trees. Sometimes in the early mornings or late evenings groups of monkeys would swing their way through the trees. The bush was constantly alive with noises of animal and bird calls and rustlings. Sometimes I would walk into the village to buy a loaf of bread just as it was being taken out of the mud beehive ovens. It was very good bread baked by a Foulah people who came originally from Guinea. What a shock it was to discover when we first went to Guinea that we were unable to get good bread! The market itself was tiny with just a few items such as pepper or okra spread out on rickety tables. Every few days a cow would be killed and cut up and you could buy meat, if you did not mind seeing the cow's head with its tongue hanging out gazing reproachfully at you from the ground. Everyone was friendly but I could not speak to the many people who only spoke the local Mende language.

My sharpest memory of our time in Mattru Jong is of M. We employed him to carry water. We lived in one of the houses built on the compound for staff. It was posh by local standards, and by ours since we've been in Sierra Leone. It even had rubber-tiled floors. However, as the station was still in the process of being developed, there were pipes but no water. So M went up and down between the river and our house with buckets. At the house he climbed a ladder carrying the buckets and emptied them onto the rooftop tank. He fell off the ladder once, and although nothing was broken, he seemed in a state of shock. We gave him some tea and he rested a bit. M spoke no English or Krio but had a lovely sweet smile. We had assumed he was a little short upstairs until one of the Ministry students came back from Freetown with a chess set. Suddenly chess became all the rage. Everyone on the compound learned it and Shidan had some good games. It was quite a shock when M, having just learned how to play, beat everyone else, including Shidan, hollow. And we had thought he was slow-witted!

Mattru Jong is where boats leave for Sonthe Island. Shidan had to go there once a fortnight or so because a station was being built on the island. I think it was nearly finished by the time I joined him but I went on the boat trip once. It was a long, lazy boat ride of from four to five hours and not all that comfortable as it was very crowded. One had the choice of frying in the sunshine on deck or baking in the stuffy heat of the cabin with hundreds of women who all got quite nervous when we passed the choppy bit at the mouth of the estuary just before arriving at the island. One character on board enjoyed talking to us and aligned himself with me, saying we were both 'educationists' while Shidan was a 'mere engineer'. This as a result of six months of teaching at the institute! I still refer to Shidan as 'M.E.' whenever I am annoyed.

In the small village of Mano we saw *Tarzan Goes to India* in three spools which only got mixed up once. We sat on

wooden benches in the 'theatre'. The driver and Mr
Camara were in the 20-cents seats while we were in the 30-
cents. There were only two other people there. We watched
Tarzan escape from the crocodile by jumping on the back
of a passing hippopotamus. All this in the steaming heat of
a Mano night with the mosquitoes biting away at us in a
frenzy.

Next we went to Kenema, a real town. It took all of five
minutes to walk from our house on the edge of town into the
centre, but it really was a town with a busy market every
day and a shop that would sometimes sell butter, a terrific
luxury. There was quite a lot of electricity in Kenema and
water in the taps! Now, twenty years on in the capital of
Guinea I don't have water in the taps. We became cinema
addicts in Kenema. We went often and cheered loudly and
made remarks with the rest of the audience. It was always a
devoted and witty crowd. One man in Kenema liked the
Black Star (an Italian cowboy series) films so much that he
strode around in black trousers, shirt and cowboy hat all
the time and became known as 'Blackstar'.

It was from Kenema that we made our first trip to
Liberia, longing to see other Bahá'ís. We'd been in Sierra
Leone for nearly two years and we were hungry for Bahá'í
company. We'd had some wonderfully supportive letters
from our national spiritual assembly secretary in Monrovia.
This was the assembly of West Africa with ten countries
within its jurisdiction. Shidan had been supervising some
water stations way up in the northeast near the Liberian
border of Kailahun and Coindu. There was a big
international market up there so he knew the road well. He
had heard that once you crossed the Liberian border it was
only a hundred kilometres or so to Monrovia. We decided
to go one weekend. It took several hours to get to the
border. Halfway along the twisting, bumpy road, Shidan
turned to me and said, 'And now for the motorway.' I

stared at him, thinking what a poor sense of humour he has, when the motorway duly appeared. There, in the middle of nowhere, was about twenty miles of beautifully tarred dual carriageway. Then it was back to the usual bumpy, dusty road.

We crossed the border without, as far as I can remember, having to show any documents and set off on what we presumed would be a short trip to Monrovia. We went on and on for the better part of eight hours and as nightfall approached felt really quite desperate. We were happy to find a Bahá'í pioneer from Sri Lanka who was managing a large tea plantation about 50 kilometres from Monrovia. We realized at this point that Shidan's friend had been talking about another place on the Liberia-Sierra Leone border. The Sri Lankan pioneer was wonderfully hospitable and put us up for the night. He was deeply interested in numerology and much of what he said completely mystified us. The next day, realizing how far from home we were, we just had time to dash into Monrovia, find the house of a Bahá'í family and then start the long trek back to Kenema.

The family we met were an elderly West Indian couple who had an American Bahá'í with them as their guest. We learned from them the other route and that the Bahá'í community at Bomi Hills was not really all that far from Sierra Leone. Having had just this brief taste of being with other Bahá'ís, we were addicted now and determined to soon have us another fix. We were already planning our next trip.

It was not many months later that we started off along the other route to Liberia. We were in exuberant spirits, especially when the route was much shorter and we arrived at the border in only about five hours. But no one had thought to mention that the border was a wide river. We left the car with the driver and were paddled across in a canoe. In Liberia we saw an official called the Collector. (He was nothing like the Fowles's character.) He studied our passports with great interest, one Persian, the other English, then handed them back with a smile. 'Are you Americans then?' I don't know what Shidan said. His mind works so much faster than mine. I put it down to being brought up in Iran for the first and formative years of his life. I'm sure Bournemouth has nothing on Iran when it comes to sharpening the senses.

We found a taxi heading for Monrovia. The road was good and wide but very dusty. We travelled with a huge boiling tail of dust. Overtaking another vehicle was a nightmare. We ploughed ahead through someone else's huge cloud of dust, hoping we would not meet someone coming the other way. There was no way to tell until we'd cleared the tail and were abreast. And taxi drivers never listen to anyone's instructions. This one dropped us at the Bomi Hills junction and we found ourselves in the late afternoon by the side of the road, in the bush, alone, hoping for a taxi to Clay and then to Bomi Hills. Eventually a taxi did come by and just on sunset we bumped up a hill to the Bomi Hills Bahá'í centre. Mama Weston, who had been there for 17 years and who had built the centre herself, was sitting in the main room writing something. I think she simply said, 'Well, hello there!' and smiled. We both felt immediately and absolutely at home even though there was nothing familiar about the surroundings.

It continually surprises me how different the external trappings are in the countries along West Africa. Liberian houses and furniture are very different from those in Sierra Leone. Each country has been greatly influenced by its colonizer. In the case of Liberia, it's America. Mama is American and was then in her late 70s. She is the darling of so many fellow pioneers. We had to leave the following noon but were enormously refreshed. We felt that now we knew the way to a very supportive place, a place that felt like home.

One of the first meetings we attended in Monrovia stands out clearly in my memory. It was a crowded meeting with about 30 people. An elderly man was giving a slide show with a small ancient slide projector into which he had to hand feed the slides. Just as the show began the pile of slides got knocked over and so were entirely out of sequence. Not in the least daunted, he put the first slide that came to hand in the projector. It was a quotation from the Writings and he asked us all to repeat it. The second slide turned out to be a prayer and again we all recited it aloud. We could not believe it when the third slide turned out to be a prayer for the dead. 'Well,' said the intrepid speaker, 'you all know someone who is dead, so let's say this one too.' The rest of that meeting is just a merciful blur.

At a later meeting in the new centre, an American pioneer burst into emotional song at some high point in the programme which absolutely paralysed me with embarrassment. Never in Great Britain had I ever heard any Bahá'ís sing, let alone a spiritual, emotional song. What a good thing that beggars cannot be choosers. For we were beggars as far as Bahá'í companionship went, so it was simply no use thinking all this carrying on was shockingly un-Bahá'í. Very quickly I realized that the British way of conducting Bahá'í meetings was not *the* Bahá'í way, just the British way. Doors were opened in our minds and our conception of the Faith must have grown enormously at that time when we were so dependent upon spiritual brothers and sisters from other countries and cultures.

Our visits to Monrovia became more frequent as the months went by and we made it to convention. Before we knew what had happened, Shidan was on the national spiritual assembly, a daunting prospect when you consider that the NSA was responsible for ten countries from Mauritania to the Ivory Coast to Mali. This would involve even more regular visits to Monrovia. Soon after there was a by-election and I joined Shidan at the national assembly meetings, which were lively to say the least. I sat through the first meeting chaired by Mama Weston and it seemed like riding a bucking bronco. I literally held on to Shidan's shirt tails in order not to burst into tears. I could not believe this was what NSA meetings should be like. Before I knew what had happened, Shidan was translated into an auxiliary board member and I was alone with the bucking bronco. But it's amazing what you can do if you have to and before long I was in the seat, having been elected vice-chairman in a year when the chairman never made it to meetings. The only good thing was that it gave Mama Weston a much-needed rest. Shidan is the one who enjoys gadding about but it was I who had to face the almost monthly trek to Monrovia and back.

After we settled in Freetown, the trips to Monrovia were by air. I flew to Monrovia Friday nights after school and returned on Sunday afternoons. The ride from Freetown to the airport took three hours. Then it was a 45-minute flight to Monrovia and another 45 minutes on the road. We marvelled that no matter how many times I made the trip, something different happened each time. I usually expect disaster but never more so than on this particular F28 flight: the pilot got out, after having taxied to the end of the runway. He put down the ladder, descended and walked all around the aircraft, inspecting it from all sides with a very puzzled expression. He got in again and took off, despite my interior monologue which went something like, 'Don't be a fool, man. If you have any doubt, don't let's go.'

Then, of course, during the rainy season there was always a storm on Friday night. On one KLM 707 we were flung from side to side and up and down like match sticks in a whirlpool while the lightning flashed all around us. The only reason I was not hysterical was that there was someone beside me who was even more scared than I. I felt dreadfully guilty at deserting the crew as they had to go back through the storm to Freetown.

Those trips taught me something about prayer and asking for things. The late night flights to Monrovia were always a bit nerve-racking as there were so few passengers – the airport was way out in the bush and I had to find my way to Monrovia. Looking back, I realize I was probably safer there than in any other place on earth. But at the time I was often frightened.

One night we arrived particularly late and I was nervous about getting a taxi alone. I contemplated saying the 'Remover of Difficulties' prayer but thought perhaps it was just too trifling a matter to bother God with. I deplored my own feeling of weakness and inadequacy. Finally I did say the prayer. Within minutes of landing, another passenger offered me a lift, whisked me into town and deposited me on Laura's doorstep before midnight. No one was home. It was the night of the commemoration of the ascension of 'Abdu'l-Bahá, a time when many Bahá'ís traditionally gather at 1 a.m. to recite prayers. I had been so concerned about my late-night transportation from the airport that I had completely overlooked this aspect of things. I think it had not really occurred to me that anyone would traipse from Monrovia in the middle of the night, especially since so few Bahá'ís had cars. It seemed unlikely they would gather at the centre at 1 a.m. I thought, 'Damned Americans always take everything so seriously!' I could have taken a taxi to the Bahá'í centre if I could have found one at that hour but the streets were quiet and pitch black.

I sat at the top of the steps being bitten by hordes of hungry mosquitoes. Time passed. I was so tired I decided to go down into the yard and sleep in the big derelict

American car that seemed always to have been there. No sooner had I put my head down on the seat than I heard strange rustlings and stirrings. I thought of cockroaches, rats, snakes! I shot up the stairs again and sat waiting and waiting. Finally, sheer exhaustion sent me back to the car again, no longer caring if I was bitten by a snake just as long as I could put my head down. I was asleep when the headlights of Laura's car swept into the yard around 4 a.m. I staggered out, blinking, and was met with roars of laughter from the carful of people.

I'm very careful these days how I use the 'Remover of Difficulties'.

16

Snow Has Many Faces

Wendy Ayoub Lind

Wendy Ayoub Lind, a British/American pioneer in Sisimiut, Greenland, was an actress and a singer in her younger days. As a song writer and composer, she is a member of ASCAP, but nowadays she is more apt to describe herself as 'an artist, a writer and sometime poet'. She works in ink and charcoal to reproduce the likenesses of the animals and birds of the Arctic. She has been a Bahá'í for thirty years and pioneered in the Bahamas, Denmark and Holland before pioneering in Greenland where she is an assistant to the auxiliary board for promulgation and a member of the Greenland National Spiritual Assembly, first elected in 1992. She has five children, nine grandchildren, one great grandchild, four pet birds and a cat. Wendy writes:

Ever since I became a Bahá'í, I'd wanted to pioneer. My first opportunity came in 1963 when the Universal House of Justice issued its first call for pioneers. On that occasion I went to the Bahamas with my husband and four of my children. It was a wonderful place to be. Sea, sand and sun *and* they spoke English!

Almost twenty years later, single again and under circumstances very much beyond my control, I found myself manoeuvred into a short-term pioneering post by the past master of pioneer manoeuvering, Mary Lou Suhm. I was between jobs, so I was free to attend the twenty-first birthday celebration of my daughter, Helea, in Holland. I was in Europe when Mary Lou finally caught up with me.

'We must have someone in Denmark before Riḍván,' she said. 'You are so close; would you consider going for us? It will just be for a couple of months.' And knowing my diffidence about learning a new language, she quickly added, 'You won't even have to speak Danish.' Then, as a bonus, she promised, 'We need pioneers in the Virgin Islands, so when you get back, we'll work on that.' Ah, the Virgin Islands! Warm, sunny and very British! And, I thought, rather exotic. Much more like the sort of pioneer post I had in mind. Well, since it would only be for a couple of months, how could I refuse?

Denmark in early March turned out to be a picture postcard. Snow-clad landscapes of glistening fir trees rivalled anything I have ever seen. Currier and Ives would have wept, it was so beautiful. Most people speak some English and the romantic in me felt so at home. And too, there seemed to be an air of destiny about this move. So, since I had no compelling reason to return to America, I decided to stay in Denmark and see what happened.

What happened was that three months later I met Carsten Lind, a Danish pioneer in Greenland, who was visiting his family in Denmark on his way to the Dublin Conference. We both went to Dublin. Two months later I was visiting Greenland and considering accepting his offer of marriage. Two months after that we were married. Greenland was now my home.

I don't mind saying I was a little apprehensive about the whole thing. It had not been my intention to marry again. Settling in a place so totally foreign to anything I'd ever known seemed like an act of idiocy. The weather to begin with! My previous experience with snow had been an occasional flurry in London, snow resorts in the Nevada mountains and winter holidays in the elegant and some-times elite ski resorts of Europe. Not forgetting the picture postcard view of Denmark that had got me into this in the first place! Snow may be tolerable for a week or two as a feature of a holiday but as a year round prospect it was most undesirable, especially for a sun-worshipper like me.

My doctor was alarmed and warned that at my age and in my condition it would be the death of me. I wasn't sure if he meant the marriage or Greenland. But since for several years I had been under his care, having been seriously ill in my early 30s and not expected to see my fortieth birthday, he confirmed that he meant the country not the man. Well, I've seen my fortieth birthday and added a few more years. Besides, thanks to him, I felt like a young girl. I also felt I was ready to face whatever the future might hold, particularly as I would be filling a much-needed and difficult pioneer post.

I honestly thought that I might die and I'll admit I was worried about that. However, to the amazement of most of my friends and the disappointment of a few, and to the consummate horror and concern of my family, placing my whole trust in Bahá'u'lláh, I sallied forth to settle in Greenland.

I am not sure what I expected. I had not really given it much thought. In spite of the few weeks spent in Nuuk, the capital, the summer before I was married, I knew very little about the Arctic region. I knew it was an ice cap covered with snow and that Eskimos lived there. I knew it was the home of polar bears, with vast unpopulated areas and nights that could last six months. I had heard the people lived in igloos, houses made of snow. I was told the people were uncivilized and nomadic and that we would probably have to hunt for our own food. My father envisioned me fishing through a hole in the ice. My clothing, according to other well-meaning, self-appointed advisors, all trying to dissuade me from making the move, would be made from the furs of indigenous animals, including seals, dogs and polar bears which, once caught, must be prepared and sewn by me. All the tales from all the outdated geography books were related to me in lurid detail.

Well, it was not like that at all. But let me tell you what life here is like, from the viewpoint of an English lady. My life before Greenland had been pampered. I'd had little opportunity to break from my high heels, nylon stockings and designer clothes. The high heels went first! When I had visited Greenland before we were married, Carsten bought me a pair of comfortable walking shoes, which my children aptly named 'beetle crushers'. Flat and inelegant, I was none too pleased with them at first, but they have become my favourite friends. Skirts, dresses and frilly blouses were quickly replaced with quilted trousers, fleecy T-shirts and bulky sweaters. My underwear resembles the sort worn by my grandfather, including long johns. The only warm coat I possessed, a mink, now hangs in the closet, an overkill that lost face to a heavy down coat and jacket. Nowadays when I am dressed to go outdoors I feel like a pregnant snowball.

The country itself, when first viewed from the air, appeared bleak, barren and cold. Generally it *is* cold. Barren it is not. It teems with life. And although much of the year it is snow-covered, it is anything but bleak. Nature impressed me immediately.

This is a country where everything is either very small or very big. There is very little in between. The mountains are granite and dominate the landscape. Words like 'majestic', 'powerful', 'awe-inspiring' spring quickly to mind. I was soon to learn that the oldest rocks on earth, dating several millions years, come from Greenland. Greenland is volcanic and we have had a few rumbles in the not too distant past. Beautiful Disco Island, north of where I live and where the Arctic University is situated, is an extinct volcano and a paradise. If we had such things here, it would be the holiday resort centre of Greenland.

There are no trees in Greenland. Although a few scrawny
shrubs, defying the wind and snow, pose as trees in
southern parts, trees as we know them in the south, are
non-existent. Strangely, there are hundreds of varieties of
flowering plants. Some of them are so small and low to the
ground they could easily escape the eye. But take the time
to look and you will be entranced by the miniature beauty
of the world at your feet. Several varieties of berries and
roots grow wild and in the summer when the snow has
gone, you can gather them and make flavourful jams, pies,
cakes and other delicious desserts.

Ah, you didn't miss 'when the snow has gone'. It does go
here in Sisimiut for about four months of the year. Where I
live, just above the Arctic Circle, we have two seasons:
winter and summer. The winter starts mid-September and
finishes mid-May. It is long and cold. The temperature
reaches 30 to 40 degrees centigrade below zero. Daylight
hours are reduced to three or four for a month or so. The
constant darkness can be depressing. The weather changes
suddenly and drastically. Winds of such velocity they can
knock you off your feet can arise in a moment and cease just
as quickly.

Snow has many faces. Some days fine snow can ring the
mountains, creating lacy swirls that lie like a coverlet
turned down on a bed. The tops of the mountains appear to
be suspended in space. On other days the snow can be
falling so thickly that the mountains cannot be seen. But
they are there and they sit like sentinels, encircling Sisimiut
and protecting us as we shelter in our valley below them.
Sometimes the snow is so fine it looks like talcum powder,
at other times like white feathers as it softly drifts
earthward. Snow storms can come without any warning. If
we do get a warning it is in the heavily-laden, grey sky,
which casts an eerie light, portraying its own brand of
beauty.

Light is one of the special features of the Greenlandic sky. Generally the skies are very blue, year-round. Clear and brilliant. And the sun shines most days. We get more sunshine hours than Denmark or England. Sunsets here give birth to glorious colours. Reds, oranges, pinks, peaches, greys, turquoises, golden, hundreds of tones and combinations, creating pictures an artist can never capture. Often the reflection of the sun paints the snow on the mountains in the most delicate pastel shades and one thinks of the icing on a special fairy-like cake.

Other captivating phenomena are the northern lights. These are seen in the winter skies, usually between October and March. Glorious curtains of transparent colour move across the night skies like giant gossamer wings. Magical and breathtaking. I remember the first time I saw them. I went outside wrapped in my warmest clothing and lay on the ground to watch this incredible show. Often I have awakened at night and looked out and seen the lights and stood fascinated in the dark until I was quite stiff. Yes, nature here, often so formidable and unpredictable, is unspeakably beautiful.

Sisimiut is the first town going north to have Greenlandic huskies. They are magnificent creatures, very intelligent, and contrary to popular belief, they are friendly and affectionate. They are working animals. The Greenlandic attitude towards the animals is very different from mine and perhaps yours. One doesn't make pets of animals here, although the children play with the puppy dogs, as all children do; they soon lose interest as the dogs grow older. The young dogs are allowed to roam free but as soon as they reach a year they must be chained and special places are set aside for this. Roaming dogs are shot!

Not so long ago dogs played an important role in Greenlandic life. They pulled the sledges – every family had a sledge and a dog team. The team was usually from twelve to twenty dogs. The dogs worked every day carrying the hunter, his family and his supplies over the ice, wherever they needed to go.

In Sisimiut there are several dog teams and it is a thrill to see them running. It's an even greater thrill to ride with them, an activity that most tourists have high on their list of priorities. Late in March we have the annual dog sledge race. It's a major event. Everyone turns out to cheer their favourite team. The exhausted dogs and their drivers are the heroes of the day. The dog team has the right of way on our roads and it's an eye-opener to see motorists patiently waiting while the dogs pass.

The life of the dog is changing. It's very much a repetition of what happened to the horse when the automobile was invented. The automobile has a restricted use in Greenland but the snow scooter or snowmobile, a vehicle on skis, is capable of covering the icy terrain very rapidly and is fast replacing the sledge and the dogs, particularly in more populated areas.

In the past the Greenlander was a hunter, but he did not hunt for fun. Hunting was an intrinsic part of life, providing food, skins for clothing and boats, as well as bones to make tools, jewellery and games and thread to sew the skins. No part of the animal was wasted. Everything that was needed came from the sea or land creatures.

In the far north, life continues much as it has in the past. Hunting is still an art. But as modern methods are introduced, some of the old ways are being replaced. The hunter, like the dog, plays a smaller role in the Greenland of today. In a society where most of one's needs can be satisfied by a trip to the local shops, there is less need to hunt and for many hunting has become a recreational pastime.

In Sisimiut there are not many making their living in this way, but for those who do, there is an open market where they can sell their catch. It's something to pass by and see whole seals, caribou and ox heads complete with antlers and horns, eider ducks and birds, all with their feathers on, lovely white rabbits and an incredible variety of fish, some over a metre in length, waiting for a buyer, and all of it is fresh!

The caribou was introduced to Greenland from Norway some 50 years ago. I was surprised to hear this. There went the myth of Santa and Rudolph and the reindeer sleigh! Since caribou is not an indigenous creature, I reasoned, Santa either does not live at the North Pole or if he does, my guess is that the reindeer pulling his sleigh are really huskies. The song might equally well have been about Horace, the red-nosed Husky! The reindeer introduced were a new strain and brought here to boost the dwindling caribou population. Caribou seem to be abundant now but can only be hunted for about six weeks at the end of summer.

While writing about hunting, I must share with you an experience I had during my first year in Greenland. We had a boat at that time and took one of our Greenlandic Bahá'í friends out on the sea to hunt for seal. Carsten shot a few birds. Our friend, Knud, was perched on the front of the boat, most precariously I thought, looking for seals. When one was sighted, we chased it with the boat and he and Carsten took shots at those foolish enough to pop their heads above water. I was not at all happy about all this and sat in the back of the boat silently praying they wouldn't hit anything. I don't know if it was my prayers or simply that they were lousy shots but we didn't get a seal. It was bad enough having to look at the birds in the back of the boat – I knew I couldn't look a seal in the eye as well. They have the most adorable faces and eyes that speak. The birds? We gave those to a friend. There was no way I was going to pluck and eat them. Although I accept hunting as a reality of life here, my heart still aches when I see an animal that has been caught.

The seal, basis of the Greenlandic diet, is hunted year round. The skins are still worked to make kamiks, the traditional fur boots, and other articles of clothing, many for purchase by tourists.

Tourism is a relatively new industry here and is developing slowly but positively. More and more people are coming to experience the wide open space and natural beauty. It is, unfortunately, quite expensive to come here, and because of uncertain weather and the great distances involved, one needs to be able to spend considerable time to make it worthwhile. But a trip to the Disco Bay, where icebergs the size of a city block majestically drift on a sea of blue, is a sight to take your breath away and certainly worth the time and expense. To see the bergs break off the ice cap, as one does every two minutes, and hear the thunderous crack is a thrilling experience. Should you be fortunate enough to see one turn over, it's a sight you will never forget.

The snow melts towards the end of May and, almost overnight, a green haze covers the ground and skirts the mountains. Within days bright yellow, purple and white flowers magically dot the landscape. The days are clear, the sky blue and cloudless. Everyone takes advantage of the warm weather by going inland, either to fish for delicious fresh water trout from the lakes and fast-flowing crystal streams, or to walk the uncharted paths and view the breath-taking scenery, or perhaps to enjoy the solitude and untamed splendour.

Camping and hiking are national pastimes, or you can sail the fjords and enjoy the pleasures they and the sea have to offer. Sea fishing is popular. You sink your line and within a very short time you are pulling in succulent fresh fish. In one day of fishing you can fill your freezer for the long winter months ahead. But no one thinks of winter. We are all too busy enjoying the beauty of the short but prolific summer. We water ski and some brave souls even swim in the inland waters. Life seems to hang suspended. It is difficult to get anything done. Everyone wants simply to be off somewhere enjoying the beautiful weather. And it is the time to travel.

Within Greenland, the only transportation between towns is by helicopter or boat along the coastline waters. Most of the inland sea is frozen in winter, so travel by boat at that time is impossible. We in Sisimiut are lucky, for although in winter our harbour is frozen over, a supply ship can usually cut a path through the ice to bring our supplies. Everything we need must be imported, mostly from Denmark. We are the last town going north that receives regular service of commodities during the winter. Those living further north must wait until spring. Since I have been here, they have begun to fly in fresh products but these are exorbitantly expensive. Most cannot afford to buy them. We depend upon the helicopters for mail and transport in the winter, and they, in turn, are dependent upon the weather. So, mail delivery can be unpredictable and few people choose to travel during this time.

The population of Greenland is 50,000 and that of Sisimiut only five thousand. It is the second largest town in Greenland. We have three main stores and many smaller businesses catering to the needs of the populace. We have a post office, banks, a court house, a city hall, schools, a hospital, an excellent library and in 1989 our own radio and television studios were opened. This year, in 1991, a satellite dish has been erected in our town and we expect to start receiving transmissions from Canada in the spring. We are not deprived of the necessities of life and the newly-installed telecommunications centre keeps us in close touch with the rest of the world.

Forty years ago, Greenlanders were living in small settlements all along the coastline, living the way they had lived for hundreds of years, happily hunting and fishing as their sole means of survival. Life was very hard but it was one they understood and could cope with. Suddenly their world was turned upside down.

An agreement was made with Denmark to centralize living, so these freedom-loving people were made to live in a way completely foreign to them. They were moved from their villages and forced to live on top of each other in centrally-heated concrete blocks of flats. Suddenly they had electricity, hot and cold running water, flushing toilets – conveniences that they didn't appreciate or want.

Since they no longer needed to hunt and fish, they were given money to buy food and clothing. Their children were sent to school and, sadly, for many years, because there were no Greenlandic teachers, their language was also taken from them. Everything it was thought they needed was given to them. Unaware it was destroying their identity, a well-meaning society thought it was doing them a favour and providing them with a better way of life.

No longer needing to hunt, life became a strange, hostile and bewildering day-to-day experience. From boredom, or a sense of loss, unable to adjust to the new way of living, many turned to drugs or alcohol. These addictions destroyed the lives of many families. All the attendant alcohol-related problems have now invaded this once peaceful land. Violence has increased. All forms of child abuse are a frightening part of life and Greenland has the highest suicide rate of any country in the world.

Just ten years ago, in 1981, Greenland received its independence from Denmark, and elected its own government. They have made remarkable achievements in a relatively short time. The government has initiated the establishment of agencies to help those disabled through drug abuse and several campaigns have been launched to educate the people in all areas of social development. Already can be seen a renewed sense of pride reestablishing itself within the collective consciousness.

Along with the desire for a better life, a sense of world consciousness among the younger generation is emerging. The young people feel the need to travel and experience other cultures. Opportunities undreamed of just a decade ago are now becoming possibilities. The ties with Canada are being strengthened. Canada is not only closer than Denmark, but the Northwest Territory Indians have a very similar cultural heritage and language. Several Greenlanders have already attended the Arctic University in Iqaluit, Frobisher Bay, and exchange programmes have been arranged between high school students there and in Sisimiut. This has opened up many new possibilities.

An outstanding characteristic of the Greenlandic people is their closeness to nature. It is one that we who grew up in the teaming cities of the world have never experienced. This closeness gives them a deeply spiritual sense.

The people are friendly and naturally cooperative. Their culture and survival has depended upon their willingness to share. Everyone in the group had a part to play and everything was used for the benefit of all. The people were hard-working and life was extremely difficult. The weather was, and still is, the greatest enemy.

As hard as they worked, they also played hard. This characteristic is evident in the modern society. Greenlanders have a sense of fun that others have long lost. They have an almost child-like approach to life. They are basically very shy and they keep their feelings somewhat secret. They have not yet acquired the degree of self-control that we have had instilled in us and some still find it difficult to sit confined in one place for any length of time.

They are a very talented people. There are a greater

number of artists than are to be found in more 'civilized' countries. I feel this is because they have a special affinity with their environment – a closeness that parallels a closeness to God, resulting in a natural, uninhibited display of creativity. Stone and bone carvers, painters, poets, lyricists and mime artists abound. They are also beginning to develop musical abilities and already there are many talented groups and performers.

The national language is Greenlandic. Danish is widely spoken but there is a strong move to learn English. Many Greenlanders speak English and it is now a compulsory subject in the schools from the age of twelve. The speaking of English will open many doors, allowing the Greenlander to enter the world stage more readily where, we know from the Bahá'í Writings, they have a special destiny and part to play in the new world order. I started teaching English to adults four years ago. Two years ago I started in the public school with children from nine years old.

I think Greenland is one of the best places in the world to live. It would have been impossible for Carsten and me to have the life we have been able to achieve here in most other countries. We built a lovely home during the development boom in Sisimiut a few years ago, and although we are now faced with the problem of paying for it in a society where the cost of living is very high and continually escalates while income, on the other hand, seems to be like the weather, frozen, I still cannot think of anywhere I would rather be.

The Faith has grown rapidly in Greenland. It first reached these shores in 1951. Today in Sisimiut we have a community of 37 believers, including our children. One other Dane, who embraced the teachings here in Sisimiut, my husband and I are the only non-Greenlanders in the community. When we came here six years ago, there were five believers. There had been an assembly a few years previously, but when the pioneer was forced to leave, that precious institution was lost. Now we have a thriving community with Bahá'í children's classes, which are the individual initiative of one of our believers. We have another assembly in the capital, Nuuk, and will be forming our third this Riḍván.

I have learned a lot from my experiences here, not only about others but about myself. I came here with no idea what it was like and with the thought that I would probably not stay here more than a few years. I hoped to be off to a warmer climate as soon as the opportunity presented itself. I have learned that weather generates one kind of warmth and people another. I have grown to love these people and it is my fervent desire to contribute something worthwhile to this land I have made my home before, for one reason or another, I am forced to leave. I did bring my love for Bahá'u'lláh here and some of that will, no doubt, grow in others.

You don't have to know everything there is to know about the Faith to be a good teacher. You don't even have to talk very much. What you must know how to do is to love your fellow man. This is not always easy. I have come to the conclusion that the best teacher is the one who comes to know what it means to worship and serve God. When one does that, one sees beauty in all things, discovers one's own reality and hardest of all, perhaps, accepts oneself.

It has been no bed of roses here in Greenland. Tests have been many and severe. At times it has been very lonely. And sometimes so frustrating that I have felt overcome with grief and sorrow. Being away from family has been the hardest test of all. My children are scattered around the globe: in England, Yugoslavia, America and the Marshall Islands. I haven't seen them in years and I miss them and my grandchildren more than words can tell. My health has deteriorated. My body has aged and weakened. In contrast, my faith has soared and my spirit has grown and my understanding developed in ways it never would have had I stayed at home.

I see life as a series of exchanges. You give something and you receive something in return:

'Whatsoever ye have offered up in the way of the One True God, ye shall indeed find preserved by God, the Preserver, intact at God's Holy Gate.'

The Báb

17

Our Home Was in the Himalayas

Thelma and Ron Batchelor

Ron and Thelma Batchelor of Surrey, England, pioneered in the Solomon Islands in the 1970s but their longest period of pioneering was in Nepal where they were accompanied by their children, Simon and Suzanne. Thelma writes:

We have pioneered twice overseas. The first time was to the Solomon Islands in the South Pacific where we stayed from October 1970 until March 1973. As a child I had always dreamed of going to the South Pacific and read avidly about that vast area. I first heard of the Bahá'í Faith in 1963 at the age of 21 when I was living and working in Montreal, Canada. Several months later I declared at a fireside in San Francisco, having had the privilege of listening to and meeting with the Hands of the Cause Leroy Ioas and William Sears.

I met my husband, Ron, at an international youth summer school in Berlin, Germany, in 1965. He had heard of the Faith one year previously and was pursuing it, though he did not in fact become a Bahá'í until five years later when we were on our way to our first pioneering post in the Solomon Islands. We married in February 1970 and soon after he applied for and was selected for a post with the Crown Agents in the British Solomon Islands. The place he chose to make his 'declaration' was in the Shrine of the Báb as we had chosen to spend three days visiting the Shrines on our way out to the South Pacific.

The Solomon Islands were beautiful and the island people lovely. In many ways it is a magical place. Ron was fortunate to buy photographic equipment from a Chinese man who was leaving Honiara early in 1971 and he absorbed himself in photography. He became extremely successful, both in producing black and white postcard photographs of the Solomon Islands, several thousands of which he sold in the local tourist hotel, and in photographing expatriate children. He was well-known for his photography. I worked as a secretary in Honiara, first for the one and only solicitor (attorney) in the islands and afterwards for a Japanese mining company. Our first child, Simon, was born in Honiara in June 1972 – our greatest blessing during our time in the Solomons.

While we were in the Solomons, we had the bounty of visits from Hands of the Cause of God Enoch Olinga, Collis Featherstone, Dr Muhajir and John Robarts. They were each so different. Each made a deep impression on us. At the time of John Robarts's visit in March 1972, I was six months pregnant with Simon and the Hand of the Cause said a special prayer for him. That was a very special moment!

We left Honiara on March 19, 1973 and spent some time visiting New Caledonia, Australia, Singapore and Malaysia before flying to Iran. I stayed with a Bahá'í family there while Ron went on to Haifa as one of the photographers of the third International Convention.

One person Ron met while working at the World Centre was David Walker, a film-maker who was with Kiva Films as a soundman. When Ron and David finally left Haifa, neither guessed that they would meet again in Nepal. After leaving Haifa, David Walker was to go down the Amazon

River with Rúḥíyyih <u>Kh</u>ánum filming the Green Light Expedition.

We spent the next three-and-a-half years back in England and our second child, Suzanne, was born in June 1975. During this period Ron continued to apply for overseas positions and was offered a post in Calcutta, which fell through, and one in Germany that fell through at the very last minute. Finally he was offered a post in Nepal as a construction advisor to the Nepalese government with the Ministry of Overseas Development in London. Nepal, at that time, was the third poorest country in the world. On our way out to Kathmandu we visited the World Centre for three days and the Universal House of Justice assured us of its prayers and support in our new pioneering post.

We arrived in Nepal in December 1976 with two very small children. Simon was four-and-a-half and Suzanne one-and-a-half. Had we known of the continual ill health we were to suffer throughout most of the nine years of our stay in Kathmandu, we might not have had the courage to accept this post. But we did not know. In retrospect this was a blessing because in no way would we wish to have missed the experiences of living in a country as beautiful as the Himalayan Kingdom of Nepal. The people were so gentle and wonderful.

Nepal is a country of extreme beauty. Kathmandu is a valley surrounded by the highest mountains in the world, the Himalayas. It is hot in summer and pleasantly sunny in winter. But from the middle of November through early February the night-time temperatures drop to freezing.

Ron's job with the British government was as a construction advisor to the Nepalese government, responsible for the building of several grain stores throughout Nepal. The difficulties and frustrations of working in any developing country can be enormous and Nepal was no exception.

Ron worked tirelessly during the nine years, with the assistance of the Nepalese, in an effort to construct the grain stores to the high standard necessary to afford long-term storage of food grains. The grain stores were needed to house the rice harvest for a buffer stock against any crop failure.

Nepal was beset with problems, chief of which was rural poverty. Hunger, malnutrition, premature death, inadequate housing and poor sanitation were rampant. There were only three doctors in Nepal, for every 100,000 people and only one per 100,000 outside of the Kathmandu Valley. The capital was expanding and in the villages the Nepalese had nothing of any material value. At that time, the life expectancy of a Nepali was 37 years and approximately 50 percent of the children died before the age of five owing to illness, mainly through water-borne diseases. Life for the Nepalese was extremely hard.

In the midst of all this we were trying to survive too! Shortly after we arrived we succumbed to the various sicknesses which continued afterwards to plague us and other pioneers in Nepal. At the same time we had to find a place to live. Eventually we settled for a house beside the Bagmati River, a tributary of the Ganges. What we did not know was that there was seldom much water in the river save at monsoon time. Corpses of animals were often thrown into the river only yards from our house, separated only by a wall, and the river bank was used as a public toilet by all passersby. Our house was adjacent to a Hindu temple, which was overrun by monkeys. These monkeys often invaded our house and garden in search of food and we were advised by the British Embassy to move for fear that we could be bitten by a rabid monkey. The incidence of rabies was high at that time.

My son had stomach trouble all that first year, my daughter had permanent diarrhoea and I got some mediaeval form of typhus. I was very ill for a year and ended up in the hospital run by missionary aid under very primitive conditions. Eventually I recovered enough for our family to go home on leave after our first year-and-a-half.

A positive note in the midst of all our troubles was meeting the Bahá'í community in Kathmandu. A wonderful group of people, both the Nepalese and pioneers. Soon after we arrived we met Penny and David Walker, pioneers who had arrived six months previously. David had worked in Nepal with the American Peace Corps and since becoming a Bahá'í had decided to return with his wife. When we met David in Kathmandu he was a bright yellow colour from hepatitis. The disease lasted for months and nearly caused the Walkers to return to the United States. Penny and David, along with Mahsheed and Bharat Koirala, became our greatest friends.

Mahsheed had originally left Iran to pioneer in the Philippines and to study broadcasting there. She then carried on her studies in Bombay where she met Bharat, a Nepalese studying journalism. Bharat was not a Bahá'í at that time, though he became a Bahá'í shortly afterwards. They were married in India and then came to live in Nepal in the early 1970s. Mahsheed began to suffer from asthma in Kathmandu but for the sake of the Faith decided to stay on. In 1976 when we first met them, Mahsheed and Bharat had two young children, Samir and Shabnam, who were about the ages of our two children. Over the years they were all good friends. Tragically, a year after we left Nepal, Mahsheed died during a severe asthma attack.

When I was ill in hospital at Kathmandu, wondering if I would ever feel well again, I received a letter from the Universal House of Justice asking me to serve on the National Administrative Committee of Nepal. At that time there was no national spiritual assembly. The letter made me think there was some reason for staying in Nepal and for continuing our service there. So often we could have easily given up and returned to Britain. But when we thought of our other pioneering friends in Nepal who continually sacrificed to stay at their posts, we felt we should support them for as long as we possibly could. Many times it seemed as though Ron's contract would end, but miraculously, it would be renewed.

Among our pioneer friends was Larry Robertson, an American who worked in the field with UNICEF. Larry married a Nepalese Bahá'í, Shyama. Dick Birkie was an American pioneer from New Mexico where he had spent time with the Navajos. He moved to the village of Pokhara but frequently stayed with us on his trips to Kathmandu. He married a beautiful Nepalese girl, Sarita. Rama Chandran was a Malaysian pioneer who arrived in Kathmandu without a job in 1980. He managed to keep going for a long time working as a pathology technician for the Canadian clinic. Rama was also to marry a Nepalese girl.

Joanne Pach was another remarkable Bahá'í pioneer who arrived from the United States in 1981. She suffered continually from ill health, as did all the pioneers at one time or another. She became a close friend and was a teacher at the British Primary School, which our children attended. Later they attended the American International School in Kathmandu since we did not intend to send them back to boarding school in England. We always felt it was best for the children to be with us, experiencing life as a Bahá'í family. The international schools provided a good educational experience as our children mingled with children of many nationalities and religions, including Hindus, Buddhists, Christians, Jews, Muslims and even some Zoroastrians.

The Nepalese Bahá'ís in Kathmandu were few in number but were absolutely dedicated to the Faith. Such

Bahá'ís as Golay, Bharat, Shailendra, Narendra, Bhakta Raj were spiritual giants and will always flood our memories with love. There were many Nepalese Bahá'ís who came from villages in the terrai, the area bordering India. We met them as they came to Kathmandu for conventions or national spiritual assembly meetings after the NSA was re-established there in 1982.

It was a rare privilege to share our lives for nine years with the beautiful Nepalese people and to learn to appreciate their traditions and culture. We were able to learn at firsthand something of the Hindu and Buddhist faiths which co-existed harmoniously in the Kathmandu Valley. As the one and only Hindu monarchy in the world, anything new was regarded with suspicion. No one was allowed to change religion. Bahá'ís had to tread warily and be most cautious about teaching the Faith. Some Nepalese did become Bahá'ís and we realized how difficult it was for them to make this change in their lives. When they made this commitment they were often ostracized by their families. The Nepalese Bahá'ís stood firm but wisely adhered to custom so as not to offend their families.

Ron fortunately had a secure job with the British government. Usually the greatest test for other pioneers in Nepal was finding work. We saw Bahá'ís come without jobs and all were sorely tested for a long time before they found work and with it a visa which would enable them to stay in the country. Those who persisted were eventually rewarded with jobs which gave them good standing in their communities and an opportunity to serve with distinction in their particular fields.

All was not hardship by any means. We had so many especially wonderful moments. Hand of the Cause Rúḥíyyih Khánum spent one week in Kathmandu in October 1977 prior to the Bahá'í Women's Conference in New Delhi. She spent time with us in our home and was driven around in Ron's project Land Rover. In the summer of 1982 we were privileged to host Hand of the Cause Collis Featherstone and Mrs Featherstone for a week, a truly rewarding and memorable time.

Once Ron brought back with him from leave in England one of the first video cameras to be seen in Nepal. We had recorded many movies from the BBC while in the United Kingdom and had brought them back with us to watch again and again. This was a novelty for the Bahá'ís in Kathmandu, both pioneers and Nepalese. We would gather on Bahá'í Holy Days and other occasions for a potluck supper and would watch a video film with as many as 40 friends, a time of great comradeship and fun.

Having servants was a luxury and at times we did not know how to deal with certain situations that arose with them. Our first housegirl claimed to be a goddess and her uncle had to feed her with fire to bring her out of her goddess trance. Over the years we had some very devoted helpers for whom we cared a great deal. There was Tej, our cook; Bahini, our housegirl; Prem, our tailor; and numerous chowkidars who 'guarded' our property, not all at the same time! They all became our friends. We learned that, as Westerners, our servants would look to us for advice and help. We would look after them and their children whenever they became sick, which was often. We miss them. We miss Nepal.

Pioneering, of course, means different things to different people. Some Bahá'ís go to their pioneering posts with the intention of staying for life. Others go for a set period of time, while others go for an uncertain length of time and wait to see what transpires and how long the 'pioneering doors' stay open for them. This was the case with us. We went as a family to Nepal for two years and those two years turned mysteriously into nine. All pioneers encounter tests and difficulties but ultimately the rewards are so richly plentiful you are left with the desire to stay with the Bahá'ís of that host country forever.

We do have one major regret: that we never persevered in learning Nepali. We had lessons when we first arrived but these lessons were interrupted by our young children wanting attention and by the debilitating effect of sickness. Since originally we thought to be there for only a year or two, we did not make the effort we should have made. As the years went by we were often embarrassed by not being able to speak Nepali. Kathmandu is an international capital and the language among expatriates and the educated Nepalese is English. But when it came time, as Bahá'ís, to communicate with the local Nepalese, we couldn't. If we were to have another chance at pioneering overseas, I know we will try a lot harder.

Nepal will always be special for us. It was our pioneering post par excellence. The pioneers were united. The Bahá'í community was united. Friends made there, we feel, are bound to us forever.

18

Once a Pioneer, Always a Pioneer

Shirley Macias

Shirley Macias confirms the adage 'once a pioneer, always a pioneer'. She began her Bahá'í life in California, then travelled to Honduras, Argentina, Haifa and back to California, where she now lives in Los Angeles. As she now says, 'And who knows where next?'

One day in late 1959, reading the *Bahá'í News*, I saw a plea for pioneers to fill extremely important goals of the Ten Year Crusade. A deputization fund offered aid to those needing monetary assistance to fill those specific goals. I immediately wrote and offered to go wherever I was most needed since I had no ties, was single and was anxious to serve. A telegram arrived saying I was to go to Honduras by Riḍván 1960.

I had never even heard of Honduras at that time. I read everything I could find, which was very little. I sold my possessions, packed my books and clothes and arrived in Guatemala City on a layover. There I stayed overnight at the Bahá'í centre, which was run by Artemus Lamb and his wife.

The next day I arrived in San Pedro Sula, on the north coast of Honduras, and was warmly greeted by George and Vivian Haley, who had a hotel there. They had been pioneers there since the beginning of the Ten Year Crusade. I stayed at the hotel for a week or so waiting for the Honduras Teaching Committee to decide on my post.

At that time Honduras had but three local assemblies. Because of the importance of strengthening this community to prepare it for the formation of its national assembly, some ten or more pioneers arrived simultaneously, but not all were able to stay. Ruth Yancy, after leaving her post in Puerto Rico, came to Honduras. She and I were to go to La Ceiba, on the north coast, to help it form its first local assembly.

We took the train from San Pedro Sula through Tela and then to La Ceiba. The train ride of perhaps 50 miles took many hours since it stopped at every little village and took on passengers and their livestock. It was hot and humid, the area being mostly banana plantations, and the smell of warm vegetation was prevalent. Ruth and I arrived at La Ceiba and stayed a few days with pioneer Bob Ancker, whom I had known in California. He had married a lovely Honduran and they had a small baby.

I remember the first night there, just before going to sleep. There was a photograph of the Bahá'í House of Worship in Wilmette and before falling to sleep I mused on the fact that I had travelled so far, yet had never visited the Temple in Wilmette. That night I had a beautiful dream. I was walking through the gardens at the Temple, with 'Abdu'l-Bahá as my guide. He was telling me things about the Temple, its purpose, its construction and so on as we sat on a bench in one of the nine gardens. Since I had never been there, I didn't know there are no benches, something I did not learn until several years later when I worked at the National Centre. When I mentioned my dream to someone on the Temple staff, I was told that originally the plan had been to have benches in the gardens but because of financial restraints they had not been included.

The pioneering committee had said I would find Honduras rather primitive, but I was pleasantly surprised. Yes, it rained a lot, but that helped to cool us down. There was no hot water in our living quarters but the houses all had rain tanks on the roofs, warmed by the sun, and showers were not uncomfortable at all, which was fortunate as we had to shower several times a day because of the humidity. There were bugs of many kinds but one learned to ignore them. We saw huge spiders, large cockroaches and flying termites everywhere, not to mention the flies. The markets were open without walls and the hanging meat attracted many unsavoury insects. But the fresh fruit was delicious, especially the bananas, cooked in so many different ways. Our basic diet was rice and beans with a most delicious 'crema' placed over the beans and, of course, warm and freshly-made corn tortillas. An umbrella and raincoat were constantly needed since it always rained for an hour or so every day – strong, torrential, drenching rains.

La Ceiba is right on the coast and we could wade out for a long distance still standing in water to our knees. The sand flies were very hungry and it did not do to loll around on the beach.

Ruth, having pioneered in Puerto Rico, had learned Spanish, which I had never studied. She was a wonderful teacher and refused to give me the translation of any word, insisting that I look it up. Ruth and I found a lovely little house built on stilts, as were most of the houses. We formed study classes, studying at first *The Dawn-Breakers*, which resulted in several declarations, and by April 1960 we elected the first Spiritual Assembly of the Bahá'ís of La Ceiba. Learning Spanish was especially easy for me, since we studied the Bahá'í books with which I was so familiar.

I took one trip to the Bay Islands, just off the Honduran coast, and spent a week with some delightful and simple folk. There were no automobiles on Roatan, one of the islands, and practically all the people there were Methodists. I spoke to a few about the Faith. Now there is an active

Bahá'í community on the island. The people were warm and friendly. When you are introduced to them, they will say, 'Now we be no longer strangers.' I stayed with the sister of a Bahá'í on the mainland and she was most gracious. We walked all around the island, which is very small, and it is truly a bit of paradise. In the evening the town's one electric generator would work for a few hours. People would gather in an outdoor restaurant to dine and dance in the open air. They even had a movie house. It may have been primitive but it was very comfortable and easy-going.

Ruth went to Panama for the regional convention in 1960. Upon her return, she decided to join Hooper Dunbar, who at that time was in Bluefields, Nicaragua, to help with the teaching of indigenous people. The Honduran Teaching Committee then asked if I would consider moving to Tegucigalpa, the capital city, to help that community and I accepted. There were friends I had known in Los Angeles there, Wanita George and her daughter Maralynn, who later married Hooper. I stayed with them for a short time and then found a place with a delightful lady, Mercedes Castillo, and her five sons. I rented a room from them and was exposed to Honduran culture and the Spanish language, since none of them spoke English. I served on the Local Assembly of Tegucigalpa. We had a Bahá'í centre located in Barrio La Ronda. When the family who had been living there moved, Wanita and Maralynn took up residence in the centre, which had a separate apartment upstairs.

Tegucigalpa is a lovely city surrounded by mountains and at that time still retained its colonial architecture and narrow streets. The climate is ideal since it is about 2,300 feet above sea level. In early 1961 the Tegucigalpa community was asked to host the first national convention and I was on the committee to prepare for this event. At the same time, twenty other national assemblies were to be elected in each of the Central and South American countries which for several years had been under the guidance of the regional assemblies of South America and Central America. We selected the best hotel in town as the site for the convention, sent invitations to embassies of other countries for the reception, organized publicity and held the convention. Ruth Yancy, who was now living in Nicaragua, came to Tegucigalpa to help us before returning to Managua for its convention.

It was a wonderful time and a wonderful convention. Hand of the Cause of God Collis Featherstone had been sent by the World Centre in Haifa to be with us. There is a photograph of the first National Spiritual Assembly of the Bahá'ís of Honduras in the 1954–63 edition of *Bahá'í World*. I was honoured to be elected to this institution and became its corresponding secretary. My command of the Spanish language was still very poor but acting in this capacity surely helped, as I found myself translating many-paged messages from the Hands of the Cause residing in the Holy Land, who were at that time the chief stewards of the Faith worldwide. Our assembly meetings were conducted both in English and in Spanish, since at least half of the membership spoke English – the Hondurans living on the north coast for the most part spoke English rather than Spanish. I also served as secretary of the Local Assembly of Tegucigalpa.

We had a small community but endeavoured to fulfil the goals set for us by the World Centre. One goal was the transfer of the Karbila endowment – a beautiful farm and Temple site on the outskirts of the capital city – from the former regional spiritual assembly to the National Spiritual Assembly of Honduras. This was easily accomplished. We also managed to get official recognition of Bahá'í holy days in schools, if only informally. We went to the Ministry of

Education with our request and were told that if Bahá'í children remained out of school on Bahá'í holy days there would be no problem. We also met with the government to obtain permission to teach the Faith in Honduras, which was warmly granted. We were to double the number of local assemblies from six to twelve by the end of the Ten Year Crusade. We not only doubled our numbers but were third only to Bolivia and Panama in the number of assemblies and groups formed by Riḍván 1962.

Shortly after the convention we were honoured with visits from Hands of the Cause of God Zikrullah Khadem, A.Q. Faizi and Enoch Olinga. They had been attending other national conventions and visited us soon afterwards. I was privileged to go to the airport to greet our visitors. I made such good friends with airport staff that whenever anyone came to visit us I was permitted to enter the customs area to await them and the friends were not even required to open their suitcases.

Visits with the Hands of the Cause of God while pioneering are among the highlights of my life. Mr Olinga stayed at the pension I was living in and we spent one night studying the guitar and practising some songs he wanted to learn. He and Hooper and Maralynn Dunbar went to the north coast and visited several villages, one of which, El Triumfo (The Triumph) responded with such enthusiasm that there were 30 or more declarations.

From the moment I met Mr Faizi at the airport I felt I was greeting a long-lost relative. He brought much joy to us all. On the afternoon of his departure, while at the airport, he suddenly realized that he had left his important black book at the hotel. The book was filled with photographs of the martyrs, of whom he constantly talked, relating their stories. He was most anxious not to lose this precious volume. I called the hotel; they found the book in his room and sent it to the airport by taxi. When my name was called on the intercom, Mr Faizi and I went to collect it. As we walked down the stairs, he began mentioning the various Hands of the Cause and how each was endowed with one of the qualities of the beloved Guardian. He said he himself was deprived of these qualities and continued to mention the various Hands, enumerating their wonderful services. I had only known Mr Faizi for a couple of days but was so overwhelmed by his qualities of loving-kindness and humility, that I said, 'Mr Faizi, you have the greatest quality of them all.'

He so sweetly replied, 'And what is that?'

'You have the quality of love.'

Then he said, 'Well, I guess I do.'

From that day, Mr Faizi was one of the most important influences in my life. He wrote to me from Mexico, his next stop, and for many years thereafter, until he died in 1980. I was but one of many to whom he wrote wonderful and inspiring letters.

The first International Bahá'í Convention was held at Riḍván 1963 and members of all the national spiritual assemblies then in existence were the delegates to the election of the Universal House of Justice. As a member of a national spiritual assembly I was privileged to attend this historic occasion.

We were a group of people from all over the world, representing 56 national communities, and many of us were pioneers. The election took place in the Master's House on April 21 with Amatu'l-Bahá Rúḥíyyih <u>Kh</u>ánum presiding and in the presence of all of the Hands of the Cause. The atmosphere pervading that house was incredible. One felt the presence of the Supreme Concourse. All of the friends were seated alphabetically according to country. I was seated in an alcove along with representatives from Guatemala, India and Iran. Just outside the window were to be seen <u>Kh</u>ánum's peacocks in full feather. On the other side of the room, seated in an alcove, were all of the Hands of the Cause who were praying as we filled out our ballots. As each country was called forward to post its ballots, there was applause. At one moment while filling in the ballot, I looked up and saw Mr Faizi smiling and blowing me a kiss.

After the convention we all travelled to London and the Royal Albert Hall where some 6,000 Bahá'ís gathered. What a celebration this was with the newly-elected Universal House of Justice greeting the friends from all over the world.

On the afternoon of the last day, Amatu'l-Bahá Rúḥíyyih <u>Kh</u>ánum went to the podium and shared with the friends the last days of the life of the Guardian. Much of her talk is now a part of her epic book *The Priceless Pearl*. It was a moving experience. At one point during her talk, she was overcome with emotion. Suddenly, some African believers arose and sang the now famous 'Alláh-u-Abhá'.

So ended one of the most incredible experiences of my life. The feeling was one of overpowering joy at being privileged to serve the Cause in this time and to be present at a moving part of Bahá'í history.

I returned to Honduras and learned several months later I would have to return to California because of illness. I felt guilty at leaving because the Guardian had asked pioneers to remain at their posts. Back in Los Angeles, my physician told me I needed surgery for cervical cancer. After recuperation from the surgery, I wanted to return to the pioneer field but could not do so immediately. Instead I became a homefront pioneer in California.

Then I met Ricardo Macias. We were married in September 1965. Early in 1966 a letter came from the international pioneering committee asking whether Ricardo and I would consider pioneering to Argentina. My immediate response was to say 'yes' but Ricardo felt he needed to work and save some money, as we had financial obligations. So I wrote saying we would be happy to go once our obligations were fulfilled. The committee wrote back saying how happy it was that we had accepted to pioneer in Argentina and could we be there by Riḍván 1966?

When Ricardo came home that evening and read the latest communication, we both said some prayers and then said, almost simultaneously, 'Well, what can we sell?' Within a month we had settled our affairs, packed up our books and belongings for shipment and travelled to Argentina. We arrived in Buenos Aires on April 1, 1966. We were met at the airport by Maralynn Dunbar, my dear friend from the Honduran days. We went to a hotel and in a couple of days met with the National Assembly of Argentina to find out where we would settle. We looked at the map. Practically the entire country was available for settlement and we had to decide where. We chose to go to Mendoza. The assembly asked us to open the adjacent provinces of San Juan and San Luis as well.

We took a bus to Mendoza, arriving after six hours watching the landscape of the western frontier of Argentina and its backdrop of the Andes. We walked for miles around the city until we found a room in the back of a house. Several other tenants shared with us a common courtyard, bathroom and kitchen. We stayed there for a while, then found another room in a house, but this too was not really appropriate.

Mendoza is a lovely city nestled in the foothills of the Andes. It is a green lush place and is a well-known wine centre. There were vineyards everywhere, even in court-yards, with channels on the side of the roads for the water from the melting snows of the Andes to nourish the vineyards and other agricultural endeavours. During the harvest season the entire city has the aroma of grapes. The area between Buenos Aires and Mendoza is dry and not very fertile. But when you approach the city of Mendoza, the highway is suddenly bordered by tall green flowering trees.

We took frequent walks to look for better housing. All I wanted was a small place with two rooms and a small kitchen but it had to have a fireplace because the winters are cold. The houses do not have central heating and can be quite damp and dank. One day I fell asleep with the kerosene heater on. The fire went out and I was nearly asphyxiated.

We found a small apartment in the neighbourhood at a very reasonable rent. It had a living room with a fireplace, a bedroom, a small bathroom with a shower, and stairs that led up to the roof. A friend gave us a mattress, since we had no furniture. Little by little we got things for the house. Since it was winter, we used the window for an icebox.

We made friends right away, since Ricardo was very outgoing. He met some people who had a television programme. They asked to interview us. Ricardo was a hairstylist and they interviewed him on that subject. However, before the programme Ricardo told them that he wanted to share the reason we had come to Mendoza and to speak about the Bahá'í Faith. They agreed on the condition that I would speak about the Faith and, in turn, sing a song with my guitar. I had never sung in public, other than informally in coffee houses in Hollywood. I sang an old folk song, then spoke about the Faith and its principles and showed some photographs of the centenary celebration in London as well as a photograph of 'Abdu'l-Bahá. I did not learn until after the programme was over that for almost the entire time I was being interviewed, 'Abdu'l-Bahá's photograph was on the screen.

After the interview, I heard someone singing the song I had just sung, not realizing it was me. They had taped the song and I must say it sounded pretty good. I was then asked to sing on live television on a show called *El Especial* that aired every Saturday evening. I did so and was hired. I worked for several months, every Saturday, singing one or two numbers. I was subsequently asked to go to San Juan, the neighbouring province, to sing and be interviewed and I was able again to mention the Faith on the air in that city, thus fulfilling, in a way, one of the goals given us by the national spiritual assembly.

Ricardo visited the province of San Luis, the other goal, and was able to give the message to several people there, so that goal, too, was accomplished.

Ricardo met several people in his profession and in a short time opened his salon on a very nice street in downtown Mendoza. We began to establish ourselves. The television programme ended and I found a job as a bi-lingual secretary for a company jointly owned by American and Argentinean firms.

Our small apartment was used well. We had firesides every Friday night and it was soon too small to hold everyone. We made many friends and had two declarations from lovely ladies who were well-known and respected in Mendoza. It was during the fast of 1967 when we found a beautiful large house for a reasonable rent (at that time, $100 a month). The house had a large living room, four bedrooms, kitchen, full bath with tub, gas wall heaters in all rooms, a large courtyard and another small bathroom off the courtyard. It did not have a fireplace but it didn't need one. March in Argentina is still high summer, much like August in the northern hemisphere, so it was quite hot. Our friends Felipe and Sylvia, who had been attending firesides and reading Bahá'í books for several months, helped us load our belongings. When they saw how hard Ricardo worked, never breaking the fast, and they realized our move was to enable us to accommodate more people at firesides, they were so touched, they decided to become Bahá'ís.

Ricardo moved his salon to the garage of our house, decorating it beautifully, and used the courtyard and the room off the courtyard to make leather goods such as sandals, purses and belts. The leather in Argentina is plentiful and he did quite well at this trade.

Firesides were well attended in our new home and more and more Mendocinos were attracted to the teachings. We received tremendous publicity in the newspapers and any time we had a visitor we were able to have him or her on a television programme, speaking about the Faith.

Felipe and Sylvia decided to get married and have a Bahá'í wedding. This was held in our home. Since we did not yet have an assembly, the national assembly sent two representatives to witness the ceremony. The house was packed with friends and relatives of Felipe and Sylvia and the wedding was covered by television and radio news channels. On the evening news, as the programme began, the announcer recited the words, 'We will all, verily, abide by the Will of God' in Spanish and then proceeded to show a tape of the wedding. It was the first Bahá'í wedding in Mendoza.

One day we received a telegram from Hooper Dunbar saying that he and Hand of the Cause Enoch Olinga were coming to Mendoza for two days. We immediately got our friends at the newspapers to come to the airport to receive them and Mr Dunbar was interviewed. That night Mr Olinga and Mr Hooper came to our home for a special meeting – standing room only and it too was televised. Our friends and acquaintances were absolutely enthralled with Mr Olinga and when we left to take him and Mr Dunbar to the airport a huge crowd gathered to see them off.

Right after that we had more declarations but were still short of the required nine for the assembly. However, the community was growing and was strong, with many friends supporting the Cause.

Ricardo caught a virus which affected his respiratory system. There was an epidemic of this virus, causing several deaths. Dr Baura, who later accepted the Faith, took care of Ricardo. It looked as if nothing could be done since they couldn't find any medicine to counteract his condition. We had round-the-clock nursing care and had to have oxygen to keep him breathing. They filled him with antibiotics and finally he pulled through, but remained very weak and unable to work. The only funds we had at that time was my salary, about $100 a month, an average salary for those days in Mendoza. We had some help from the deputization fund, which is occasionally used to help keep pioneers at their posts, but we did not like to have to do this. After much consideration and prayer, we decided we should leave Mendoza and sell what we had to pay our debts. This was a painful decision but there seemed no alternative. The Bahá'í community was strong and we knew it would prosper and grow. When we left Mendoza in 1971 we left a portion of our hearts there.

We returned to Los Angeles and then were asked to serve at the national centre in Wilmette. After many years of illness, Ricardo died during surgery. His remains are buried at the Inglewood Cemetery in an honoured spot at the foot of Thornton Chase's grave. He suffered for a long time but his loving attitude and desire to serve the Cause never diminished.

Six months later, I was invited to serve at the World Centre. I stayed there for five years. In May 1989 I returned to California specifically to assist my mother, who was then 85.

I still want to pioneer again. Being a pioneer for the Cause of God is a state of heart and mind. The bounties one receives are tremendous. When you are out there relying solely on the assistance of Bahá'u'lláh, anything you do to further the Cause comes with little effort. In fact, when one makes the tiniest effort on His behalf, oceans of recompense are given and the way is found. Doors just seem to open, one leading to another.

It is said that Hand of the Cause of God Enoch Olinga was once walking with some pioneers in Panama on a hot humid day. One of the pioneers, who was very tired, said he was looking forward to the next world and some rest. Mr Olinga laughed and said he would get no rest there, for once a pioneer, always a pioneer, throughout eternity.

19

In Bolivia

Bruce Maxwell Fox

I had only been a Bahá'í for one week when I became the caretaker of the Pueblo, Colorado Bahá'í centre. For an entire year I confronted the local spiritual assembly with question after question. The following year I was elected to the assembly.

Now as I write these pages, sixteen years later, I am reminded of that time. I spent two years in the Ḥaẓíratu'l-Quds in Pueblo, deepening and working and looking for a way to go pioneering. The *American Bahá'í* advertised for people to go as travel teachers for six weeks in Bolivia. I responded and was not turned away.

When I left that lovely little house I expected to return. I commanded but four words in Spanish, yet I resisted learning more because I really only expected to be in Bolivia for six weeks.

At the end of my six weeks, I attended a pioneer class. Bolivia urgently needed pioneers and the Bahá'ís wanted me to stay. I arbitrarily decided I would, kidding that, 'They do not have papaya in Colorado.' Other members of the team agreed to stay on too. The American international goals committee wrote to the National Spiritual Assembly of Bolivia asking them to send us back since we were only travel teachers and not pioneers. The national spiritual assembly said no. I stayed. The assembly in Pueblo was kind enough to pack up my belongings and send them on. I was a health food nut – the grains, beans, honey and herbs they sent were enough to feed a poor Bahá'í family for over a year.

I wound up going to Cusco where I met Rúḥíyyih Khánum. She said to me, 'I hope you are not one of those pioneers who has promised to stay and then goes home.' The essence of true pioneering, of course, is to stay at your post, through good times and bad. Travel teachers do short term service in an area and then leave. It was not expected I would stay, but I felt I had found the one true place where I could actually be of service.

I attended the Bahá'í conference in Bahia, Brazil where I met Hand of the Cause of God Enoch Olinga. I was wearing a day pack, so when they spoke of the need for travel teachers in Paraguay, Mr Olinga said, 'Here is one ready to go right now!' As it turned out, I was the only one of the Bolivian pioneers who did go to Paraguay on the teaching trip. I spent two months travel teaching through-out Paraguay, learned a little more Spanish and had simply a great time getting to know the people.

When I returned to Bolivia, I was asked by the Bahá'í community not to wear my fire engine red suspenders for fear the Indians would think I was some sort of a clown. I obeyed. The only belt I could buy had the letter 'J' on it. Since this was not my initial, people kept asking what it stood for. I told them it stood for 'justice'. The answer in fact was that this belt was the only one in my size that I was able to find.

I was six months in Cochabamba getting my permanent visa and trying to structure goals for my service to the Cause. In each place that I went I was able to connect and communicate with waiting souls. In Beni, a jungle in northern Bolivia, I spent six months with Fernando Huerta, the only member of our travel teaching group who was expected to stay for a year. He wound up staying two years more than the original plan. I went to Potosi for eight months and lived with Garth Pollack, another member of a travel teaching team who overstayed the period of time set by the international goals committee. Garth is now in Villa Montez in Tarija, the head of Esperanza (Hope) in Bolivia.

I travelled around for three years teaching all over Bolivia. On one of these trips I met Hand of the Cause Dr Muhájir in Cochabamba where he invited all the Bahá'ís to his hotel to enjoy watermelon. About five of us went. This was just before he went to Ecuador, where he passed away.

I became a member of the National Spiritual Assembly of Bolivia for two years in 1981–3. I then went home to the United States for a visit. Before I left, I made promises to different people as a means of ensuring that I would return to Bolivia. Many people had told me of a Bahá'í who went home for a visit and never came back. While on that visit, I met a girl I thought I might marry, but I decided that first I had to return to Bolivia and fulfil promises to people there. Immediately I got off the plane in La Paz, I felt as if I had returned to my real home and my real service to the Faith. I knew I could not go back to the States. I asked Mr Khamsi where I should pioneer. He suggested Chuquisaca and the national spiritual assembly concurred. So Fernando Huerta helped me get an apartment in Sucre. I have been here ever since.

I felt I was ready to be married and set about finding a wife. I met a Bahá'í girl who had been in the Peace Corps in Africa and wrote to her extensively. She seemed a likely candidate until she said she thought pioneering in St Louis, Missouri, was the same as pioneering in Sucre, Bolivia. I began to feel it would not work out with her but she came for a visit. All the other pioneers were enchanted with her. I was in a panic, thinking she expected this to be a serious situation, while now I was convinced that it should not be.

Before she came down, I had met on several occasions another girl, Maria Teresa Palacios, but felt she was a bit young. There was the language barrier as well. Yet we seemed to communicate quite well with only a few words. Almost all of the pioneers felt Maria was not the one for me and that the other girl was. I ended up marrying Maria Teresa anyway. We married a month after I had come down with hepatitis and my skin was still a most unattractive yellow. We weren't really in love but she was active in the Faith and we had much in common. We have learned to love one another and our marriage has become a good one.

Many Bahá'í travel teachers, visitors and pioneers came to Sucre over the years. Susie Zalaya (Millard), the youngest of our original group of travel teachers, was here in Sucre when I arrived, although she soon left. Next Noel Coq (Jost) came. She helped me start Fox Language Academy but when her husband finished his studies here, she returned to the United States. Carol Pena (Terry) was here for a number of years but when her Bolivian husband could not find a job here they both went to the States. Jurgen Bruckhoff was here but had to return to Germany. Bernardo Fritzche returned to Germany with his Bolivian wife when he finished studying medicine. Margi Mendel also helped with the Academy but went to Santa Cruz, Bolivia, and married a Bolivian there.

In 1982 Teresa and I took our first trip together, to Ecuador to a Bahá'í conference. The trip by bus took six days. Teresa kept asking me, please, to allow her to include one more bag which she said she would help carry in Ecuador. But once there, she told me she was unable to help so I ended up carrying around 17 different bags of different sizes and shapes. I felt like her personal donkey. But a highlight of that trip was that we met Hand of the Cause Paul Haney.

Teresa worked in the cooperative of rural school teachers for a year-and-a-half and her salary was used to help advance the work of the Cause in Bolivia. She went back to teachers' college, had some difficulty at first, but eventually became a grade school teacher.

As a member of the national spiritual assembly, I was eligible to go to the Fifth International Convention in 1983. While there I met Hands of the Cause Ali-Akbar Furutan and Dr Ugo Giachery, who told me he liked my jacket, a tartan of green, blue and white. On my way to the convention, I stopped at La Paz to see a baby, as Teresa and I hoped to adopt a child. We were unable to have our own children. Teresa was surprised when I called her and said I had seen a baby and that if she liked, she could come and get him. That was Jamal Fox Palacios, who was born on March 21.

My mother gave me $2,000 so I could attend the convention, stating that she would give me the usual yearly stipend as well, but if I did not attend the convention I should consider this money simply an advance. My mother, though not a Bahá'í, has helped me remain in Bolivia in full service to the Faith with her financial aid. She has helped my brothers and sister – none of them Bahá'ís – in the same way, treating all of us the same. In my case, the money she has given has been enough to live on here.

The dollar was worth a great deal at that time. I had started a bilingual school, the Badi School, which we ran while also continuing to run the Academy. I was making five dollars a month, considered a good salary. With this salary and the money my mother gave us, we lived like royalty, Teresa, Jamal and I. A year later we went on pilgrimage to Haifa and it cost but $1,200 round trip, business class, on Lufthansa. My mother came to visit that summer and began thereafter to send $20 every now and then in her letters, which was a big help.

During the six years we ran the Badi school we gained a lot of practical experience in teaching, far beyond anything a textbook could provide. This was of enormous help later in our work teaching Indians the Faith.

In March 1986 we were given a baby girl, Navvab Fox Palacios. Another Bahá'í pioneer had wanted to adopt this child but was unable to maintain her. Navvab was nine months old when we brought her into our family. Her first weeks were difficult on all of us, but she is now happy in our family. We adopted another baby girl on Valentine's Day 1990, Tahirih Gildersleeve Fox Palacios. Each of our children is a great delight to us. They are happy and healthy. We teach our children at home with materials from the States.

Our family life is a real bounty as is the opportunity to teach the Faith here, although there are many hardships encountered on teaching trips. Much of the time it has seemed as if I have opposed accepted practices, but much of what I have learned has been by trial and not always by error. Sometimes it seems just a stroke of luck that what I have done has turned out to be right for the situation. Pioneers have to learn to go with the culture of the country in which they live. Sometimes learning this culture takes a bit of time. Then, suddenly, you gain comprehension of things you could not understand at first.

We made contacts all over Sucre and today we are known as 'the Bahá'ís of Sucre'. Any stranger arriving here looking for Bahá'ís is immediately sent to us. We sold the Badi School to the teachers because we felt we could no longer work effectively in education/school administration in Bolivia. We decided we would do better in the countryside.

Every time there are conferences, summer schools or

special classes we have been able to attend, sometimes travelling in jeeps, trucks, buses or on burro, horseback and often on foot. On one trip with another travel teacher we decided there would be no trucks that day, so we walked. Just as we were sitting down to rest, a truck came by and we hitched a ride. On the return trip, I got on a 'Noah's truck' with every kind of farm animal in it – goats, sheep, pigs, cows, horses, dogs, cats, donkeys and chickens. It was an interminable ride. It took 48 hours to cover what was normally a ten-hour route. The smells were amazing and both the smells and incessant bleating and braying made it impossible to sleep.

That experience reminded me of the first teaching trip I made into the country, into the mountains. I slept outside because I did not like the smell of the shelter. Others slept inside. In the morning we found out what the powerful stench was: dead llamas that had been there a while. In addition, a donkey had died sometime during that night. In the morning there were nine condors circling about.

When in the jungles of the Beni with Fernando Huerta, one day I chose to wear a pair of lederhosen, my suspenders and no shirt. I offered to play frisbee. Fernando refused but other kind neighbours accepted. A drunk passing by asked Fernando if I were an illusion or what.

One auxiliary board member said jokingly, 'The only time Bruce does not have his foot in his mouth is when he is changing feet.' Another told me I didn't have to sign my letters because my spelling and grammar were so bad that he knew who had written the letter. Once I asked one of the counsellors if my clowning with the Indians was a good idea. He thought not. But on pilgrimage, I asked another counsellor who introduced me as the pioneer who jokes with the Indians in Bolivia and 'they love him for it'. Many believe that as Bahá'ís we must present a dignified – even solemn – demeanour. Yet I have found that humour is a form of communication that allows me to break down barriers.

One day in Paraguay I was well off the beaten track. An Indian Bahá'í offered to escort me back to the main road where I could get transportation back to Asunción. His horse was short for me in the first place. We had no common language. Sign language had to do. He forced me to put on the stirrups which he extended to their greatest length but they were still too short. I felt like a misaligned daddy-long-legs and couldn't move. I had my backpack on with its metal frame. There was a tree limb hanging out over the trail. I tried to duck but my legs were anchored in the stirrups and my movement was restricted. I got my head under and the metal frame over and was stuck. The Indian came to my rescue, making the horse move back. He also allowed me to take my feet out of the stirrups for the rest of the journey.

On one trip into the interior of Chuguisaca I was walking with a travel teacher who said I could stay with a Bahá'í family that day because he had personal things to attend to. I had only recently returned from a pioneer training institute in the States where I was told that no matter what anyone offered me to eat, I should accept it. Here again it was the old story in my life of doing things backwards. I attended a training institute three years after I began pioneering. I got a great spiritual uplift from attending and much practical advice. However, for me, it seems that I have to learn the hard way, to just bungle along, trying this and that. The advice to accept offers of food fresh in my mind, I accepted this family's offering. Since I did not speak their language they fed me and fed me and fed me. Every time I said 'Thank you' they thought it meant I wanted more and they kept heaping my plate with potatoes.

On that same trip I had to hike up the mountain with my

full backpack. I was tired and kept asking how much further. Each time I was told it was just a bit further. This went on and on until about 1 a.m. I was given the only bed in the community. I was too exhausted to eat or even to talk.

I continue to learn every day, aware of the many merciful blessings bestowed upon my family and me. Growth in the Faith has been tremendous here but it falls so far short of what needs to be done. One solution might be the establishment of an educational institute or centre in the countryside so Indians who are Bahá'ís will feel it is theirs. A part of the solution is having more capable pioneers and development of the capabilities of the native people. All this will require great spiritual growth within the Bahá'í community.

20

Essentially a Homebody

Patricia and Frank Paccassi, Jr.

Patricia Jane Butler and Frank Edward Paccassi, Jr. met in Detroit, Michigan, in 1949. Frank was attending Wayne State University and Pat was working in a music store. They were married in October 1950 and their first child, Lynn, was born in December 1954 and their second child, Judith Ann, prematurely in April 1957. Frank began working with the Chrysler Corporation in the aerospace division, a job that required a series of moves. So far, the life of typical Americans. But soon, all of that was to change.

They became Bahá'ís in Carmichael, California in March 1964 and made their first pioneer move to Puerto Rico in October 1965. Subsequently they moved to St Thomas in the Virgin Islands, 1966–71; Barbados, 1971–6; to Dominica, 1976–7; St. Lucia, 1977–90 and in 1990 to Trinidad, where they now live.

Moving to many places was normal for Frank but nothing in my life had prepared me for the amount of moving around we were to do. I soon realized, in dismay, that I am essentially a homebody addicted to familiar routines. The many moves we have made for Bahá'u'lláh still amaze me.

We became Bahá'ís in 1964. As we deepened in our knowledge of the Faith, it seemed inevitable that we would become interested in pioneering. An article in the *Bahá'í News* was the turning point. It was a plea for pioneers and in it was a challenging quotation: 'Let the doubter arise, and himself verify the truth of such assertions.' Accepting challenge was a way of life for me. As for Frank, moving, especially for the Faith, was no problem. We began a process of writing letters and sending resumés all over the world. Unlike missionaries who are sent out by churches, Bahá'í pioneers pay their own way by working in the new country and within the new culture of that new land, thus becoming, as much as possible, a part of it, at one with the new land and its people. So our resumés went out and we sat back and waited and waited and waited. We came to realize that if we wanted to go, it would not be with a job waiting for us. We would simply have to go and find work once we were there.

I began to have second thoughts. As a result of her early arrival on this planet, Judy, our youngest daughter, was in special education. What would happen to her education? Grandma Snyder had come to live with us in December 1964. She had become a Bahá'í on her eightieth birthday but was a lot younger than her years – active, lively, gregarious and with an inquiring mind. How would she react to living overseas? I had just started back to college to get my degree. The need for each individual to acquire as much education as possible is emphasized in the Bahá'í writings. Also, we were actively teaching and working for the Faith in our community. Perhaps this was enough, then. In addition, the foreign goals committee stressed we were to have jobs before we left. But no one answered our letters.

We had told everyone we were going pioneering and had actually planned to go with another Bahá'í family. We had decided to go to the Caribbean as there were many goals for that area. It was also closer to home than other outposts and it had a warm, balmy climate. What should we do? We had been Bahá'ís for a year and a half. Were we really ready? The question loomed before us and haunted each hour of our days.

The answer came quickly and decisively one night after a

fireside. Frank, who is normally easy-going and who usually says things such as 'Whatever you want to do is all right with me', surprised me when he announced firmly, 'Tomorrow I am going into work, quit my job and we are going pioneering!' People who were there have told me I went pale. I remember going weak. But that was it. We were on our way. As Bahá'u'lláh says, the best provision for one's journey is trust in God.

We finally decided to go to Puerto Rico. It had many industries and we felt that Frank, with his engineering background, would be able to get a job. Ignoring the fact that they spoke Spanish and we did not, we shipped our goods to Ponce, Puerto Rico, and departed. What a crew we were: Papa, Mama, two girls, aged nine and eleven, two Raggedy Ann dolls, an 80-year-old Grandma and a registered French poodle.

We were met at San Juan airport by the Heath family. I can still see their lovely brown-skinned, golden-haired children. How gracious they all were! We left the same day aboard a small plane for Ponce. Flying low over the middle of the island we could see the mountains and the rainforest with its rich foliage. Everywhere it was green.

In retrospect, I think it was probably a saving grace that we gave every appearance of being tourists and were not expected to speak the language. Everyone was very helpful. We checked into a charming, older hotel with large rooms. All five of us, six counting the dog, in one room, for $15 a night. But late that night, I lay awake, the heat so oppressive it was hard to breath. From deep inside, I wondered, what in the world are we doing here?

It seems to me that just about everything one does when pioneering becomes a lesson. Some are quickly obvious. Some take longer to learn. But they just keep coming. I had never thought tests came in one's weak areas. I had always participated in areas where I was strong. If you are not good at it, why bother? I was now to find new answers about the value of tests on a daily basis.

Almost immediately we perceived we had to find a car and another place to live. We decided to first find a car and then to drive around to look for a place to live. We started making the rounds of used car lots. Every car we looked at was priced outrageously, even the battered ones. Our tourist image was now backfiring. At a small lot we told our tale of woe to the manager. We said we had little money, no job, etc. He rubbed his chin, looked around the yard and his eyes fell on an older car painted in many shades of blushing pink. 'Well,' he said, as we all moved towards this apparition, 'I really haven't checked this one out good, but you can have it for $200.' Frank, who had received quotes for three and four times more money for cars looking no better than this, said, in surprise, 'Two hundred dollars?' The man very quickly said, 'Okay. You can have it for $150.'

Frank looked under the hood, kicked the tyres, opened the trunk with a screw driver. Up to this point, I had said nothing. This is a macho-oriented society and women do not enter into business dealings. But now I snuggled up close to Frank and whispered, 'We said lots of prayers this morning. Get in the car and see if it runs.' The car ran and we bought it. It lasted for the nine months we stayed in Puerto Rico. The lesson? Prayers are answered, sometimes not as we envision, but . . . prayers are always answered.

As soon as we ran out of money, Frank found a job. We moved into a lovely apartment. Leonard Ericks, another young pioneer from California, moved in with us. I took an intensive Spanish course with nuns and priests and laymen at a Catholic university. Life, as we had never known it, had begun.

We were soon found by our first two new Bahá'ís. One was Noel Robles y Robles. The second, Iris Guinalls de

Maull, was a law student at the university and lived upstairs from us. Iris has remained a steadfast, devoted Bahá'í and has served on the National Spiritual Assembly of Puerto Rico for years. Iris was the first Puerto Rican to go on pilgrimage. In 1973 Iris, Frank and I and Rose Perkal Gates were together in the Holy Land in Haifa, as we were all delegates to the International Convention. I was beginning to learn the answer to my question, 'What in the world are we doing here?'

Frank's job soon turned sour. The man who hired him did not like him being friendly with his underlings and accused him of proselytizing on the job. He knew he had either to quit or be fired. We moved to the San Juan area. Many jobs for engineers were advertised, but Frank could not find one. Our money was again low. We sadly wrote to the foreign goals committee back home about our situation. We acknowledged they were right about employment and wrote we regretfully felt we would have to leave our post. A loving letter came back. The committee would subsidize us until Frank found work. A postscript to this letter reported that a new national spiritual assembly was being formed in the Leeward, Windward and Virgin Islands. If Frank could find work there, it would be very helpful.

Dorothy Behar, another pioneer from California, had moved with us to San Juan. She decided to move to St Thomas as well. We consulted, pooled our money and sent Frank first to St Thomas where he found a job the very afternoon of his arrival! Joyfully, we looked ahead to the move; yet it was tinged with sadness for we had come to love Puerto Rico. Another lesson we were learning was to love but to be detached.

It's a short air hop to St Thomas on a small airplane and by this time we felt like veteran travellers. The flight was fantastic, full of symbolism for me. A large brilliant rainbow seemed to cover the plane and it was with us most of the way. The sign of the Covenant! The waters around St Thomas were clear, with gradations from a deep blue to light green. What a welcome to the West Indies!

St Thomas was an interesting post. It had been opened in the mid-1950s by Knights of Bahá'u'lláh Charles and Mary Dayton. They were followed closely by Ellerton and Marjorie Harmer. In the '60s other pioneers began to arrive in response to the call of the Nine Year Plan. The Harmers were the welcoming committee. This wonderful family eased newcomers into the community. Whatever kind of help one needed, the Harmers were there. I imagine there are many who remember them as godparents in the pioneering field. They are still there and I am sure doing the same things today.

As St Thomas is a United States territory it was relatively easy for Americans to get jobs. Because of this many prospective pioneers to other posts remained on St Thomas. This was, in one way, a good thing but it also deprived the rest of the area of help that was badly needed. It was five years before our family moved on to Barbados.

In 1964 the National Spiritual Assembly of the United States informed the area that it had been asked to help with the formation of the first National Spiritual Assembly of the Bahá'ís of the Leeward, Windward and Virgin Islands. This territory ranged from St Thomas in the north to Grenada in the south. It encompassed five different languages, four currencies and 600 miles of small pieces of land surrounded by large bodies of water. The national assembly was formed in 1967 with five local spiritual assemblies as its foundation. Many new national spiritual assemblies, especially in developing areas, receive financial assistance from the Universal House of Justice. But this national spiritual assembly was supported almost entirely by the St Thomas Bahá'ís.

As we settled into this community a lesson was given to

us that confirmed us as pioneers. It started when Frank soon lost the job he had when we arrived. It seems he had a bad habit of telling his bosses they were double billing the government for work they had done. Obviously, he had to go.

Then began a period of adjustments. Frank could not immediately find another job. It became apparent that I would have to look for work. I was not happy with this idea because I had not worked for years and I also felt strongly that it was best, whenever possible, for women to remain home to take care of the children. Women are then available to do a lot of teaching during the day. But there was no money coming in. It was time for me to find work. I quickly found a job in a jewellery store. Merchandise sold on the island is duty free, making it a good spot for tourist shoppers. On Christmas Eve, for example, there are usually ten to twelve cruise ships in the harbour. The salary, while adequate for single girls, did not begin to cover a family's needs. It paid for food and that was about it. The end of the month was coming and the question was, how would we pay the rent?

When we left Carmichael, our house was not sold. Our friends Maxine and Marty Roth took care of renting it out for us. It was a full week before our rent in St Thomas was due when we received a letter from the Roths. Our garage door had been damaged by a hit and run driver. The Roths had put in an insurance claim but decided to fix the door themselves. In the letter was a cheque which covered the rent with one hundred dollars to spare! We were saved by a hit and run driver several thousand miles away, and, of course, by the attention of caring friends.

The next week we received another letter from the Roths. Could we send $90 to cover costs of repair to the hot water heater? The message was clear. We would receive what was needed, nothing more. The principle has worked for us ever since. We have never been without what was needed. All we had to learn was the difference between needs and wants.

Soon Frank got a good position with the government. He was head of a one-man department of research and statistics. He made a good salary and had very little to do. I moved to a larger jewellery store, managed by a Jewish couple who visited Haifa frequently and always visited the Bahá'í Shrines while there. They were sympathetic to the Faith so I was able to work and still take time off whenever I wished to go travel teaching and also on Bahá'í holy days. I usually took Judy with me on summer teaching trips. For a long time I was known as 'Judy's mommy' in the Windward Islands.

We seemed to be settling into a routine. The girls were both in the government school system. Judy, with her sweet nature and iron will, was doing fine in school and had picked up a West Indian accent. The adjustment was harder for Lynn. She was now twelve years old. Other pioneers have told me that it is most difficult for children in puberty to make the change from one culture to another. The younger the child, the easier it seems to be. Grandma, on the other hand, loved the Caribbean at once and everyone loved Grandma.

The latter part of the 1960s saw the beginning of mass teaching in the southern part of the United States. We were as excited and enthralled as the rest of the Bahá'í world. The national spiritual assembly immediately began to consult on it. Was our area ready? Were we ready? Could we afford to put on a mass teaching project? Two out of three is not bad. We would get the money somehow.

The national assembly began to put together an international mass teaching project. The counsellors were asked to send an auxiliary board member, Ruth Pringle, if at all possible, to assist. The National Assembly of the

United States was asked to send an experienced, multi-racial team to work with us and show us what to do. And I was asked to coordinate it. Guiding bravely and praying madly, I started.

The first choice for the project was Nevis, a small island in the Leeward Islands. However, I was unable to find anywhere to rent as a base. I then thought of Barbados as I had been teaching there the previous summer and the people were very receptive. A trip to Barbados solved the problem.

Barbados has a large sugar cane industry with housing facilities for workers during harvest time. I saw one of the cane houses and thought it was perfect – large rooms, a lot of bunk beds and a good-sized kitchen. Jim Taylor, a black member of the team from the States, looked at it, turned to Shirley Yarbrough, another black team member and said, 'Well, we've come full circle.'

Oh, but what a marvellous project it was. The balance of people working as a team was impressive. West Indians from several islands were there: Don Providence, a youth from St Vincent who had been teaching with me the preceding year on Barbados and has remained close to us and to the Faith all these years; Shirley Howard, also from St Vincent, came, bringing her newly-born son; Errol Sealy, who was appointed in 1990 as the first counsellor from the Caribbean, was there as a 17-year-old youth. There were people from sophisticated areas and from rural villages – white people, black people, brown people. And wonderful Ruth Pringle giving us guidance and communicating our progress and our needs to the Universal House of Justice.

Working with her was a real education for me. I learned more from her in six weeks than I had learned during my six years as a Bahá'í.

Starting in the summer of 1971, the first stage of the

project lasted six weeks. There were 500 enrollments in the first weeks and 1,500 by the end of the project. Ruth Pringle put together a follow-up and consolidation plan that was outstanding. Back-breaking, it is true, but outstanding. The plan, however, depended upon the Bahá'ís being able to use the government schools as meeting places in the various villages. It was not to happen. The government refused permission and the deepening efforts suffered.

Jim Taylor stayed after the project until December but was not able to stay any longer. It was obvious that the valiant and hard working pioneer family, Philip and Karen Wood, along with a few other devoted souls like the Haynes family, Diane Bourne and Hazel Beckles, the first youth enrolled on Barbados, would be unable to cope with this huge influx of new believers.

Frank and I consulted and then volunteered to help. Frank left his job in St Thomas and the family moved to Barbados in October 1971. It became apparent that the only job that might be available for Frank would be a teaching position in the government schools. Although he had never been trained as a teacher, his BS degree was sufficient for him to teach physics and general science. It took a year for a teaching job to open. Our visitors' visas ran out before a job materialized. We went to the neighbouring island of St Vincent to wait and received financial assistance from the foreign goals committee.

The growth of the Bahá'í population in the region resulted in the formation of another national spiritual assembly, for Barbados and the Windward Islands, with its seat in Barbados. In April 1972 Hand of the Cause Rúḥíyyih Khánum, representing the Universal House of Justice, was present for the election.

Our move to Barbados started us on a new way to serve the Faith. There were so many new Bahá'ís in so many different parts of the island that we had to visit as many places as possible. Not having meeting places was a real drawback. In spite of all that was done it always seemed to be a case of one step forward and slide back a few. It was like working with quicksand: you can get it together, but you can't hold it together.

The time from the mid-70s on was hard. It was exhilarating and frustrating at the same time. Rapid growth and slow consolidation. We were all learning new skills and while we got very good at the first step of enrolling people, the remaining steps of consolidation were elusive. We banned the 'are they Bahá'ís or aren't they?' 'paper assemblies' and 'rice Bahá'ís' stage as being counter-productive. We kept on teaching and the growth continued.

It was in Barbados that our family continued to receive help in such unusual ways that it could only be part of God's bounty.

One of my favourite examples is how I got to attend the International Convention in 1973. Frank and I were both delegates that year and we only had enough money for one air fare and expenses. I had been on pilgrimage and had taken a teaching trip around the world the preceding year. It was clearly Frank's turn.

When we had travelled from St Thomas to Barbados, we had shipped all of our goods air freight. Everything had arrived except two boxes. Eventually we received a call from Eastern Airlines telling us that our boxes had been found. We went to the cargo hangar, they took us outside and there sat our two boxes. They had been there the whole time, out in the weather. We opened the boxes knowing that whatever was inside must be ruined. In one box there were old clothes and miscellaneous goods. In the other was Frank's collection of early Marvel comic books. They were water soaked and had lost their collector's value. Frank put in a sizeable claim based on catalogue prices but as the insurance cheque did not arrive by return mail, it faded from our memories. Yes, you guessed it. That is just what happened. The cheque arrived in time for me to travel to Haifa for the International Convention. My only regret is that I made such unkind remarks to Frank about dragging around with us this large bunch of comic books.

During the four months that we were in St Vincent waiting to return to Barbados, two events resulted in many changes for us. The first concerned Lynn. She would have to switch from the American to the British system of education when we moved back to Barbados. Essentially what it meant was that she would have to go to the United States to finish her high school education. During this period we had a young travel teacher in St Vincent, a granddaughter of Curtis Kelsey, who became a good friend of Lynn. After telephone calls back and forth it was decided that Lynn would live with this girl's family in Indiana and finish high school. A sensible decision but I was to miss my oldest daughter acutely.

The second event concerned Grandma. Still active, she was now 87 years old. One day she fell and broke her hip. When we returned to Barbados, she attempted to walk again but one leg had become shorter than the other. She was now confined to her bed. She remained cheerful and whenever I travelled she would pray and pray for me. In August 1976 she had a cardiac arrest and three months later at the age of 90 passed away peacefully in her sleep. She is buried in Belleplaine, Barbados, the first pioneer to die at her post in the Windward Islands. A loving cable was received from the Universal House of Justice, assuring us of its prayers for the progress of her soul. The marker on her grave identifies her as a Bahá'í pioneer and quotes the first line of her favourite prayer by 'Abdu'l-Bahá: 'O God! Refresh and gladden my spirit . . .'

Frank had worked at two schools in Barbados but he was let go from the school in Belleplaine. In spite of endless efforts to find another position, still there was no job to be had. We had received an extension to stay until after Grandma died. We asked for and received another extension to settle our affairs, but we still hoped to find a job and to remain in Barbados.

The national spiritual assembly asked Frank to look in the other Windward Islands for a job. Its first choice was Dominica as this island had just recently been transferred to its jurisdiction and needed help. Two months later we left for Dominica. Frank was hired as a mathematics and science teacher at St Mary's Academy, filling in for a Dominican who was receiving more training overseas. Could there be a pattern developing?

We had lived in two islands, each the seat of a national assembly. I had served as recording secretary in both places. In Dominica I was elected corresponding secretary which involved an even greater investment of time. Eventually, the only way I could manage was to spend two weeks in Barbados and two weeks in Dominica every month. Was this the same woman who had been such a homebody, such a creature of habit? It was ironic but many of life's little ironies proved opportunities for personal growth for Frank and me.

Dominica was lovely. It is the largest of the Windward Islands and the least populated. It has a large mountain range in the centre of the island and the tourist brochures say they have one river for each day of the year. The people are wonderful and, to my ears, their West Indian accent is the most pleasant in the Caribbean. They have a real sense of honesty. This is evident in the market place, where the women sell fruit and vegetables to me for the same price they charge everyone else. Believe me, that is not a common practice in the islands.

Frank's salary was 540 East Caribbean dollars per month or roughly $200 in American money. Even in the late '70s, this was not a lot of money but it covered all of our needs. We had a comfortable house in an estate up on a hill overlooking a beautiful valley and the sea beyond it. Hand of the Cause Enoch Olinga and his wife Elizabeth visited that house and when a chicken passed our screened-in porch, they clapped their hands and laughed in delight, saying it was just like their home in Africa.

Roughly six months after we arrived, more pioneers came – Edith Johnson and her brother, Al Segen. Edith was a seasoned pioneer having lived in Africa. Junie Faily-Silver arrived soon after that. What a welcome addition! All were loving, devoted and hard-working Bahá'ís. The island soon came to have Bahá'í communities and many activities.

Frank had his own share of ironies. While in Dominica he went on pilgrimage and was welcomed as the first 'Dominican' pilgrim.

A year later the Dominican teacher returned and Frank was once again asking the national spiritual assembly where to look for a job. Its first choice this time was St Lucia. Except for Esther Evans, Knight of Bahá'u'lláh for the Windward Islands, who was 78, there were no other pioneers on the island. Once, on my way back from two weeks in Barbados, I stopped in St Lucia on an errand for the national spiritual assembly. While there I picked up a *St Lucia Gazette*, which is the government publication listing teaching positions and so on, and found that several schools had openings. Frank sent resumés to each one. As it turned out, all the resumés ended up in the same place, the Teaching Service Commission. A month after school started, the Commission called Frank and asked if he could teach engineering science. 'Of course,' he said. After the phone call he said to me, 'I wonder what engineering science is?' Two weeks later we were in St Lucia.

Moving to St Lucia was a step up financially. Because he had been hired from overseas, although this usually meant places like England, there was a gratuity and furnished housing provided at a reasonable rent.

As we had arrived so quickly, quarters were not immediately available but we eventually settled into a large house overlooking the Caribbean Sea. It also overlooked a small airport where a crop-duster took off with a roar at 6 o'clock each morning and small airplanes several times a day. This did not detract from our fondness of the house and its view. I even got so I would look blankly when visitors would say, 'How can you tolerate that noise?'

Frank Fernandes, who was originally from Guyana but had become a Bahá'í in Barbados, came to St Lucia at the same time as we. He stayed for a year working as a full-time Bahá'í teacher. He was dedicated and hard-working. On foot and by bus he covered the whole of that end of St Lucia. There are not many communities in the south where his name is not mentioned when you ask someone if they have heard of the Bahá'í Faith.

Later on Emily Kramer, now Greer, travelled back and forth between Barbados and St Lucia. She spent time in the American South teaching, holding children's classes and working on general consolidation, not an easy task for a single woman. Emily is another of those pioneers to whom 'car' is an important word. On advice of friends, who shall remain nameless, she bought an old clunker that looked fine. It cost endless money for repairs and provided endless opportunities for spiritual growth. The darn thing would strand her on the road, miles from anywhere, would not start on the very next day after being repaired and was at all times unpredictable. Nevertheless she decided to buy four new tyres to spare herself the aggravation of constant flat ones. She drove the car home with its new tyres, parked it on the street and came out in the morning to find that someone had stolen all the new tyres and had put on their old smooth ones.

Keith and Stephanie Bloodworth and their nine-month-old son, Ruhi, arrived from Canada to pioneer. Stephanie had filled in at the last moment for a Canadian travel teacher the year before, had fallen in love with St Lucia and now here she was with her family, ready to go to work. They became true friends. We shared the same love of teaching and serving the Faith. They were there when our daughter Lynn and her husband and sons left for Grenada. I watched them leave with a heavy heart. I had grown so close to my grandsons and now they had to leave. The Bloodworths took them to the airport. As the two families walked down the stairs, Ruhi, who up to that time had called me Pat, stopped, looked at me and said, 'Bye-bye, Grandma, I'll be home soon.' About a year later another son, Badi Gerald, was born to the Bloodworths and he became another loving grandson to us.

Beverly March pioneered from Jamaica and lived with us for about three years. She was a West Indian of radiant spirit, an invaluable pioneer. She was soon appointed an auxiliary board member. When she left to further her education, I was not the only one who sorely missed her.

Projects were started. One highly successful international project was held in memory of Grandma Snyder. Nancy Cole was one of the team members who returned with her mother to pioneer. Nancy eventually married Moses Auguste, who had been one of the first Bahá'í youth in St Lucia after we arrived. Moses and his sister Juliana were team members on this same project.

It's interesting to see how Bahá'ís get to their pioneering posts. Often it is through travel teaching, either individually or with teams on projects. It's as though it had all been laid out in advance. More often than not, pioneers say that they feel like they belong at their post as soon as they arrive.

The Bahá'í communities in the Windward Islands continued to expand. New national communities were formed. Barbados and the Windward Islands divided in 1981, each having its own national spiritual assembly. In 1983 the Windward Islands was itself divided, with St Lucia and Dominica each forming their own national spiritual assemblies and leaving St Vincent and Grenada together until the following year.

To be a part of the birth of a new national spiritual assembly is a thrilling experience. The feeling does not come from any sense of personal accomplishment but is rather one of appreciation for the great privilege of being allowed to be there, a witness to history.

Most memorable is the year St Lucia and Dominica formed their own national spiritual assemblies. As corresponding secretary I was asked to represent the 'mother' assembly at the formation of the National Spiritual Assembly of Dominica. Hand of the Cause Mr Khadem, representing the Universal House of Justice, and Counsellor Ruth Pringle were there for the St Lucia formation. Immediately after that convention, I travelled with them to the next convention in Dominica.

Another marvellous opportunity came for me during the visit of the international travel teacher Mehrangiz Munsiff. She had visited the islands before and I had a deep admiration for her. How could I not admire one who had been started on her teaching exploits by Martha Root and who had continued her work at a pace that would exhaust any ordinary person? During a trip back from the country, with a van full of Bahá'ís, we began to banter back and forth about how Mrs Munsiff needed someone to organize her time and she said to me, 'Why not come with me and organize me?' The remark seemed to have been made in jest but I soon realized this might be an opportunity for me. As we continued to discuss this possibility, I set up a criterion. As chairman of the national spiritual assembly that year, I was uncertain if I should absent myself for ten weeks for such a selfish reason. I decided I would go if the airfare was within our means and, secondly, only if the International Teaching Centre, which had arranged Mrs Munsiff's trips, gave me its approval. This sounds silly now, but it all seemed logical to me at the time.

I checked with the travel agent and was quoted a price so reasonable I could hardly believe it. But there was no answer to my cable to the Teaching Centre. I consulted with Mrs Munsiff and showed her a copy of the cable I had sent. She shook her head as she read the cable and told me that the way it was worded might lead the Teaching Centre to think that it was my idea only. We telephoned Haifa that day and she talked with Counsellor Peter Khan. He told her that while the Teaching Centre had received the cable, it felt it had insufficient information and had decided to wait. I have thought about that answer many times. It is so comforting to know the calibre of the institutions guiding our Faith.

We then spent a wonderful ten weeks travelling through Grenada, Trinidad, Tobago, Guyana, Surinam, Brazil, Uruguay, Paraguay, Bolivia, Ecuador, Peru and Panama. Travelling with Mrs Munsiff is great. I was not inexperienced at travel teaching but I had always carried addresses and phone numbers with me so that when I arrived at my destination I could then work out my schedule with the Bahá'ís. With Mrs Munsiff, as we arrived at the airport there were the Persian believers carrying large bouquets of flowers. Meetings had been arranged way in advance, the media alerted and the highest officials in the land were prepared to receive her.

Only one problem arose. Mrs Munsiff became very ill and needed rest and treatment after Uruguay. I had to continue the itinerary. It did not seem fair that the communities were expecting Mrs Munsiff and got me. But Bahá'ís are so gracious and understanding and forgiving. We muddled through and fortunately she was able to continue from Peru.

At the end of the year of this trip, Judy became very ill. We had to take her to the United States for treatment. This started a chain of events which resulted in Judy leaving St Lucia in 1988 to live in Sacramento, California.

We spent twelve years on St Lucia. Frank was eventually given a permanent teaching position; he retired in 1988. We had been given permanent resident status and had planned to spend the rest of our lives on St Lucia. We had figured that at the age of 60 our nomad days were over. Little did we know!

While we were in California helping Judy to get settled into a new culture, we met a family who had been pioneers in Trinidad, Dr Keith and Cheryl Thorpe. We had known them in the West Indies. They are a marvellous family; the Faith is their life wherever they are. Now as we compared our situations – the Thorpes with a house in Trinidad and unable to remain there, the Paccassis without a job or pension and early social security benefits about two years away – it became clear. Another move was in the plan for the Paccassis.

We have been here for almost a year. We both love it. It's a bigger island and all this space is dizzying. The Bahá'í work is exciting. We are involved in deepening institutes and working with new believers. And for the first time Frank and I can work as a team full-time. It has opened a new level of service for us which was never possible before. Now, if our energy level does not totally desert us, we shall continue to serve Him as best we can.

The West Indians are interesting people. They are friendly, generous, relaxed. They believe in God and talk about Him. They rely upon God's grace in their daily life. They are curious, born educators and are very eager to listen to the Word of God. As one put it, 'Once you're talking about God, it's my duty to listen.' They are also sensitive and emotional and for the most part still practice the principle of 'an eye for an eye'. They are a very caring people. You sneeze on your porch and an hour later someone sends a message for you to drink some lime tea and put a plaster on your chest. Carry your baby on your shoulder and someone will immediately tell you that you have to support the baby's back. Turn your car around and four men who have never driven a car in their lives will holler instructions to you. When you walk into a village people will call out and ask you 'What's your mission?' If 'you do 'em something, it will come back to you'. Feuds are carried on in families for ages. If they have two of something they will give you one and if you are really in need, they will give you both. If you are late or don't show up where you are expected, no one will say anything. They just assume you have a good reason. This relaxed attitude is wonderful to live with unless you are trying to get your telephone fixed or are waiting for the plumber.

Things are changing rapidly in the Caribbean as they are all over the world. When we lived in Barbados in the early '70s we could go to town and leave our house unlocked and the windows open. When we returned, all was as we left it unless it rained and then someone had gone in to close our windows. Today, all over the island, there are bars on all the windows, chained fences are installed around houses. Drugs are a real problem. AIDS is spreading. But still the teaching continues. The contrast between the ills of the old world order and the solutions of the new World Order of

Bahá'u'lláh is more sharp than ever. People are open to Bahá'u'lláh's healing message.

Looking back over the years, some things stand out very clearly. One is the effect the Hands of the Cause of God had on us. Meeting and being with them is one of the great bounties of being in the field, especially during the past 25 years. In the larger countries, one usually gets to see them only at conferences and summer schools. Today there are but a precious few of them left and the opportunities have become even slimmer. But for us, over the past years, Rúḥíyyih Khánum has eaten tuna sandwiches in our kitchen, Dr Ugo Giachery praised Lynn's cooking, John Robarts laughed at our corny jokes, Dr Varqá told us stories about himself and the early believers, Dr Muhajir told me to go on a world teaching trip and laid out my itinerary for me, Mr Khadem told me I was an energetic Bahá'í. All these remarks and memories are in our treasure-house. From these contacts with the Hands of the Cause and getting to know them, their spiritual power is felt in every way. Each time a Hand of the Cause would visit, it would galvanize the entire community. Unity would become stronger. Everyone made more effort for the Cause. Sympathy and understanding of the Faith increased as they visited officials and prominent persons in the country. Future historians will, I am sure, do justice to their service.

Of course it was not all easy as pioneers. We had our share of robberies, illnesses, long periods of unemployment, disappointments, disagreements, misunderstandings and frustrations but these are part of life everywhere. Would we change what we did? I don't think so. Of course, each of us always wishes we could have done more and done it better but we did the best we could at the time. I think that's what 'Abdu'l-Bahá meant when He said we grow spiritually little by little.

Did we ever regret being pioneers and wish to return to the United States? No. That was not even an option or a solution to tough situations. When you're in the field, you feel more Bahá'í. It's somewhat like the definition of the two kinds of Bahá'ís – those to whom the Faith is their religion and those to whom the Faith is their life. You are aware of being a Bahá'í 24 hours a day. All your senses are heightened; you pray more, you serve more, you end up doing things you never would have done anywhere else and you're more fulfilled. Why would anyone leave a life like that?

Yet I know there are many Bahá'ís who are not pioneers and I know they also feel all of these things. I remember a saying of Hand of the Cause Horace Holley, that pioneering is not moving from place to place but from self to self. We can all serve the Faith wherever we live. There is never a shortage of work to be done.

21

The Gardener

Nancy Casasanta

When one thinks of Bahá'í pioneering, most often thoughts are of living in remote regions under difficult circumstances, helping to bring water to dry areas, teaching practical things that enhance the quality of life, teaching the Faith by word and by living the life as an example. But for Nancy R. Casasanta of Hartford, Connecticut, pioneering meant becoming, of all things, a gardener! Many times at firesides Nancy has spoken most eloquently of her joy at tending the beautiful gardens at the Bahá'í World Centre and at the Bahá'í Shrines. When asked to write of this experience for this book, Nancy found it difficult.

I suspect I am being rather covetous about it all. Still, a part of me longs to share this story. It is not unlike having fallen in love for the first time. A part of me wants to shout it for all the world to hear and a part of me wants to protect and privately cherish it. While at my post I did not feel at all like a pioneer. I expected to do more and to affect many lives. It is only now that I am back at home, among my friends and family, after four years away, that I feel like a pioneer.

In 1979 I went on my first pilgrimage to the Holy Land. On the plane returning to America, I knew that some day I would return to Haifa. Five years later I received my official invitation to serve at the Bahá'í World Centre. I served both as a secretary and then as a gardener. At first I resented being sent out to work in boots that soon became covered with dirt, working with the sweat just dripping off me. Many of those I had arrived with were comfortably sitting in air-conditioned offices wearing dresses while I was out digging holes and developing muscles I didn't want. I felt I was being punished. Then, day after day, my friends would pass through the gardens during lunch or an afternoon break and tell me how blessed I was that I had been chosen to work in the garden, out amongst the flowers, the birds and the blue sky. It finally dawned on me. How blessed I was to tend the final resting places of the Holy Family. People would come from all over the world for just a brief period of time in order to worship at the Shrines of the Báb, Bahá'u'lláh and 'Abdu'l-Bahá. And here I was with unlimited time to go and pray or just to visit in silence. And here it was, too, seeing all those visitors from so many countries, that I began to feel the oneness of man, to feel that we are all world citizens.

Working in the gardens was backbreaking work, dirty and often tiresome, but I grew to love every minute of it. I worked with two Arab men who watched me for three months before they began to believe I would stay and endure the hot sun and continuous climbs up the terraces each day. It was difficult for these other workers to accept me in the gardens they had tended so carefully long before I arrived, to accept me doing what they believed was not woman's work. They were not Bahá'ís. They were very respectful towards me but they could not understand why I chose to wear 'pantaloons' and to work like a 'donkey' instead of sitting in the marble building with the rest of the ladies drinking tea. I knew I was constantly being watched and judged. But as time went on they seemed to watch me less. Although I would work in silence for eight hours each day, I never felt alone. Pilgrims from all over the world would walk through the gardens and comment on the beauty of the flowers. I took great satisfaction in my work.

There was not a pebble out of place on the many paths when I finished work for the day.

The time came for me to leave Israel. Still I wanted to stay in the Middle East. I needed a job as well as a destination. I wrote to the National Spiritual Assembly of Cyprus and inquired if they had need of a pioneer. Thus began a new area of service.

Cyprus is a very beautiful island, very, very old. The Cypriots are hard-working people who live for their families and their country. In the Greek part of the island, they are of Greek Orthodox religion and are a proud and honest people. I learned quickly to speak enough Greek to get by. In the larger towns English is spoken but in rural areas the people speak only Greek.

I made many friends. They could not understand what an American woman was doing all alone in Cyprus. This gave me a perfect opening for mentioning the Faith. Everyone listened politely but never went any further in their questioning. Consequently I left religion alone and worked on being a good friend. They seemed to relate to me as a friend but there was one other obstacle. Americans, in general, were not well liked. The impression most people in Cyprus have of America is negative. I was very careful in all I did and said. I was not just representing my country but the Bahá'í Faith as well. It is a difficult thing not to be liked because of your nationality and not to be understood because of your religion. I never would have been so tested simply living at home in my own country.

I also learned there is a world of difference between merely reading scriptures and living by them. Nowhere else have I experienced the kind of transformation that comes with pioneering. The Writings took on deeper meaning and I felt watched over and guided all the time I was away.

In Cyprus I worked for a British off-shore company as a

financial consultant. The company sent me to Spain for three months where I rented a villa and searched out British expatriates who might be interested in investing in the company. Just as in Cyprus, people in Spain found it unusual for an American female to be representing a British company there. I had little contact with Spanish people. The people I met were mostly from Wales, Holland, Austria, Canada or England. Most spoke English. I returned to Cyprus without having made any sales. The market crashed and I was without a job. Wondering how I would exist with no job and no work permit, I panicked. This could mean my pioneering days were over, for the time being at any rate.

Then I received a letter from my father. He needed an operation and I was needed at home to take care of him. I have been at home now for two years. My father has recovered from his surgery. I have found a job which challenges me. I have created a lovely garden in the yard at my father's house. Many people walk by it daily and stop to admire it. As long as my father needs me, I shall remain here. But I hope one day once again to see the beautiful gardens at Haifa and to pioneer. Meanwhile, I know that I am still tending the garden mentioned in the following quotation attributed to 'Abdu'l-Bahá:

> At the gate of the garden, some stand and look within, but do not care to enter. Others step inside, behold its beauty, but do not penetrate far. Still others encircle this garden, inhaling the fragrance of the flowers and, having enjoyed its full beauty, pass out again by the same gate. But there are some who enter and, becoming intoxicated with the splendour of what they behold, remain for life to tend the garden.

22

We Were Happiest When Pioneering

Esther and Nyenti David Tanyi

In a continent as large as Africa, even homefront pioneering can take on all the aspects of pioneering in a faraway foreign country. Knight of Bahá'u'lláh Nyenti David Tanyi experienced both and writes of the 35 years he and his wife Esther spent pioneering:

I was born 63 years ago into the Banyang tribe of southwest Cameroon. After my middle school education I took correspondence courses and obtained a diploma in book-keeping and accountancy.

I was a devoted Protestant of the Basel Mission (now Presbyterian) Church and much loved by the missionaries with whom I worked first as a junior clerk and later as a shopkeeper at their bookshops in Buea and Victoria (now Limbe) from 1947 to late 1953. Southern and northwest Cameroon was then under British administration, together with Nigeria, and there were in Cameroon only three churches. From 1950 other churches began entering the country and each claimed 'ours is the best and the others are wrong'. As a person interested in religion, my mind was greatly agitated trying to decide to which church I should belong.

One of these churches preached to me that just as I am not conscious of my life in the womb of my mother, so also will I not be conscious after death. So, I said to myself, I should enjoy myself the best that I can as, after all, according to the teaching of my church, I shall neither see nor feel heaven or hell.

Then one morning as I worked at the counter at Basel Mission Bookshop, I saw a car driving in covered with mud. I remarked to my assistant that the car must have come from far off. I expected a big sale and a good commission. The occupants of the car were a white man and a white woman. The man came out of the car, walked to the shop and asked to buy film for his camera. He bought it and walked out. Soon he came back to the shop and asked for Paludrine, a malaria drug. I told him that our stock was gone but I could direct him to a place where he could buy some. He said he knew nothing of the town as he had only arrived the night before. I asked my shop assistant to take him along but the man said, no, he wanted me to go with him. I told him that as the only person in charge of the shop, I was expected to remain at my post until noon. He said he would wait and went back to his car. It was between 11:00 and 11:30 a.m. on a Saturday in the rainy season (July through August) of 1953. At noon I closed the shop and directed him to Bota, the residence of the pharmacist. He bought the drugs and the pharmacist gave him some free of charge as well for his contribution to tourism in Cameroon.

As he was driving me to my home, the man told me he and the white woman were travelling with an African gentleman. All three were lodging in the hotel. The couple would be leaving soon but the African would remain for some time. As living in the hotel was expensive, the man asked me if I could help the African look for other accommodation in the town. I said I would help.

We arrived at my home and they met my wife, Esther,

who was making bread outside of our home. After an exchange of greetings, they asked my name. I did not ask theirs – they may have told us but we attach no importance to the names of passers-by. We gave them a map to our home for the African man. They stopped by our home a couple of days later to tell us of their final departure.

The very day that I gave them the map to our home, the African gentleman appeared at our door, smiling and beaming, paper in hand, and asked if this was the home of Mr David Tanyi. We welcomed him and introduced ourselves. We were very much interested to meet someone from Uganda, East Africa, and he also expressed his delight at meeting us. This gentleman was Enoch Olinga. We conversed for a while and he asked if he could visit us on the next day, Sunday, and enquired at what hour we would be home on Sundays and when on weekdays. I told him that 10 a.m. after Sunday church services was fine and after 5 p.m. on weekdays. Enoch visited often and kept to these times. He became a member of the family. Sometimes he spent a whole day at our house when he had correspondence or other material to type. Sometimes he visited me at the shop. When he got ready to leave, he always said, 'I want to begin trotting home.' Enoch was often humorous like that, and it was from him that I first heard that expression 'trotting' used for walking.

So our friendship continued and the search for accommodation for him in town was at hand. We learned from him the names of the white people. They were Mr Ali Nakhjavani and Mrs Violette Nakhjavani.

Because Enoch knew the aim of our friendship, he did not tire of visiting us. He started teaching us the Bahá'í Faith step by step. I had a cousin who was very jovial and who sometimes would visit our home and order drinks to entertain us. He first asked us to take Enoch's order in Pidgin English, which is a sort of lingua franca here in

Cameroon. 'Mister Enoch what kan mimbo you go drink?'
Enoch would say, 'Nothing, Dickson, thank you.' Then
Dickson would exclaim in surprise, 'So you pepol for
Uganda no drink mimbo?' Enoch would reply that the
people drink, but in his case it is his doctor's advice. Then
Enoch, wanting to please Dickson, would say, 'All right.
Any soft drink for me.' Dickson would then send the errand
man away with instructions. 'Me, two trouble mata; Mister
David, two trouble mata; Mr Enoch, cocoa kream.'
Trouble mata means trouble, Martha, i.e. when you drink
and become drunk you will trouble Martha, your wife. The
drink is palm wine, sold in pints; two trouble mata is two
pints. So this became Dickson's song each time he ordered
for us. It was not until later I was to learn that it is a law in
the Bahá'í Faith not to partake of alcoholic beverages.

Another step taken by Enoch was that he offered to pay
for a meal to be prepared one day to which we would invite
some of our friends. But we told him that he was our guest
and according to our tradition we could not accept this. He
insisted and we then accepted. Esther prepared the meal
for us, our friends and Enoch on the particular day Enoch
had suggested. We later learned that this was the Nineteen
Day Feast. However, religion was not discussed at this
Feast. From the day we met Enoch until the day we went to
go pioneering, our home had been the site of all Bahá'í
meetings.

Soon after that first feast, Enoch began talking about the
Bahá'í Faith, first to me, then after some time he asked
permission also to talk to Esther. I listened and read and
asked many questions. I became attracted to the teachings
of the oneness of mankind, life after death, and the
prophesies fulfilled. I was amazed by the story and
martyrdom of the Báb, the imprisonment and banishment
of Bahá'u'lláh, the cruel torture and execution of the Bábís,
and that these events had actually occurred in our so-called

modern times. I was amazed that the teachings had reached so far despite these happenings. I then became convinced of the stations of the Báb and Bahá'u'lláh as Manifestations of God. I declared as a Bahá'í.

One day Enoch Olinga said, if the sea were to drift into town or a wild beast threaten to attack us in the town, and each and every person was concerned to build a strong wall around his house to protect himself, his family and his property; and another person called and invited everybody to build one strong wall around the whole town to protect everybody and all the property, which of these two is the wiser? Esther replied that the person asking for the building of one strong wall is the wiser because by so doing the poor, disabled, orphans and stray animals would all be protected. Esther had answered correctly. Enoch said that was the Bahá'í message calling all people to oneness and unity. Esther declared her membership at this meeting.

Our numbers at this point rose to six, Esther being the first woman Bahá'í in Cameroon. I was, of course, one of the first six. We brought new friends to our meetings every Sunday. Enoch encouraged everybody at the meetings to speak.

On one occasion when on a visit to Accra, Ghana, Enoch told the friends that 'David and Esther are the Adam and Eve of the Bahá'í Faith in Cameroon because they were the first couple to declare their faith in Bahá'u'lláh'.

Ali Nakhjavani opened the door to our hearts and Enoch Olinga introduced the Faith to our open hearts and ears. That is how I became a Bahá'í.

One afternoon Enoch brought home a cable. He read the cable to me and Esther.

URGENT ENTRY AFRICAN BELIEVER VIRGIN TERRITORIES BRITISH FRENCH TOGOLANDS ASHANTI PROTECTORATE NORTHERN TERRI-TORIES PROTECTORATE BEFORE RIDVAN. WILL ENSURE VICTORY. SHOGHI.

This was in April 1954. While we contemplated the holding of a meeting regarding the contents of this cable, two days or so later Ali Nakhjavani arrived. This time I saw him as a Bahá'í and not as a tourist. A meeting was called. At this time our community numbered nine and we were sure of forming a local spiritual assembly on April 20, 1954.

As usual, the meeting was held in our home. The cable was again read to the community. When the question was asked, everybody wanted to go to pioneer. But Ali explained that only four people were required. The best way to solve this problem was by secret ballot. The result was that the following were chosen: David Tanyi, Martin Manga, Edward Tabe and Bennedict Ebala. A prayer was said at the close of the meeting. All during the prayer, Ali was weeping. This raised some suspicion in Esther. We were married less than two years and our love was high and she was five months pregnant. Esther found it very suspicious that, in the face of my having to leave her immediately and go to the unknown, this white man was weeping so at prayer. It is unusual for an adult to weep in our society, especially on such an occasion. 'Maybe it is a deal to sell you. Find out,' urged Esther. So I enquired from Ali as to why he was weeping and he explained that he wept for joy for us and for sorrow for his country, Iran – that it is sad that Iran persecuted Bahá'u'lláh for His good message which we have accepted and for which we are willing to sacrifice by leaving our families, friends and relatives to go to distant countries to teach the very Faith for which Bahá'u'lláh had been persecuted. Esther was satisfied with this answer.

Ali and Enoch completed our travelling arrangements. We flew to Lagos on April 10, 1954. Ali obtained passports for the four of us. Esther remained with my parents because she was expecting our baby. When he was born, we named him Enoch.

Our party of five then left Lagos by road and arrived at Lomé, the capital city of French Togoland, on the night of the 13th of April. This was to be my pioneering home, so early on the morning of the 14th Ali accompanied me to the post office where I cabled the Guardian of my arrival. I was then left to settle in Lomé. One by one Ali settled each of us in our pioneering posts before Riḍván as the Guardian had instructed: Edward Tabe in British Togoland, Bennedict Ebala in Ashanti Protectorate and Martin Manga in Northern Territories Protectorate. All of these places elected local spiritual assemblies by Riḍván 1955.

Esther joined me in December 1954 after giving birth to Enoch. Teaching work progressed steadily despite our personal difficulties. Benin was even opened by Bahá'ís from Togo.

Because I had no employment in Lomé and Martin Manga was to return home to Cameroon, I was asked by the Africa Teaching Committee of the American National Spiritual Assembly to transfer to Tamale, Northern Territories Protectorate and to pay occasional teaching visits to Lomé. This was on the Gold Coast, now Ghana, in March 1957. My employment took me to other places in Ghana, namely Accra and Kumasi, until 1989 when I retired from employment, fell sick and my wife insisted we return home. We came back to Cameroon on December 4, 1989.

Looking back, it seems amazing how it was that we could ever teach. First I was left alone in Lomé, newly married and in love. I could not speak French or the local dialects. I was just six months old in the Faith. This was my first time travelling out of my native country. These and other things agitated my mind, so I wrote to Enoch Olinga and Hand of the Cause of God Músá Banání that I must return home to Cameroon. When their letters of reply came, my hand trembled in joyful expectation of their support for the return home. Instead, Mr Olinga wrote, 'I hope you will resign yourself to teaching the Message of Bahá'u'lláh,' and Mr Banání wrote, 'Physical weakness does not appear in the picture.' I then prayed for Bahá'u'lláh to open the way for me. Within a short time I met my first friend in Lomé who was bilingual in French and English. By then I had received the basic books and pamphlets from the Africa Teaching Committee. I introduced the Faith to this new friend who later became a Bahá'í. So the Faith spread in town and in neighbouring Benin through the combined efforts of this man, Esther and myself.

We made friends wherever we went. Pioneer reinforcements came: British, Iranian and American. Our happiest times were when we were out teaching or at meetings. But we suffered many trials. Esther suffered the most. She suffered acutely when I had to leave her when she was pregnant. For some reason the allowance which it had been decided she would receive was not paid to her. I sent her no money because I thought she was being taken care of. When I was alone I was paid an allowance but when Esther joined me with the child, this allowance was sliced to half, until Auxiliary Board Member Valery Wilson visited us in Lomé and intervened. Before this intervention, Esther had to accompany the Togolese women to the sea shore and help the fishermen pull the nets. She was paid in fish, some of which she would sell and some of which we kept for our own food. The other women who lived in the house in Lomé would quarrel with Esther for washing my clothes, saying they did not launder men's clothes. Esther explained that she had been trained differently. None of the women would stop our baby from crawling to the fire or taking a sharp knife. Esther was always watchful of our baby but it was hard for her to give him the care he needed and do this other work.

The Bahá'í community elected me to attend the Africa

Conference in Tunisia in 1955, but then a delegation approached me and said they would like a citizen to attend instead of me. I stepped down for the sake of unity. Then the person they chose to attend fell sick on the very evening the flight was scheduled, so he did not go. Thus Togo was not represented.

In 1963 in Accra, Ghana, the Africa Teaching Committee instructed me to prepare all necessary arrangements to attend the London Conference. I did all the preparation and reported to go but the tickets never came.

Two of our babies died among non-Bahá'ís in Tamale and Accra. When the menfolk went off to work, the women at the compound would assemble, come outside our apartment and mimic Esther's weeping. All this was reported to the landlord, who reprimanded the women and warned them that any further misbehaviour would cause their removal from the house.

When we lost our 19-year-old son in Kumasi, Ghana, in 1983, the Asare family, Iranian fellow pioneers, and the other Bahá'ís comforted us and we shall always remember this kindness.

In comparing the two sides of our lives, we know that pioneering kept us happier than we are now, back here at our home where we look like aliens in our own country and are living miserably. As veteran pioneers, Esther and I would advise other pioneers to adapt themselves to the environment in the new culture and to remain at their posts at all costs. That is by far the happiest of solutions.

23

'How Do You Go?' 'Peacefully.'

Enoch N. Tanyi

Enoch N. Tanyi, son of David and Esther, stresses the importance of learning the culture of the place to which one pioneers and also the language as quickly as possible because this 'facilitates interaction and opens doors to teaching'. Enoch writes:

At the age of four I started my primary school education at Tamale in the north of Ghana. Tamale is a predominantly Muslim area. Every Friday afternoon there was a period for religious instructions. Each pupil was free to attend either the Muslim or the Christian class. I always attended the Muslim class. The teachers were called 'Mallams' and were often strict disciplinarians who wielded the cane. I remember learning by heart the Kalima and the opening chapter of the Qur'án. This early association with Islam is probably the cause of my special love for that religion.

When I was nine or ten, we moved from Tamale to Accra and I was enrolled in a Roman Catholic school run by missionaries. We were often taunted because children called our Faith the 'by heart' Faith. Thus two non-Bahá'í factors influenced my early religious life. My parents were constant in sending us children to Bahá'í gatherings and in teaching us the Faith. It was these things and the exposure to Bahá'í pioneers, travelling teachers and visitors that were the secondary Bahá'í influence. Becoming a Bahá'í was thus a gradual process but before the age of fifteen I had already made up my mind to become a Bahá'í.

Tamale

Tamale is the northern regional capital of Ghana. I grew up considering it my home as I did not remember my previous home. I learned the language, Hausa, which is widely spoken in this area. With my parents, I spoke my mother tongue. Despite the use of Hausa, we were not really integrated into that community and were marked out by the indigenous people. I remember the scarcity of water in Tamale. My mother had to get up at 4 a.m. and go and wait for hours in a queue to obtain a bucket of water from a standing water pump. This chore was not without frustrations for her because of the queue-jumping of those who considered her a foreigner.

Twenty years later I travelled to the north of Ghana again with some Bahá'í pioneers. The custom of the people of north Ghana is to serve visitors a bowl or calabash full of water from which all are to drink. A short time after our arrival, from some distance came one of the young ladies of the house with an old metal bowl in her hands. All were silent as we each had to take the welcome sip before discussing our mission. As the young lady approached, I saw a brownish liquid in the bowl and murmured, in near panic, to the pioneer seated next to me, 'Whiu! Look at the dirty water brought for us to drink.' 'Well, you don't have to drink from it,' the young lady replied. The bowl went round and round and when it was my turn I raised it to my lips and took a sip. I thought, 'Should ordinary drinking water be such a rare commodity?' The young lady took the bowl and ambled off to her smoke-filled kitchen. Three thirsty people had drunk from the bowl but the water remained to the brim! Were we hypocrites? Were we wise?

Or were we offensive to our host who had offered the best he had in all sincerity and warmth? These questions were to haunt me for some time.

Accra

The capital of Ghana is a cosmopolitan town. There is such a concentration of so many cultures that children grow up ignorant of aspects of their own culture. It is the practice here that people seated in a group are greeted in turn counter-clockwise. Once, a group of Bahá'í friends were seated in a home. I was seated next to the door but on the left side of the room. A man entered. I was the first person he encountered so I stretched out my hand to greet him. He withheld his hand, walked to the right side of the room and started shaking hands, going around the group counter-clockwise. He shook my hand last but the feeling of hurt persisted.

When one enters a Ga home (the Ga are the people of Accra) one is welcomed with two basic questions which require certain responses: 'How about where you are coming from?' to which the answer is 'Peacefully', and 'How about the people of . . . (the place the visitor has travelled from)? to which the answer is always, 'They are well.' I made an error one time when welcomed by a hundred-year-old lady and gave the answer to the second question first. She smiled and gently tutored me in what to say to each question.

Kumasi

Kumasi is the Ashanti regional capital and its inhabitants are called Akans. There is a tradition among the Akans – and indeed in most Ghanaian homes – of being invited to eat whenever one enters a house at meal times. The host says, quite literally, 'My hand has got it,' and the guest, if he does not feel like eating, politely thanks the host. Once when visiting Bahá'ís in a village near Kumasi with my two younger brothers, who had never before been in this particular Bahá'í community, my host served food and brought a jug of water for the two of them. The host left to give them privacy in which to eat. I heard chuckles and my two teenage brothers said almost simultaneously, 'Enoch, look. Look at two golden fish in the drinking water!' Smiling, I responded, 'That's a supplement to your protein intake. Make no mistake, the jug of water is no aquarium!'

When visiting a village, one asks to see the chief, who arranges for a linguist to serve as translator so one can state one's mission. After the introductions and statement of one's mission, it is customary for the guest to ask permission to leave the chief's presence. The chief answers by saying, 'There's chance,' which means permission has been granted.

The culture calls for the use of the right hand in giving and receiving or even in pointing at things. It is never proper to give anyone anything with the left hand.

While our family was in Accra, Ali Nakhjavani visited and was invited to our home. My mother roasted some groundnuts and put them on a plate. She placed the plate in front of our honoured guest and a lusty cockroach sauntered across the groundnuts. I was standing nearby, apprehensive of what our guest would do. As if he had noticed nothing, he took a handful of the groundnuts and began to munch them in a relaxed manner. Not even a tacit lecture on hygiene!

Knowing at least a bit of the language and of the customs facilitates interaction between pioneers and those of other cultures. Basically the pioneer should just do what needs to be done without concern about the results. This does not mean that there should be no appraisal of teaching efforts to see in what ways they could be more effective. As much as possible, all effort must be made to organize three or more days of deepening institutes in a quiet place where there will be little distraction.

Other than that, Bahá'í teachers must be patient with themselves and work with sincerity, perseverance and love. God will Himself bring the results. Sometimes the results are not immediately visible, but there are times when one learns, years later, that words or actions have helped someone to declare his faith in Bahá'u'lláh.

24

Travels in India

Madeleine Klingshirn

Madeleine Klingshirn of Fribourg, Switzerland taught at the New Era High School, a Bahá'í school in Panchgani, Maharashtra, India, open to children from all national, racial and religious backgrounds. Wherever she travelled through that huge sub-continent she found people eager and willing to hear about the Bahá'í Faith.

I was born into a Catholic family in a little town named Bulle, Switzerland, in 1956. My father is a German who left his country after World War II. My mother is a Swiss. Both are sincere believers in God but they were not really attached to their religion. They never forced any form of religious practice on me. I had the freedom and space to accept something new.

At the age of 21 I met a Bahá'í for the first time, a young woman of my age, daughter of a Chinese mother and an Arab father. She had been a Bahá'í for a couple of years and was getting married. She invited me to the ceremony, a Bahá'í one. There were many people in attendance and the atmosphere was loving and warm. The ceremony was simple and yet, so meaningful and beautiful. I think that my heart was touched by this experience.

I kept in touch with Cathy until I left for the United States for a stay of one year to learn English, American English! I spent the year in California but never came across any Bahá'ís. Truth is, I never thought to look for them. But when I returned to Switzerland, one of the first friends I encountered was Cathy. I did not search for her, she came my way. Then one day when I was hitch-hiking, a man gave me a lift. During our conversation, I learned that he was a Bahá'í and that his wife was from California, from the same town I had lived in while there! He knew Cathy very well as they were living in the same community. So Cathy and I met again and became close friends.

Then once again I left Bulle to go to another city for a new job. Again I had no contact with Bahá'ís for a long, lonely time. I had the address of an American pioneer living in that city but could not reach her for an entire year. I was very unhappy and felt my life was meaningless. I prayed to find purpose in my life. And then once more, unexpectedly, walking on the street, I met a young Brazilian Bahá'í. He was going around with a little stand, explaining the principles of the Faith. I listened and this time it really clicked in my mind. There was in this Faith something I needed to investigate seriously. From that time on, I attended firesides, a feast and my first summer school. However, I did not read any books, just a few pamphlets, before I accepted the Faith. That year, 1981, one month after attending summer school, I declared my faith in Bahá'u'lláh. That was a powerful feeling, a spiritual rebirth. I knew that now a whole new life was ahead of me – not an easy one, but a challenging one, a purposeful life, at last!

I developed a great thirst to meet Bahá'ís from other countries, other cultures and races. I was seeking confirmation in my Faith. I left behind my home, my family, my friends and my job and flew to Australia where I attended the 1982 International Bahá'í Conference in Canberra. Over 2500 Bahá'ís from about 45 different countries gathered there in a spirit of love and unity that was so strong I could not sleep at night. I felt dizzy! The conference was a great confirmation for me as a new Bahá'í.

After the Canberra conference, I did some travel teaching in Australia. I met some Indian Bahá'ís who told me about Panchgani and the New Era High School, the first Bahá'í school to be opened in India. They had worked at the school, which they knew very well, and they urged me to visit. As I had the time and sufficient money to allow me to travel for a few months in India where things were so much cheaper, I bought a ticket to Bombay and decided that Panchgani was going to be my next destination. I must say, however, that at first the idea of travelling alone to that huge country was terrifying.

I had written a letter to a Bahá'í family in Bombay and had hoped they would be at the airport to meet me. They were not. Luckily, a young Indian woman, who realized I was lost, offered to drive me into town. With her husband and brothers, in a crowded car, we drove into Bombay. I stared out the car window, appalled and frightened at the hundreds of beggars and poor people, walking in the streets, barefoot, half naked, looking starved and sick. When we reached the address I had been given, we discovered that the people had moved to New Delhi. However, I was able to locate some Bahá'ís who could help me find my way to Panchgani. My first week in India was one of such culture shock, I can scarcely recall the details. Everything was different here.

When I arrived at Panchgani and visited the New Era High School, I discovered a village situated in a gorgeous natural environment on top of a plateau, surrounded by other plateaus, from which one can see in all directions. No big concrete building, only small pleasant houses with trees and gardens – a beautiful, calm and inspiring place. Even the light and the colours are special. I was warmly welcomed at the school. When I met the children I knew that I wanted to stay and serve in that special environment but I did not know if this was a possibility.

During my stay in India I had two distinctly different experiences: the time spent at New Era High School and time spent travel teaching and visiting Bahá'í communities throughout the country. Had I stayed only at the school, I would never have seen the Indian culture as I got to see and understand some of it in my travels.

At the school I taught a class in the primary section. The work was enriching but there were many tests and difficulties for me. One of them was the food, which while good, was very institutional, always the same, and this affected my mood. On the other hand, I had difficulty with some Indian cooking. The Indians love chili and put it into almost every dish. My western digestive system simply could not cope with this hot, spicy food. I suffered every time I accepted an invitation to dine in an Indian home. Yet I accepted many such invitations so as not to offend.

There was something else I found difficult while serving at the school. Living all day long in a large Bahá'í community, individuals had the tendency to watch and evaluate one another's behaviour. Each tried his or her best to serve, but each had his or her own area of vulnerability and inner struggle. I found that living in a completely different environment, having to adjust quickly to many new ways of life, created stress. I became overly sensitive at times to people's remarks.

The greatest bounty of being there were the spiritual experiences. Much was happening in Panchgani. Visitors from throughout the world came regularly to the school including Hands of the Cause of God, counsellors, great scholars, and many others. I spent about six months teaching at the school. Leaving was difficult. I had become attached to the children and the staff members. There were many wonderful friends and I knew I would miss them.

India is a vast and complex land with a great diversity of ethnic groups, languages, customs, religious communities, sects and castes. To know and understand the people of India would require more than one lifetime. As a Westerner trying to survive in this land, it was necessary to be very tolerant, patient and open-hearted and to maintain at all times a sense of humour. I found it difficult to understand people through the intellect but I could feel close to them when I opened my heart to them.

Travelling was always an adventure. Imagine sitting on a train for 40 hours, a train crowded with all sorts of people. There were always those curious enough to ask me lots of questions. This gave me an opportunity to talk about the Faith. In India people are much concerned with religion. Religion is part of their daily life. When they hear a foreigner talking about the Bahá'í religion, they want to know more. Travelling by bus and train was tiring. There were such crowds. At times it was necessary to stand for hours in a line just to get a ticket. Because of the bad condition of the roads, sometimes the bus engine would suddenly quit. Then everyone would have to get out and wait for another bus to come.

I visited in many states, cities and villages and met Bahá'ís nearly everywhere I went. It was a special event for them to meet a Swiss Bahá'í sister. They asked lots of questions and were always ready to offer their help. For many people, even among the Bahá'ís, there was some- times a reluctance to accept a single woman, even a foreigner, travelling about alone, mingling with all sorts of people. Within the strongly male-oriented Indian society, women have to struggle to find their place. There is a division between the men and women and also between women of the older and younger generations. I had several offers of marriage but the idea of being expected to stay at home, submissive to the all-powerful husband and a mother-in-law as well, was unthinkable. Yet I saw the respect Indian men had for their mothers and wives and for other women as long as the women showed great respect to them. Indian women wear clothes that cover all parts of their bodies and I followed the same rule. I wore beautiful and elegant saris which were very comfortable once I learned how to walk in them.

I learned much from the Bahá'ís I encountered. In many cities the Bahá'í centres were the rallying points for friends. I knew I would always get a welcome there as part of the great Bahá'í family. I met Bahá'ís who were such examples of devotion, hard work and sacrifice that they were an inspiration. One young man, a very deepened Bahá'í, worked for the Faith seven days a week, from early morning to very late at night and all of his work was on a volunteer basis. But for him there was never any doubt – working for the Faith was the primary focus of his entire life.

There have been many declarations in India but to deepen those thousands of new Bahá'ís is an enormous task which falls to just a few very strong and deepened believers. In India, as everywhere, deepening and confirmation in the Faith can be a slow process. In one Bahá'í home I was surprised to see a big picture of Christ in the living room and a small picture of 'Abdu'l-Bahá in another room. This was because the family did not want their neighbours to know they had become Bahá'ís.

Daily life in India can be very hard. Some mornings there would be no water from the tap. The water shortage in India is acute. A simple shopping expedition can be difficult. If you are lucky you can catch a rickshaw, a three-wheeled motorcycle with a bench to sit on and a roof to protect you from the sun or rain. Be careful how much you pay for the trip! At the marketplace you soon get lost in a noisy and smelly crowd. The market is fascinating, full of life and excitement but trying to buy sufficient foodstuffs for a few days is an adventure. Learning the techniques of bargaining is essential. Bargaining in India is somewhat of a national sport.

Emerging from the market one day in a state of exhaustion, I went to keep an appointment with a friend. I went to her house but she was not there. I waited and waited and waited. Finally my dear Persian Bahá'í friend arrived, explaining how she had spent hours going from one office to another trying to get a visa to go to Canada. She was so tired and discouraged she wanted only to go to bed. Our visit had to be postponed. I struggled to get a rickshaw to drive me home for a reasonable price. I arrived home quite worn out and wondering what it was that I had done for the whole day. In India the concept of time is very different from that in Western societies. The attitude is that if something does not get done today, then there is tomorrow or next week or whenever. It does not seem to matter.

I spent fifteen months in India, which might be termed a very short stay. Yet I felt I did get a good idea of what it means to live there. I do not think I was really a pioneer in India but I did live as a Bahá'í in that country, among the people, and I did learn what characteristics are essential for the long-term pioneer. One must have strong spiritual qualities and not be afraid to sacrifice personal hopes and desires.

At the time I was in India I was still a new Bahá'í, not really deepened and certainly not prepared to live there as a pioneer for a long time. I realized I could not come up to expectations. Local Bahá'ís always expect a lot from the pioneers, in terms of their knowledge of the Faith, strength, dedication and capability.

It was painful for me to realize my shortcomings in this respect. I decided to return home. My experience in India has changed me and my vision of people and things is very different now than it was before this experience. I will never forget the beautiful friends I found in India, their warmth and hospitality, their simplicity, their devotion to religious matters, the way they care for their family and friends.

I think that in order to be a successful pioneer one should first go on a visit to the goal country, to get a feeling for the place and people, to become informed of the conditions there, to find a place to live and a place to work. After that, if one still wants to pioneer, one must remember that he will always need a large store of patience and good humour.

25

It Used to be Called Ceylon

Pym Trueman

Pym Trueman of Kingston, Tasmania, recalls pioneering in Ceylon, just before it was renamed Sri Lanka:

It was a long chain of circumstances that lead up to my becoming a pioneer in Ceylon, in the time just before Ceylon changed its name to Sri Lanka. My daughter, Jennifer, had always wanted to go to boarding school. I could never understand why, as I had spent seven long years in a boarding school and very seldom found anything enjoyable about it. However, when a teacher from the New Era School in Panchgani came to Melbourne and spoke at a fireside, Jennifer made up her mind that that was where she wanted to go. The school presents a unique opportunity to be a part of an international student body while receiving a high calibre education. I gave Jennifer the challenge that if she could save her fare to go to India, I would pay her school fees.

She got special permission from her school to get a job. She was but fifteen years old at this time. She worked for six months and saved up her money. When her sisters realized she was off to India, they wanted to go too. So they all got jobs and earned their fares. I decided that if my girls were all going to India, then I had better go as well. This meant taking my two-year-old son with me as well.

Jennifer flew to India in July, ready to start at the beginning of the new term. Diana, Derry and young Peter went over with me by ship the following January. We landed in Bombay and travelled by train to Delhi where we stayed at the national Bahá'í centre for a few weeks until we got acclimatized.

Diana and Derry went to the school at Panchgani. Diana went to work there as an office assistant and Derry was enrolled as a student. Peter and I went travel teaching in the northern parts of India, into Punjab and up to Kashmir, then back to Delhi via Calcutta.

When we got back to Delhi, the National Spiritual Assembly of India asked me if I would be willing to pioneer to Ceylon to fulfil one of their goals. They needed two pioneers to go to Ceylon before Riḍván. One pioneer was travelling from Malaysia and they needed another. Well! How could I refuse?

Pioneering is not meant to be easy and our troubles started before we arrived at our post. We always travelled third class on the trains in India because third class was half the fare of second class and a quarter of the fare of first. The trip back to Bombay, although hot and crowded, was uneventful. I had trouble keeping people from feeding Peter foods that might give him 'Delhi belly' and tried to keep him on a diet of bananas, nutmeats I extracted from shells and boiled eggs. When he had settled to sleep in my arms, some children came through the train, singing loudly to gain a few rupees. I tried to bribe them to move into the next carriage so they would not wake Peter but there was a language barrier and they seemed to take ages to move on.

From Bombay we went to Panchgani where we picked up Derry, who had decided to return to Melbourne. She had not settled at the school and wished to return to Australia to take up nursing.

On leaving Poona en route to Bangalore, I unadvisedly

bought a piece of cake wrapped in greaseproof paper. By the time we got to Sholapur I was ill enough to visit a doctor who gave me medicine; when I arrived in Bangalore I was very sick and was diagnosed as having hepatitis, most probably from eating the cake. Fortunately my host was a medical doctor so I was given good care. After about ten days we were able to make our way on to Madras from where I had a booking on a train to take us to Rameswaram at the southernmost tip of India. This train was meant to connect with a ferry which would dock at Manner in Ceylon. From there we would go by train to Colombo.

I say 'meant to connect with the ferry' because when we arrived in Rameswaram, it was just in time to see the ferry steaming off in the distance. The next ferry was three days later. We were stuck in a small fishing village comprised of a number of small huts, a rather grand Hindu temple, a railway station and a boutique where we could purchase some food. We didn't know a soul.

We spent the first night sleeping in the railway waiting room. The station master was upset with us because we locked the door before we went to sleep. The next night he gave us a small room with one bed in it. There was also some water in the shower recess so we could wash and rinse out some clothes. The children slept in the bed and I slept on the cement floor. Owing to the kind intervention of a Singhalese family man who occupied one of the larger rooms at the railway station, a room with several beds in it, we were able to each have a bed on the third night. During the day we visited the temple, explored the beach which smelled strongly of fish and rented a couple of bikes to venture a bit further afield.

It was with great relief that we boarded the ferry on the morning of the 20th of April. After a hot and fairly crowded journey on the decks of the ferry, we stepped down onto the beach at Ceylon just at sunset. We had managed to fulfil the goal but only just in time. I knelt and kissed the sand before struggling with my luggage and a sleepy two-year-old towards the overnight train to Colombo, where we were met and taken to the Bahá'í centre.

Staying at the Bahá'í centre was an adventure in itself. I always thought of it as a 'wildlife sanctuary'. There was no glass in the windows so the birds flew in and out at will. If one went into the kitchen at night and suddenly turned on the light, a swarm of disturbed cockroaches scuttled away. It was nothing to be sitting quietly and see a mouse scamper across the floor. I was told they had got rid of the snake that used to reside there. There was a hole in the roof above my bed and I was not certain what might be up there so I always slept with a lump of wood the size of a baseball bat alongside my bed in case something ventured out in the night.

My life as a pioneer in Ceylon was a mixture of riding in buses and trains, tramping over rice fields and up mountains to the tea plantations, visiting fishing villages and rubber plantations and always being on the move. My standard travelling equipment was a tin of powder to sprinkle on mattresses to repel bed bugs and a packet of mosquito coils. Black tea was three cents a cup and white tea ten cents so I quickly learned to appreciate black tea.

There was a period of some months when I did not stay in one place for more than four days at a time. The National Spiritual Assembly of Ceylon certainly knew how to utilize its pioneers. It was at this time that I learned the true meaning of freedom. I was crossing over a bridge at the Colombo railway station, intent on catching the next train to Galle, with a suitcase in one hand and Peter hanging onto the other. I realized that if a national assembly member had come up behind me and said, 'We don't want you to go to Galle; we want you to go to Jaffna', on the other end of the island, I would have changed direction and cheerfully gone to the other platform. It was exhilarating to know that I had reached a state of mind where I could be wholly intent on serving the Faith and teaching the Cause of Bahá'u'lláh with no personal desires or ties to restrain me.

There were many memorable times during my eighteen months in Ceylon. One was the time I spent with the Rodiya people at Waduressa. These outcasts of Ceylon, because of their isolation from the rest of society, are so pure-hearted, like the pearl protected within the shell of the oyster. I still have a strong love for Noni who would cook and bring me breakfast of yams and who would sleep in the cottage with me if Peter and I were on our own. If Jenny was with me, then her husband, Ippiya, would come down with his sleeping mat and spread it on the verandah. I would hear the clang of his machete on the concrete floor and felt sorry for anyone who might dare to disturb us in the night. I have a very warm feeling every time I remember Peter and Ippiya sitting together on the verandah with an English picture dictionary, Peter saying the word in English and Ippiya saying it in Singhalese.

I remember the family who brought their table and chair down for me to use. It was probably the only one in the colony. I remember the farewell they gave me with a spread of food such as they could manage and the gift of a piece of jewellery, a chain with a few stones missing. It was a royal offering from such poor people. And the procession through the colony in the light rain which seemed to blend with the tears that were shed at my leaving.

By far the most precious of memories are of my travel teaching with Hand of the Cause Mr Samandari, that wonderful soul who had been able to attain the presence of Bahá'u'lláh. He was in his nineties when we met and still travelling the world with all his worldly goods packed into one suitcase. The only material things which he took from his stay in Ceylon were some pieces of bamboo which he said were excellent for making calligraphy pens.

While we were in Ceylon and India Peter had many uncles, as this was the term he used for most of the men we got to know. Mr Samandari was always called 'best uncle'. There was a lovely bond between them.

Mr Samandari was travelling with his son Dr Samandari, and Peter and I travelled with them by train to Galle and Jaffna. From these towns we would travel by car to the little fishing villages and to the tea and rubber plantations. One day we visited a tea plantation with a tea factory on the top of a hill. Dr Samandari said to his father, 'I don't think you should try to get up there. I think you should wait here while we go to the factory.' However, with the aid of his walking stick, Mr Samandari made it right to the top of the hill and walked around the factory, showing great interest.

I recall one fairly typical day of his time in Ceylon. He always rose early for prayers and then wrote some letters. After breakfast we set off to meet with some Hindu leaders in the town. Then we took a hired car to one of the fishing villages where he spoke to the people in a way that reminded me of Jesus with His disciples. We came back to town where he spoke to students at one of the colleges. In the evening there was a meeting with the Bahá'í community.

Mr Samandari was tireless in his efforts to spread the Faith of Bahá'u'lláh. There were times when he would flag but he always seemed to be able to rally his strength and gave freely of his time when people sought to speak with him. His life was an inspiration to other people. My life is richer for having been with him in Ceylon.

26

The African Bees Were Aggressive

Timothea Sutton

Timothea Sutton was 16 when she wrote this story. It won first prize in the 15 to 18 age group in the Write Time competition sponsored by Herald of the South *and appeared in that magazine its April–June 1990 issue. Pioneering in Tanzania was a dramatic change of lifestyle for the young American.*

Ring, ring, ring. Oh, no, it's the phone, again!

'Hello . . . Good-bye.' How many more times do I have to hear that word. Not many for we leave tonight.

'Are you packed yet?'

'Timothea, phone for you.'

'This is the last shopping trip. Is anybody coming?'

'Hey, I need some gum for the plane.'

Doors slam and footsteps echo off into the distance. Whew! I'm alone! My God! We are leaving tonight, now I do NOT want to go. Whose stupid idea was this anyway? Finish packing. I feel like a robot, my mind is numb.

'We're back. Are you ready to go? The cars are here to take us to the airport. Start loading the bags up.'

'Wait! I need to make one more call . . . Dee? We're leaving . . . yeah, I love you too. Write to me. I'll miss you. I love you!'

Damn! There's not even time to cry. Here come more good-byes.

'Timothea, get out some ice cream for your dinner. Hurry.'

'Okay, mom, ice cream.' Force it down. Why does it taste so funny? Is this adrenaline?

'Good-bye, I love you!' Car doors slam. My heart's going to explode. Don't cry. Smile, talk. It's not over yet. I'm going to choke. What's wrong with my throat? Eat something. Carrot sticks? One after another. Eat, eat. Chew, chew. Chew, chew. We are at the airport. Unload the bags. Check in.

'Who has the tickets?'

Then, more good-byes.

Now it's only Kathy, Michael, Rachel and us. Upstairs. More food.

'What would you like?'

'Ginger ale.' There, that goes down easily. I have another and another. I have to go to the bathroom now. Kathy is going with me.

'May I have your attention, please. Flight 347 Logan to Heathrow has been delayed until 10 p.m. Thank you.' That's us! Kathy, Michael and Rachel are leaving.

'Timothea, if you need or want anything just write me and I'll send it.'

'Thanks, Kathy.'

More good-byes. Go through the metal detector. Now there's no turning back. Sit down and try not to cry.

'Flight 347 is now boarding.'

Good-bye, America. Good-bye, home. Good-bye to my old life. Hello?

'Fasten your seatbelts and prepare for lift off. Please extinguish all cigarettes. Enjoy your flight on British Air.'

Suddenly I feel tired. I'll try to sleep. We'll be landing in London soon. Bump, bump and we've landed. Get the bags out. Do we have them all? Count. Okay, let's go. I have to go to the bathroom. Oh no, we are changing airlines. Pick up our bags, count again. Twenty pieces? How will we ever move it all? We will have to take a bus to another part of the airport. How will we ever get all the bags on?

'You sure have a lot of luggage. May I help you? Are you moving there?'

'Thanks. Yes, we are.' My God, WE ARE! Stop. Don't think about all that just yet.

Get off the bus. Check in.

'Who has the passports?'

Tickets ready. Onto another plane. Gosh, it's noisy. Is it going to explode or something? Landing in Paris. Poor Dad, he's sick with a cold. I'm so tired! We have eleven hours here but everyone is too tired to go out. We've found some benches to sleep on. Oh my God, look at the time! And we are in the wrong part of the airport! Run, run, RUN! Onto a bus. Hurry up!

'Okay, this way.'

'Are you sure?'

'No.'

Phew! We're here. Just in time. Get on. Yes. *Another* plane. Sit. Take off. Good-bye Paris. We land in Nice for fuel. Take off again. Where is the gum? My ears hurt. Try to sleep. Oh, why are we doing this? Why are we going? I miss home already. But I'm so tired I don't have the energy to cry. I'll get dehydrated at this rate.

Stop in Saudi Arabia.

'Excuse me. Please put on a skirt before the inspectors come on board.'

What? Inspectors? Oh, bomb inspectors. Under the seats, into bags, check, peer, poke and pry into everything.

We're off again. This was the last stop. Now we're really stuck on this plane. Next stop, Dar-es-Salaam. Hey! Let me off! Lunch. Food? How can I eat? My tear ducts are working okay now. I'll have to start paying them for working overtime.

Oh my God, we are landing. This is Dar-es-Salaam? The major city? All I see are grass huts and dirt roads. Dad's laughing at my face. I guess I look as surprised as I feel. Landing. Now I have to get off. Please, God, wake me up from this nightmare. One more step and I'm off the plane. Well, maybe not. Mom grabbed my arm just as I turned to get back on. Darn. It's so hot. Well, I am here and I want to go home.

Hot. Steamy. Millions of black faces. Dirt. Flies. Children shouting 'mzungu' (white person) and 'give me money'. A man with leprosy. Poverty. Strange smells. Yuck! That is food? No thanks.

Night. Our first night. What? All five of us in one room? Our bathroom was bigger than this. Sleeping for the first time with mosquito nets, I feel caged in, trapped. Oh, why me, Lord, why me?

Morning. Into the truck. Going to someone else's house. 'Hello, Jambo. Habari.'

Americans! A pool. Swimming. The water is hotter than a bath, but who cares? Two girls, Bahá'ís. Americans, they're nice. We are leaving for Iringa, our new home.

Five big people in a jeep. Squeeze in. Long endless stretches of bumpy, dusty roads. What? This is the best road in Tanzania? Ouch! My head just hit the roof. Going through a game park. Wow! Elephants and zebras, right on the road. Drive, drive, drive. My legs are dead. What, we're here? Eleven hours in that car.

Unload. This is our new house. Will it be our home? Bugs, bees, cockroaches, dirt, dark, cold. *That* is a bed? *This* is really our house? I am crying. Stop. Dig out mosquito nets, sheets, blankets. Make up the beds.

Sleep. Where am I? Oh, no! So it is real, not just a bad dream? I feel sick. So this is pioneering. Cold showers, bugs, off and on electricity, feeling sick, smelly bathrooms, feeling lonely and waiting for mail? How long can I live like this? Two years is an awfully long time.

One Year Later

Wow! I survived a year! Even more amazing, now I like it here! This past year was the hardest of my life but also the most rewarding. The year seemed to go on forever, yet it was over before I realized it had started. I've learned a lot about myself and about life. I've learned that if I rely on God I can rely on myself. Other pioneers say to me: 'It's not always this hard; you're just having a bad time. Sometimes things *do* work out!'

Yes, we are having a bad time. We will be unable to stay here unless my father finds another job. I do want to stay here. Even though the times things have gone wrong outnumber the times they have gone right by 20 to one, we still are alive and we want to continue. Pioneering has become my favourite word. It represents what I want from life. That I, a far from perfect Bahá'í, can serve Bahá'u'lláh every day. Well, you can't get much better than that. The thoughts and worries, the tests and difficulties, both physical and spiritual, that constantly beset us, they seem so important. But once in a while you can see with clear eyes how unimportant they really are. Every time you go out of the house you are saying 'I am a Bahá'í' just by being there.

Racial prejudice is a big problem all over the world. When I attended a local school here in Africa, I experienced first hand what it is like for someone to treat you according to your skin colour. I was the only white person in the class of 40 or more people. There were only two other whites in the entire school.

In history and geography and most of the other classes I was taught how bad white people are. How all of the problems, personal and national, are the fault of the whites. Well, if you were taught that, and the only whites you ever saw were rich, living apart and better off than you, what would you think?

From that example you can see how one Bahá'í coming for one or two years could make a big difference. They would see you coming to help them, working with them and not living like a king with a lot of servants, but simply. It's through things like this that people will realize the truth about men. That we are all equal and connected. And that for world peace to be achieved, everyone must work for it. Each in his own way.

It was very hard for me to have people dislike, even hate me, just because of my skin colour. My hair was pulled. I was slapped, small stones and other things were thrown at me, my books and pens were grabbed. There was constant harassment. It was very upsetting but seeing it from their point of view, I can understand it. I also understand a little better how minorities feel. I think that is what pioneering is all about, learning how the other guy feels.

When the situation is reversed, and you experience the other side of things, that is how you become a whole person. Going to school here was a very difficult experience but I learned a lot from it and now I have many new friends and a new perspective on prejudice.

We had two beehives in our house when we first moved in. One was about four feet long and two feet wide and the other was slightly smaller. One hive was in the ceiling of my parents' room, the other was in the living room ceiling. The African bee is unique as it is very aggressive and hostile and attacks without much provocation. The noise of the bees droning was keeping my parents awake so we decided to do something about it. First they sprayed kerosene on the hives. This was a bad move. It enraged the bees and they swarmed out all over the house ready to attack anything. We managed to get all the animals out of the house and then we ran to the safety of a friend's house where we spent the day.

That night when it was time for bed we had to creep in slowly with towels over our heads. We went straight in and got into bed. We could not use the bathroom or put on any lights. Luckily by morning the bees had mostly quieted down and we were able to come out from under the covers. During the next few days there were many scary moments when the still angry bees attacked many people. Lots of ducks, rabbits and chickens were killed. One of the teachers got 30 stings on her face, head and neck. Finally we brought the local exterminators down and they sprayed a very strong poison all over the house. We weren't supposed to go in for 24 hours, but had nowhere else to go so we went indoors. Everything in the house had a coating of a clear, whitish poison. We had to wash everything, dishes, clothing, furniture, walls and windows. We had not had sufficient time to prepare the house before it was sprayed. Nobody felt clean for weeks but it got rid of the bees.

Next some men came and tore out the ceilings to get the honeycombs out. They were very messy and got the poisoned honey all over the place. They rebuilt the ceilings and left. We cleaned up as much of the house as we could but apparently we did not do this well enough for some new bees smelled it and came to live in our house. So it was sprayed once again and all the wood that had honey on it was taken out and burned and the ceilings were once again rebuilt. Mom says she will never forget the sound of thousands of angry bees droning over our heads.

Harry, my younger brother, had been taken on a hunting safari with a friend. On the day they were due back I was alone in the house. I heard a horn tooting outside. The door opened and Harry burst in struggling under a mound of bloody meat. My breakfast immediately rose to my throat.

He dumped the meat on the counter and with a cheerful 'Hi' went back out. Before I could start having hysterics he was inside again with another huge piece of meat, this time with some of the hoof still on it! Next, Hashim, the hunting companion, came in with another huge piece. They deposited the meat on the counter, told me that it was Cape buffalo and impala and that I needed to get it into the fridge soon. Then they were gone, this time for good.

What was I going to do? The cats were going crazy. There were flies everywhere, blood was all over the kitchen and there was a horrible smell of raw, warm meat in the air. I knew that it must go in the fridge but it wouldn't fit. How would I ever get it into the fridge without getting covered with blood? Just the thought of touching it made my stomach churn.

I emptied out the fridge, took out the shelves, got a big plastic tarp from upstairs, wrapped it around the meat and made three slow, bloody trips to the fridge. Finally it was all in and I had started to mop up. There was blood everywhere, with a trail of bloody footprints leading to the fridge. Suddenly I heard my mother arrive home.

I rushed out and said, 'Mom, we've got a buffalo in our fridge!' Judging by the expression on her face, I should have broken it a bit better. Seeing her eyes glued on me, I looked down. My clothes were covered with blood in different stages of drying. My hands, arms and face looked like I had been in the sun too long. When I had cleaned myself up, mother and I sat down and discussed our problem. Our fridge was full of two tons of raw meat and the electricity was unpredictable.

Our solution: first cut it all up and give everyone here a gift of meat, then take the rest and have a buffalo barbecue! Three days later we were all gathered around big fires cooking shish-kebabs and buffalo and impala steaks. We invited 20 people and we all began to eat. I could not forget how it had looked sitting in a bloody lump on our counter. Still, I took a taste and it was surprisingly good.

When all had eaten as much as we possibly could, we sat and watched the sun go down. Then we all said prayers from many different religions and in many different languages. It was a wonderful evening.

Out here we are almost completely cut off from the rest of the world. When we hear of something happening in Europe or the United States we feel almost as if we are on a separate planet. Our lives are so different and seemingly unrelated to those people in the news. Yet every day the world draws closer, taking step after step, going towards peace. To think that we are all longing and striving for the same things brings us closer together so that you can call anyone brother and know it is true. These days when the youth of the world are disillusioned, disheartened and with no hope for the future and living as if there were no tomorrow, it is very hard to go against the flow. It is up to us as Bahá'í youth to choose what we want for our future as our destiny. When the Universal House of Justice said, 'Youth can move the world', it was no idle statement. It is up to us whether we wish to take up the responsibility given to us by Bahá'u'lláh. We must choose whether we want a bright future or a dark one and once we choose we must act on our decision.

We must scatter to all ends of the earth, spreading the message of Bahá'u'lláh. I am not saying it is easy. I was scared out of my wits when I left the States. Often I still am. But even though it is hard, it is a necessity. If we lose a tooth we don't stop eating. Without food we would die. A little pain is better than starving. Once we have made the effort and eaten, our stomach is comfortably full. When we arise to make an effort towards world peace, our lives are full.

27

Kabu of the Purari

Sue and David Podger

Shirin Sabri, a poet and writer now living in Australia and a long-time pioneer, sent this story written by her parents, David and Sue Podger. It appeared in Herald of the South, *which granted permission for its use in this book:*

Some parts of the world shrug off the existence of man. The giant river systems of Papua New Guinea seem like that, scaling man down to a tiny, barely tolerated presence. Forming great deltas, the rivers sprawl and intertwine for hundreds of miles. Heavy rain, which comes often, will send them heaving over their banks to spread flash floods through gardens and settlements.

The Purari is one of the largest of these river systems and is the home of over 20 Bahá'í communities, living in stilt-legged houses on its banks. Our story is of how these people came to be Bahá'ís, what prompted them to it and why they remain so to this day.

The day-to-day life of the Delta people is dictated in many ways by the huge river. Fish may be trapped in it, and crabs. The riverside swamps have sago palms which provide the staple diet. Malarial mosquitoes breed and spread out from these same swamps, afflicting everyone. Less prevalent now, but still dangerous, the crocodile provides the stuff of dreams and myths. These days, too, the houses are square and small, nothing like the very large, tall houses of pre-war times in which whole communities lived. In those days, symbolic designs of great force and wooden carvings bursting with life adorned the great houses and men carved ornate wooden racks to display the skulls of their enemies.

When the war was over a man named Tommy Kabu returned to his home on the Purari after serving in the navy overseas. He was able to improve the lot of his people by starting a large cooperative sago business. However, in an accident, his boat was burned and this, combined with the negative attitude taken to his efforts by the administration, destroyed the venture. A man of good faith, he kept his standing with the people and established the famous 'Sago Camp' in the capital, Port Moresby. A large vegetable garden and a tea shop were two more of his community ventures. He was an immensely popular and respected man and became one of the most important early postwar leaders of Papua.

In 1965 my wife Sue and I met Tommy for the first time. We were newly arrived in Papua New Guinea and only told him of the Faith at the urging of a friend who was visiting us at the time. In response, Tommy asked for a book to study quietly by himself.

How well I remember Tommy's words when we diffidently presented ourselves at his house and after awhile asked how he liked the book. He had read and reread the first page, for it seemed to have a message addressed to him:

> Let us look back over the past of our people. We have had great men and great chiefs. When a great man lives he is good for his people. He makes them better. He sees further than they can see.

And further on, on the same page:

But the best man is the Great Man who is the Prophet of God
and tells men of the life after death so they may no more be
afraid. He is the man whose eyes see all, what is plain and
what is hidden.

These are the words of Rúḥíyyih Khánum written in her
booklet *The Good Message*.

Tommy Kabu's response to our question was: 'A very
good page. It is true.' I asked what had interested him and,
regarding me calmly, he said again, 'A very good first page,
a truth.' He said this and then smiled a wide, beaming
smile, and kindly looked straight into my eyes. We were an
unlikely pair, myself an office efficiency and computer
analyst, and Tommy Kabu being, well, Tommy. A man
who defined himself. But we seemed to reach a conjunction
of souls, as I looked into his seemingly age-old eyes, and we
became friends for life.

It was Tommy Kabu, the modern-day leader of the Gulf
people, who first taught the Bahá'í Faith along the Purari.
On his first visit there as a Bahá'í in 1966 we went along
together. The visit arose out of Tommy's success in
teaching the Faith to the tribal people in Port Moresby
whose home was Poroi, a village far up the Purari. Tommy
and I had promised that we would one day go to their
village and tell the story of the Faith directly to their
kindred.

We flew by small plane from Port Moresby to Baimuru,
hired a motor driven canoe and set off. Travelling from
village to village, we met with his many friends and talked
into the night with them about the coming of a new
Prophet, Bahá'u'lláh.

The coming together in unity of peoples of all colours
had been prophesied in one of the myths of the Iai people,
Tommy Kabu's tribe. Unused to the climate and the
fatigue of travel, I would sometimes drift off to sleep while
a group of Iai people discussed the Faith intently with

Tommy. He was a most impressive and courteous man and spoke in a heartfelt, persuasive way and his audience would not retire, sometimes, until dawn!

But the main aim of our journey was to reach Poroi, the village some 80 miles upstream. Tommy felt that the people of this village, who were Pawaias, would respond to the Bahá'í Faith. He admired their qualities and said they were honest, good people. Once we had established the Faith amongst them, he felt, it would grow healthily from then on.

Our trip to Poroi was not a smooth one. Some days after we left Baimuru we stopped at Mapaio, the village of our wiry little boatman, Kairi Api. We were forced to remain there for days, waiting for more gasoline to be brought. Rain had swollen the river and we had already used more gasoline than planned by running against its flow. The enforced stop made me appreciate the rhythm of the villagers' lives and their subjugation to events.

On the night before we left for Poroi a great cloud of mosquitoes swept in off the river and into the village. All discussions ended and everyone dived under sheets or blankets for cover. Soon the whole company was sound asleep, leaving me struggling to learn the brand new skill of sleeping with a blanket over my face. Perhaps, I thought, I could make a sort of tunnel in the blanket and breathe through that. This worked well and I was congratulating myself on having applied western ingenuity to such a simple problem when the first mosquito found the end of the tunnel. The next moment I was leaping about and snorting hard trying to expel inhaled mosquitoes from my nostrils. No one stirred. I retreated back under the blanket. The noise of my tormentors crowding outside was one continuous high-pitched hum. Even suffocation was preferable to exposure to their ministrations and with this thought I eventually found sleep.

The next morning we set off for Poroi. As one travels
further inland more wildlife shows itself. There were
breadfruit trees black with sleeping flying foxes and flocks
of brilliantly coloured birds screeching overhead. Small
crocodiles basked on the mud and on exposed logs. But the
river, the great, muddy, seemingly endless river, unwinding
slowly before us, always drew our attention back. We
stared through the light glaring down onto its rippling
surface. We trailed our eyes along the tall palisades of trees
that jammed its congested banks.

By nightfall our small motor had taken us only half way
and under the quickly darkening skies we searched for
shelter. With the dusk came the rain and when we finally
found an abandoned house we were soaked and cold. Some
dry wood under the house cheered us all up and soon we
had a cooking fire going. Everyone had a story to tell of a
similar occasion when the rains had caught them out on the
river and these stories were recounted with much laughter
and good humour. Surely a few shared miseries must be
one of the secrets of lasting friendships.

We reached Poroi in the afternoon of the following day
and were greeted by a crowd of people who inspected us
very curiously. After resting for the afternoon, Tommy
began to explain the Bahá'í Faith to the villagers over the
evening meal. Soon the whole village had come to listen.
They sat in separate groups inside the men's house, the
women and children sitting apart from the men.

Some hours of talk about the Faith went by, all conducted by the men. Nearly all the discussion centred on
the three main teachings of the Bahá'í Faith: that there is
one God, that all the great religions have been sent by Him,
and that all men are one family and should unite together.
Finally a group of women who had been silently regarding
us all the time stood up and left the room. A short time later
they returned, dressed in grass skirts and shells, to dance

and sing outside. Tommy listened to the singing and, laughing to himself, he whispered in my ear, 'They want the men to hurry and make up their minds.' A message came in from the singing women to the effect that they would give the men until tomorrow, but then, whether the men liked it or not, the Poroi women were going to become Bahá'ís!

This message was relayed in whispers and I watched it going from group to group in the big room. Excitement and tension grew. Intent, immobile faces stared out of the flickering firelight as the older men made lengthy speeches expressing caution. The noise of singing and dancing from the darkness outside became louder and louder. 'Bahá'í lifts us up,' sang the women, and they sent in another message that they would sing all night to show their serious intention.

Feeling gave our voices wings as Tommy and I entered into the spirit of this village-wide confrontation. His eyes glistening, he redoubled his efforts to present in a loving way the message that heals hearts and souls, the message of Bahá'u'lláh.

Gradually, the crowd of talking, arguing men grew smaller, as one by one, they fell asleep where they were. By first light the next morning the old men of the village were still hard at it, talking about the Bahá'í Faith with a seemingly untiring Tommy. I saw the women slip away in the dawn light, their vigil completed. With sunrise the village was completely still and the morning passed very peacefully, with neither Tommy nor I venturing to say any more. We rested and swam in the river.

By the afternoon we had our first Bahá'í community in the Gulf of Papua! Individual men and women and married couples began to approach us, asking to become Bahá'ís, and after giving some further explanations, we wrote out their membership cards and witnessed their marking. No one could sign his name, for the entire village was illiterate.

From this humble beginning in 1966 the Faith spread slowly to other villages. John Francis, a Bahá'í from the highlands of New Guinea, visited numerous villages and attracted nearly a hundred people to the Faith. Later visits by my wife Sue and myself, by Violet Hoehnke and Ruhi Mills, by Emete Pamudi, John Gapo and Erena Ari all went to build up the community numbers and knowledge of the Faith.

From the very beginning one of the attractions of the Faith for the Gulf people was its system of administration. They approved the idea of elected local assemblies, they rejoiced in the fact that in the Bahá'í Faith they ran things themselves. Every year they elected delegates who travelled to the city of Lae to take part in the national convention. At the first of these conventions, when a Pawaia delegate rose to tell the story of his village and its Bahá'í community, he was warmly applauded and encouraged. In the audience of delegates, too, was Kairi Api, our faithful boatman on that first river journey.

At the time of writing it is only eight years since Tommy Kabu, the first Papuan Bahá'í, travelled amongst his people telling them of this new Faith. The hard existence imposed by the river has taken its toll in that short time. Tommy is dead and with him all the old men we met in Poroi. A stone memorial to Tommy Kabu's memory can be found in Port Moresby and close by it is another living memorial, a community of Pawaia Bahá'ís who live in a settlement Tommy founded. And the book *The Good Message*, which first attracted Tommy to the Faith, is now being translated into Hiri Motu, the common language of Papua.

Bahá'ís in the Gulf District are more active than ever, as their community approaches a thousand in number. They are happier and more resourceful and more active in all aspects of life. Visiting among the villages, attending schools on the Faith and developing their communities, they have not neglected the message placed in their hands by their renowned leader, Tommy Kabu, and nurtured in its humble beginnings by the remote village of Poroi.

The lovers of mankind, these are the superior men, of whatever nation, creed, or colour they may be.

'Abdu'l-Bahá

28

Like Every Place You've Never Been

Mariette and Ho-San Leong

Ho-San Leong, a Chinese from Malaysia, and his wife, Mariette, of Australian background, pioneered for twelve years in Papua New Guinea. Ho-San writes of those days:

We had been living in Sydney, Australia, for just over two years in a two-bedroom apartment and had assisted in the formation of the first local spiritual assembly in Canterbury. Our daughter, Mei-Ling, was starting to walk and we felt that it was time to move on, to find a place to settle where there would be trees and open space instead of the confines of Sydney suburbia. And so it was that when Mariette and I saw an appeal for caretakers for the national Ḥaẓíratʼul-Quds in Lae, Papua New Guinea, which appeared in a small column of the Australian *Baháʼí Bulletin*, we immediately jumped at the idea. We knew very little about the country, but we had spent a day in transit at Port Moresby when we were on the ship heading for Australia near the end of 1971. We had met several of the pioneers who were living and working in that city at the time.

Mariette and I had married in Malaysia at the end of 1969, a marriage of two distinctly different cultures – she of an Australian background going back some four or five generations and I a third generation Chinese born in Malaysia.

My family was among the handful of early believers in Malaysia when the Faith was first introduced in the early days of the Ten Year Crusade into Malacca, our hometown. My father learned of the Bahá'í Faith and its teachings through an advertisement for a Bahá'í meeting in the local papers and his life was transformed. He was not content to be the only Bahá'í in the family. It was his strong conviction that the Faith was intended for the family unit too and he persisted in his determination to make us all Bahá'ís. All seven children and my mother accepted the Faith one at a time, with mother the last to declare.

As a Chinese family moulded in traditional ways, we grew up praying to many gods in the home and mother felt that she could not abandon them without an auspicious religious ceremony to send them back to heaven in peace. So a special day was set aside for this. A priestess from the Buddhist temple was engaged to officiate at the ceremony to break the nexus with the gods and thus enable my mother to begin her new life as a Bahá'í, having come to terms with her gods in this manner.

Mariette came from a Bahá'í family and grew up in Adelaide, South Australia. In 1944 her parents were living in Woodville, an Adelaide suburb. A friend who lived in the same neighbourhood taught them the Faith and they very quickly became involved in the community and the work of the Faith in Australia and the Pacific. In those early years the Australian community was still very small and was engaged with the goals and tasks assigned to it in the Australasian-Pacific region.

Papua New Guinea is the large island nation lying just north of Australia, with a population close to four million, made up of almost 700 tribal groups and languages. It is a beautiful, rugged country with very high mountains forming its backbone and clusters of islands scattered over a vast area in the western Pacific region. The country gained independence from Australia in September 1975 and since then has undergone enormous changes as it attempts to come to grips with rapid modernization and technology.

As it turned out, we did not take up the caretaker job in Lae but instead I succeeded in obtaining a data processing officer position with the Papua New Guinea University of Technology, based in Lae. Mariette had this romantic notion, out of a sense of adventure into unknown territory, that we would be given basic accommodation, possibly a grass or bamboo hut, with no running water and electricity and that we would have to cook our meals on open fires. Imagine her surprise when we were taken from the airport to a freshly-painted three-bedroom house on the university residential campus grounds and she discovered that it had all the modern facilities. It was almost too much for her to bear. She kept saying that this was luxurious pioneering, not the rugged kind that she had expected in a place like Papua New Guinea.

That first year was a slow learning curve for us, as we adjusted to life in a new, very tropical environment, got to know the local people and learned to speak in 'tok pidgin', the Melanesian Pidgin language which is still widely used and spoken by all the different language groups in the country. It was an exhilarating experience as we grew to know their customs and attitudes and cook their kind of food. Our second daughter, Su-Yin, was born two months after our arrival and in our girls' early years they adapted very well to the place and made many friends.

The following year, after a very happy and exciting visit to Madina village in New Ireland to attend summer school, we had the idea of adopting a Papua New Guinean child to enhance our experience of the country and its people and also to have an older sister for our kids.

Madina village is part of the early history of the Faith in Papua New Guinea, having formed the very first Bahá'í community and elected the very first local spiritual assembly in the country in the 1950s. Today a good number of the children of the village, now adults and second generation Bahá'ís, serve on the national spiritual assembly and other institutions of the Faith.

Seff was twelve years old when she became part of our family. She came from the Homerang family in Madina, from amongst the earliest and most dearly-beloved believers. Michael and Tivien Homerang were happy to have their daughter become part of our growing family. According to Papua New Guinean customs it is quite usual for a child to be adopted into an extended family without undergoing formal adoption procedures and it is accepted as proper and correct in every way. So to all intents and purposes, Seff became our daughter and we in turn, became her parents.

Over the years she managed very well to maintain the delicate balance and harmony between her two families. We fostered a very close spiritual connection which has not been severed despite the fact that we no longer live in Papua New Guinea. Seff today works at the Bahá'í World Centre and we are so proud and happy for her. Her letters to us from the Holy Land are filled with the spirit and wonderment of the environment she works in and she feels overjoyed and privileged that she can render her services to the Faith at its very heart.

The year after Seff joined us we had the bounty of going on pilgrimage. We could not take the three girls with us and therefore had to find a simple, workable solution as to how to care for them in our absence. We came up with the idea of asking Seff's natural mother to look after them.

Imagine the looks of surprise from our expatriate neighbours on the campus when they learned that we were going halfway around the world and leaving the children in the care of a simple villager! They felt that we were definitely odd and were not convinced by our assurances that everything would be all right. There was another Bahá'í couple on campus and they kindly agreed to provide support and assistance to Tivien and the children while we were away.

Six weeks later we returned to Lae after the wonderfully happy pilgrimage and visits to several other places. We found the family in good shape. Tivien had taken it all in her stride, had befriended her expatriate neighbours and had quite won them over with her love and friendship. She had made straw handbags for the women and taught them how to cook native style and they just loved it all! They were full of praise for her and told us they understood now how we had no qualms about leaving the children in her care. Our campus neighbours knew that we were Bahá'ís and that it was no mere coincidence that had brought Seff into our family and her mother to look after our home and children while we were away.

Our girls befriended our hausmeri's daughter (hausmeri is pidgin for domestic help) and invited her to stay overnight. While we saw nothing unusual in this, one of the data processing supervisors working with us remarked on it. She was curious to know more about the Faith and its teachings about race unity and the oneness of mankind. Today she is a Bahá'í. She named her second son Olinga after Hand of the Cause Enoch Olinga, who visited the country many years ago.

In the years we lived in Lae we managed to visit villages up in the Highlands and to meet with many Bahá'ís living in remote places. Informal meetings and gatherings were held in the open. Teaching the people about the Faith by telling stories about Bahá'u'lláh in a simple style often brought good results. People were happy to hear about the new 'lotu' (religion) and God's plan for uniting the peoples of the world. Many people were illiterate but they could readily understand the essence of the Faith. It was an experience to see how they accepted the tenets without intellectual judgement on their part.

In teaching we were also learning and being taught constantly. It was a joy to see souls responding to the glad-tidings. There were, however, physical difficulties. There was the time I slept in a round hut and spent the whole night awake and itching. The Highlanders love pigs very much and look after them as well as they care for their children. The hut was alive with pig fleas! For days I had to use medication to heal the sores that appeared all over my face, hands and legs.

Sometimes we ate food that was not properly cooked and served in none-too-clean utensils. Invariably we would get sick. We had to watch the water we drank because that too caused some problems. Still, it was good to be part of the teaching that went on, month after month, year after year, in all corners of this vast country.

One year both Mariette and I happened to be on the national spiritual assembly and we were able to participate in the International Convention in 1978 in Haifa. It was especially thrilling for us because her parents were there too. We shared many happy times with them.

Being in Papua New Guinea was not easy for Mariette as her family was not close enough to visit on a regular basis. While there was always enough activity to keep us from being bored or depressed, there was nonetheless a feeling of isolation. Papua New Guinea is billed by Air Niugini, the national airlines, as one country 'like every place you have never been'.

Towards the end of each year, in November and

December, the planes were filled to capacity with thousands of expatriates making their annual exodus to their home countries. Some years we managed to get to Australia or Malaysia but many years we visited Bahá'ís and made travel teaching trips. There were very few roads and air travel was expensive. But each time we called on the Bahá'í friends in their village homes and assisted with the development of community activities and consolidation of the local spiritual assemblies – which had sprung up in all 20 provinces, including Port Moresby – we found it a happy and rewarding experience.

In October 1985 when *The Promise of World Peace* was released, we used the occasion to proclaim the Faith in Port Moresby and other major townships. We were sent two books from Canada and were able to present one to the governor-general of Papua New Guinea on October 24, United Nations Day, and one to the prime minister. We had befriended the editor of *Niugini Nius*, one of the national newspapers, and managed to get his agreement to print the entire statement over a period of five days.

There is so much to remember and this short account of those days has brought it vividly back to us. We are so grateful for those twelve years. Some pioneers have been there much longer and are still there, serving the Faith with strong dedication and love. The Faith is well-established in the country and is growing rapidly.

Papua New Guinea is indeed like every place we have never been. Our connection will always remain. Our children grew up there and will always remember the people of that land with love. Perhaps one day we can go back for a nostalgic visit, see those dear friends in the villages and partake of their kindness, love and hospitality.

29

The Fitzners of Portuguese Timor

Graham Hassall

Graham Hassall is writing a book about the Ten Year Crusade which saw thousands of Bahá'í pioneers travel throughout the world, many to remote regions, to take the message of Bahá'u'lláh to all peoples. Graham agreed to share this particular story with us:

The announcement by Shoghi Effendi late in 1952 of plans for a Ten Year World Crusade drew the Australasian Bahá'ís out of their insular concerns and gave them a wider perspective and purpose. As one of the twelve communities with a national assembly when the decade-long plan began in 1953, the Bahá'ís of Australia and New Zealand were asked to send pioneers to seven virgin territories and to six consolidation territories. Of the virgin territories, four were in the Pacific Islands – the Admiralty, Loyalty, New Hebrides and Society Islands – and three were in southeast Asia – the Cocos and Mentawei Islands and Portuguese Timor.

Some details of the plan were already known to the Australian Bahá'ís when they travelled to attend the fourth intercontinental conference of the Crusade in New Delhi in October 1953. Harold and Florence Fitzner of Adelaide were determined that they would seek to enter Portuguese Timor. They were among many who made their decisions to pioneer known at the conference.

At this time only Portuguese could obtain visas for entry

to the colony. The granting of entry permits for non-Portuguese was highly unlikely, yet the Fitzners began their campaign to secure them. Harold wrote to the Australian consul in Dili on July 9, 1953 and received a discouraging reply in October. He then began a lengthy exchange of letters with the Australian consul and with the Department of External Affairs before departing for New Delhi. The campaign for entry continued in India where Harold and Florence were told when they visited the Portuguese Consulate in Bombay that their application could only proceed when lodged in Australia.

Following their return to Adelaide they were visited by Australian security officers who were curious to know why an Australian couple nearing retirement were so desperately attempting to gain entry to a poor, remote, neglected and all-but-forgotten Portuguese-speaking colony.

Shoghi Effendi advised that if Timor seemed impenetrable the Fitzners should consider pioneering to one of the other goals. Irene Jackson had already attempted to enter Portuguese Timor and, finding it impossible to do so, had moved to Fiji. Harold did write letters of enquiry to the government officials for Cocos Island, Loyalty Islands and even the Chagoa Islands but none of these met with success.

Providentially, the Australian Department of External Affairs sent the Fitzners' application direct to the governor of Timor in November, and just as miraculously, the authorities finally granted visas for temporary residence. Harold explained to his manager at the North British Mercantile Insurance Company where he was chief clerk that he wished to retire early so he could move as quickly as possible to Timor. Although somewhat bewildered by the request, the company consented, and despite the fact that Harold was five years short of being eligible to receive a full pension, agreed to pay 90 percent of his salary from the date of his retirement on March 21, 1954. When informed that permission to enter Portuguese Timor had been granted, Shoghi Effendi wrote to the Fitzners through his secretary that this success was clearly the working of a great spiritual law in which the state of the heart of the believer attracts a divine outpouring of aid.

Harold spent the remainder of March combing Adelaide's libraries for information on his adopted land. In one he asked about translations into aboriginal languages and was told that there was no point in making such translations because aboriginal races were dying out and in twenty years would be extinct. Influenced by this advice, he wrote to Hand of the Cause of God Collis Featherstone that it was thus 'foolish to worry about translations' for the Timorese, adding that many of the tribes in New Guinea were also dying out. The Australian Bahá'ís of the time knew very little about the non-western and truly indigenous peoples living in their region.

With preparations complete, Harold left Adelaide on April 4 by train for Perth. He stayed for five days there with the Fitzners' long-time friend, Mrs Miller, who had become a Bahá'í during Clara and Hyde Dunn's first visit to the capital of the Western States in 1924. Harold's ship sailed, first for Singapore and then Jakarta, where he was met by Persian Bahá'ís, including Mr Payman, who had already been in Indonesia for four years.

After a few days spent with the Bahá'í friends in Jakarta, Harold travelled by train to Surraleya, then by plane to Kupang, the capital of Indonesian Timor. Late in June he flew to his final destination, Dili. Florence remained in Adelaide until the end of the school year and arrived on October 5. A Portuguese Bahá'í, Jose Marques, arrived in Timor from Lisbon on July 28, 1954. All three were named Knights of Bahá'u'lláh.

Timor was at that time divided almost equally into two

parts, half belonging to Indonesia, the other half being a Portuguese Overseas Province. Approximately half a million people lived there. Most were Timorese but there were also Malays, Indonesians, some eight to twelve thousand Chinese, 60,000 'misturas' (mixed races), two thousand Portuguese, two hundred Arabs, and three Australians.

Harold explored his new environment for two weeks before sending his first report to the Asian Teaching Committee on July 16, 1954:

> I have been in Dili for over two weeks and I have been able to survey the position. The town itself is not very big, two long streets, one facing the sea and harbour and the other at the rear. The first street has business places, customs and administration buildings. The second street has Chinese and Portuguese shops and dwellings. Everything here is very costly, a small cake of Lux soap is 1/5; biscuits 32/– for a four-and-a-half-pound tin; hotel is two pounds per day and accommodations are almost impossible for Europeans. I have the only room available at the hotel, about the size of one of our Australian bathrooms. The food is Portuguese, very oily, buffalo and goat's meat, and fish, which is plentiful but does not seem to have any taste.

The quality and cost of housing were also noted: a four or five room plaster house cost about £1,000 to £1,500 and a brick house close to £5,000. Harold had travelled to the interior of the island by road and reported the roads so rough that he felt 'like jelly'. He felt that employment prospects were impossible unless he learned to speak Portuguese or established a business of his own.

Very few residents of Dili spoke English. There were one or two Dutchmen and two Germans with whom Harold conversed in broken English, while there were a few Portuguese present on temporary visas who spoke English more fluently. He reported to the committee that he had not met one Chinese yet who could speak English, adding

that they all spoke in Chinese and some Malayan. Harold
found the Timorese to be very friendly, but 'they are lazy
and probably thieve when they get an opportunity. We will
have to plan carefully to get the message to them, as they
only speak a little Portuguese and their own Timorese
language.'

As 80 percent of the Timorese lived in hamlets spread
across the territory, secluded from Dili and other towns, the
Fitzners indeed found that it was difficult in later years to
contact them. Most were Catholic. As well as being the
predominant religion, Catholicism had been the official
religion of the territory since the coming of the Portuguese.
The church was influential within both the administration
and the educational system. The social pressures on the
population were sufficient, the Fitzners felt, for them to fear
for their jobs were they to become Bahá'ís. The Catholic
bishop was a member of the ruling cabinet, and Portuguese
officials, who had no experience of other religions, viewed
the Fitzners with 'distrust and opposition'. Harold wrote
on July 2, 1954:

> The police asked my religion and I told them Bahá'í but they
> could not understand. I then explained we believe in all Faiths
> but he wrote down 'Protestant-Bahá'í'. They only know two
> religions, Catholic and Protestant. I will go carefully and keep
> you posted.

It was about this time that Harold spent a night in jail.
There had been much confusion over the status of the
Portuguese pioneer, Jose Marques, who, since he could not
obtain a job when he arrived in Dili, had appealed to the
Australian National Spiritual Assembly to assist him
financially. The presence of a continental Portuguese in
Dili, having no employment but receiving regular payment
from Australia, drew the suspicion of Timorese authorities
on both Marques and Fitzner. It was all a 'ghastly mistake',
Florence wrote to the Featherstones in November, not long

after her arrival, 'and of course Harold and I are his friends, so we are classed together. We have heard that they want us to go back to Australia.'

Around August of 1955 the authorities intensified their investigations. They insisted that Marques leave the territory. When he cabled to the Bahá'í World Centre for advice they intercepted the message, searched his accommodation, seized his Bahá'í books and interviewed Harold for four hours. The situation was delicate. By October 1955 the Fitzners were expecting news of their deportation and Harold's reports to the Asian Teaching Committee were filled with requests to find other Bahá'ís ready to replace them until they could re-enter. The Fitzners' application for permanent residence was denied in November and Harold, feeling his worst fears had been confirmed, commenced plans to leave Dili on a Royal Australian Air Force flight to Darwin the following January.

Then, quite unexpectedly, news came in December 1955 that they could stay after no less a personage than the Bishop of Timor, Jaime Guolard, intervened to prevent their deportation. By chance, Bishop Jaime had viewed the references that Florence carried detailing her teaching experience in Adelaide and had recognized on one the handwriting of the mother superior of Loretta Convent whom he had met while in Adelaide during the second world war.

Permission to stay was accompanied by the strictest of conditions: the Bahá'ís had to promise the Governor, Colonel Themuda Barata, that they would not contact the Timorese. The pioneers interpreted the regulations to mean that no active proselytizing was allowed, such as going into the villages to gather people together to tell them about the Faith, but that they were still permitted to invite into their own home friends who, should they enquire about matters of religion, could be told about the Bahá'í teachings.

Only after months of uncertainty did the Fitzners learn details of a rift between the governor of the Colony, who displayed friendliness towards them, and the administration in Lisbon, which had been pressing for their expulsion. With this final obstacle removed, they were free at last to concentrate their energies on settling in, establishing an income and building a Timorese Bahá'í community. Marques was also permitted to stay. By February 1956 he had obtained a government job. In June 1957 he married Miss Menexer and in 1958 moved to Turascai, about a hundred miles from Dili.

When Florence arrived she and Harold established English language classes. By April 1955 there were nine students learning English. They came to the Fitzners' house in the morning between 9 a.m. and noon, then, after a siesta, from 2 to 5 p.m., and again from 6 to 8 p.m. The hours were long but Harold wrote:

> In between lessons, we have callers who wish to consult us, Bahá'í friends and others, some of whom are sick and want our prayers, or want food or money or assistance in arranging business agencies or help in filling out forms for visas for Australia, Hong Kong, Singapore, etc. Sometimes we have tourists who pop in for tea. All these friends are interested in our work and want to know about Bahá'í. Weekends are devoted to Bahá'í work, calling on friends, Saturday evening firesides, Sunday morning youth classes, writing letters, which now seem to come from all over the world. We have many Bahá'í friends who have migrated to other countries and quite a number of pupils who are now living in Hong Kong, Macau, Singapore, Australia, Formosa and even in the USA.

Despite Portuguese Timor's underdeveloped political, social and economic institutions, Harold and Florence saw their new home as rather idyllic. But Timorese society was very different from Australian society and it was difficult to teach the Timorese about the Bahá'í Faith. Harold wrote that they were dealing with 'people in a semi-civilized state, with in most cases no education and a limited vocabulary even in their own tongue'. He felt that Bahá'í pamphlets were best prepared 'almost in a kindergarten language'.

Florence wrote that:

> Timor is really a beautiful island and at the present time one could hardly imagine a more peaceful, law-abiding country, all races, classes and creeds mingle together in good fellow-ship. Drunkenness is rare. Fighting hardly ever occurs and theft is also a rarity. Food is difficult, on account of short supplies but a lot of tinned goods are being imported from Singapore and Hong Kong and Australia. The native people seem to make up shortages with their home grown native food, beans, mandiola, vegetables, etc.

To Florence, Timor was 'God's island'. The people were 'living in a very primitive way, growing grain and fruit for their daily needs and meeting once a week, usually on Sundays at the local market to sell or barter their wares'. Yet during this period the Portuguese empire began to crumble and Timor felt the first effects of those movements towards independence which were so hard-won in the Portuguese colonies.

Within the growing turmoil, however, Harold and Florence methodically consolidated their position. Although quite isolated from other Bahá'í communities physically, they received communications from Bahá'ís in diverse places. The Honolulu and Lisbon local spiritual assemblies, Bob Meissler of São Paulo in Brazil and Grace Saunders all wrote letters; Bill Motteram sent books and literature from Adelaide; Carl Scherer supplied literature in Portuguese from Macau; the Adelaide-based Asian Teaching Committee corresponded frequently and supplied copies of the American *Bahá'í News*, the *Geneva News* and their own production, *Koala News*, while the North American Asian Teaching Committee sent copies of its publication, *Newsgram*. Comfort came also from Dr Muhajir (later a Hand of the Cause) and Mrs Muhajir, who at that time were pioneering in somewhat similar conditions elsewhere in the Indonesian archipelago, the Mentawei Islands.

In addition to this moral support from around the world, the Fitzners relied on the encouragement given by Shoghi Effendi, architect of the Crusade. One letter of his dated 1955 concluded:

> May the Almighty guide every step you take and fulfil every desire you cherish, for the promotion of His Faith, assuring you of my deep and loving appreciation of your high endeavours and historical services and of my fervent prayers for your success in the days to come. The light of your spiritual teaching will bring the far distant areas close together, because it will create a bond of unity which knows no separation. The persecutions in Persia seem to have opened new doors of spiritual confirmation, and if the friends will seize their opportunity they will be surprised at the results they can now achieve. Now is the appointed hour for the spread of the Faith throughout the world.

Another letter written on behalf of Shoghi Effendi stated:

> The beloved Guardian has been deeply touched by these contributions, as they link the Faith of Timor with the Holy Land. He will pray fervently for each and every one and for the success of their labours, that the seeds they sow will grow and bear rich harvest! You should weary not in well doing but continue on, steadfast, feeling assured of the blessings of Bahá'u'lláh.

The environment in which the Fitzners now lived was far from peaceful. Yet despite the many forms of restriction and the growing unrest in the colony, the Bahá'í community slowly grew. In March 1955 Miss Irene Nobae De Melo Benaox, a young Portuguese nurse, aged 24, was the first in the colony to embrace the Cause, having studied it for eight months. She later married the administrator of Dili. Other new Bahá'ís included Nevis, a solicitor and director of the Economic Department of Dili, who became a Bahá'í in April 1957. In that year the Bahá'ís of Portuguese Timor came under the jurisdiction of the Regional Spiritual Assembly of Southeast Asia. In October a Chinese youth, Young Kie Kong, joined the community.

More declarations quickly followed. By February 1958 there were eleven adults and seven youth in the community, allowing the first local spiritual assembly to be formed in Dili at Riḍván 1958. Those who became Bahá'ís endured misunderstandings and intolerance just as the Fitzners did. In July 1959, for instance, Harold reported to the Asian Teaching Committee that one of the Portuguese Bahá'ís had come to a meeting very distressed and said he was being persecuted by his chief because he was a Bahá'í. Azevido, the first Bahá'í in the Dili Hills, was harassed and questioned by the police and died the following day. His widow was sick and without a pension, and the family, because of both poverty and social duress, withdrew from active participation in the Bahá'í community.

With the Bahá'í community expanding, the need for a local Ḥaẓíratu'l-Quds became increasingly evident. The Fitzners approached the Australian National Spiritual Assembly early in 1959 for assistance in purchasing a suitable house in Dili, which cost the equivalent of £1,500. They had heard that funds to assist the various pioneers had been pledged at the 1957 National Convention in Australia, but upon inquiry found that most of it had already been earmarked. Seeing no other alternative, the Fitzners mortgaged their own house to raise sufficient capital, while generous Australian Bahá'ís also assisted with contributions.

In 1962, with some money finally saved, Harold and

Florence were able to leave the one-bedroom dwelling that had been their home for six years for a larger house built to accommodate their specific needs: lounge and dining rooms, three bedrooms and three bathrooms and a 'school-room' in place of a garage. Subsequent additions included another garage, a separate classroom for Florence and a four-roomed cottage at the rear for the houseboys. In addition to English language instruction, Harold began to teach accountancy. One tourist later published a travelogue of his experience in Portuguese Timor, describing Harold as 'perhaps one of the most extraordinary men' he had ever met.

In 1966 Goro Jorgic, a member of the Australian National Spiritual Assembly, visited the Fitzners and the Bahá'í community in Dili and afterwards wrote about the procession of teachers, doctors, administrators, professionals and even soldiers who passed through Harold and Florence's house. 'The secretary of the Indonesian consulate and his wife revealed to me the similarity of the principles of Bahá'u'lláh to Indonesia's official five principles,' Jorgic subsequently wrote, adding, 'The Governor expressed appreciation for the English teaching services rendered by Mr and Mrs Fitzner . . . the wife of one of the directors of the public service upon study of English with the Fitzners eventually obtained a Cambridge certificate, enabling her to teach at Mozambique High School in Africa.'

The Fitzners returned to Australia on several occasions, mostly to see to Harold's health. In 1957 he was rushed to hospital in Darwin after collapsing in Dili and on another occasion he collapsed in a Darwin street. But these traumas did not keep him from his teaching activities: the month after his collapse he held conversations about religion with Rev Pearce of the United Church and forwarded to the Asian Teaching Committee the address of George Ellis who lived in the remote and accurately named Northern Territory settlement, Rum Jungle.

Harold left the hospital determined to do some effective teaching and decided to advertise in a local paper. The ad, which ran the very next day, listed the twelve principles of the Faith and attracted three responses, including Sergeant Ted Holmes, who became a Bahá'í and later introduced Ruth Sinclair to the community.

Harold died on February 3, 1969. He had been bedridden with cancer of the stomach for six months. He told Florence he wished to be buried on a hill and was thus buried in the Chinese cemetery overlooking Dili the morning after his passing. A small group of friends and the Australian Consul in Dili, Max Berman, attended the funeral. Florence decided to stay in Dili. She continued to work from 8 a.m. to 7 p.m. every day. There were changes, however. Harold's pension ceased at his death. Florence also had to endure the lack of status that came to widows in Timorese society. In the eyes of some Timorese students, it was no longer necessary for them to pay their tuition fees.

While Florence was on pilgrimage and resting in Australia in 1974 a revolution occurred in Portugal. The wars in Angola, Guinea and Mozambique were absorbing 50 percent of Portugal's budget and on April 25, 1974, unwilling to continue the struggles, the Portuguese armed forces overthrew the Caetano regime in Lisbon. Timor itself then became politically unstable as some Timorese wished for continued Portuguese rule and some for independence. Indonesia invaded and, after a brief one-sided war against the independence fighters, incorporated the former Portuguese colony as part of Indonesia. Florence lost her home and her new car. Unable to return to Dili, she settled in Unley, South Australia. In 1978 she travelled to New Zealand, Tonga, Fiji and Samoa. She died two years later on September 7, 1980.

With the invasion of Portuguese Timor by Indonesia its Bahá'í community dissolved. Some Bahá'ís had emigrated to Australia in the 1960s, feeling that the colony offered them no future. Others remained in Timor. As Indonesia banned the Bahá'í Faith, the small Bahá'í community in Portuguese Timor became illegal under the new regime and of necessity ceased to exist.

A generation of Bahá'ís in Australia and Southeast Asia know of Harold and Florence Fitzner and of the sacrifices they bore in order to take the message of Bahá'u'lláh to Portuguese Timor. But who can measure the true value of their suffering and sacrifice?

30

Wednesday is Market Day

Shahnaz Tulsi

Shahnaz Tulsi, an auxiliary board member in Africa, has been a pioneer in Tanzania for twelve years.

I was born in Tehran in 1945 into a Bahá'í family of Jewish background. I attended deepening classes in Tehran which so affected me that I yearned to go pioneering.

In 1968 Hand of the Cause Dr Muhajir and the counsellors advised me to go to India. With much difficulty, and after offering many prayers, I obtained permission from my parents to go alone to this foreign land. On October 12, 1968 I went to India and, as instructed by the national spiritual assembly, spent some time in Chandigarh. Then, again at the request of the national assembly, I went to Jaipur, Rajasthan, to try to revive the local spiritual assembly.

While there I studied at Rajasthan University and received the Higher Proficiency Certificate in English, a Master's degree in sociology and a Bachelor's degree in adult education. My dissertation 'A Study of the Methods of Communication used by the Bahá'ís in Educating Persons to Adopt the Bahá'í Faith' helped proclaim the Faith among the teachers and lecturers and promoted the Cause in the university. My viva examination – two hours of teaching and deepening in the Bahá'í Faith – provided my highest mark. It seemed to me to be a confirmation, a sign of Bahá'u'lláh's power.

In Jaipur I served as a teacher of Bahá'í children's classes, a member of the local spiritual assembly and a member of the state teaching committee for six years. However, most of my time was spent travel teaching in the villages and towns of the area, particularly in the north of India, opening to the Faith villages in the Tibetan area near the border in the Himalayas. I gave the people Bahá'í pamphlets in Tibetan. These days were among the happiest in my life and will never be forgotten.

In December 1975 I married Narendra L. Tulsi, a Tanzanian who was studying in India and who had become a Bahá'í during one of our group teaching tours to his university a few years earlier. Our wedding in Jaipur was attended by about a hundred non-Bahá'í friends and university staff – a good proclamation event for the Faith and the best fireside. The next day the newspapers published our wedding photo with a detailed explanation of Bahá'í marriage.

That same month I obtained employment in the external services division of the All-India Radio in New Delhi as a translator and an announcer in the Persian unit, a capacity in which I worked for five years.

In 1979 my husband went to Tanzania and found a job in Arusha. I resigned from my job and joined him. It had long been the wish of Dr Muhajir that I serve in Tanzania! I was very happy that his wish was fulfilled while he was still on this earth. From September 21, 1979 until April 1989 I was in Arusha, first serving as a member of the local spiritual assembly and later as an auxiliary board member. Then my husband changed his job and we moved to Tanga, Tanzania.

Tanga is the fourth largest town in the country. It is a coastal town of the Indian Ocean and was once an important port. Now it is very quiet. It is hot and humid, very dusty and there are many mosquitoes and other insects. Most of the population is Muslim, of different sects. There are also Indian Hindus and some Christians. My husband is an electrical engineer working for a textile company that belongs to a Hindu family. Our neighbours are Hindus from India.

The town is very dull without any activities or much entertainment. As there is no television station in Tanzania, there is more time to be with people and to teach. Many of the Asian families in Tanzania now have video sets so that they can see their own films and movies. This is the only entertainment and many are addicted to watching day and night. We have one cinema.

There is a post office and telephone system but most of the phones are out of order. It is rather unsafe to walk alone in the town because of thieves. I had a bad experience when I first arrived. My mother had just arrived for a visit and we went shopping at nine in the morning. Two big men came towards us with knives in their hands and tried to snatch my watch. After minutes of struggle, they took the watch and ran away. Now I know not to wear a watch, earrings or other jewellery and to carry only a little money. Every now and then houses are robbed and businesses are looted. It is not safe to be on the streets after sunset so Bahá'í meetings must be conducted and finished before dark.

Water and electricity are a big problem. When we have water we have no electricity. Much of the time we have to carry in water from outside, for when there is no electricity the water pump does not work. We have to be very careful of our health at all times as this area has much malaria and typhoid and people often get diarrhoea and jaundice. Water must be boiled. We sleep wrapped in mosquito netting. When travelling we do not eat food along the way. Despite all our precautions, we do sometimes fall ill.

Wednesday is market day. Everyone in town goes to market to get fresh fruit and vegetables – it is a social occasion. It is important to know just when the market day is in each of the villages to which we plan to travel so we can buy what we need. Sometimes we travel in a vehicle carrying books, musical instruments and tapes for use in mass teaching.

The roads are a big problem and train travel is difficult. On one month-long trip to conduct training institutes, ten of us booked tickets a month in advance so we would at least have a place to sleep. However, there was no water on the train, for either drinking or washing. At each station we would get out and buy maize, eggs, bananas, peanuts or whatever was available. The compartments were full of cockroaches, bedbugs and mosquitoes. Without water the toilets and washrooms were unclean. Yet we enjoyed this trip, teaching people even on the train. The people everywhere are eager to hear about the Faith. There are constant opportunities, so even rigorous travelling conditions cannot defeat us.

When we got off the train we had to walk and carry our luggage for about an hour before we reached the bus stand at 5:30 a.m. Then we found there was no bus on that day! We waited for two hours until a lorry came along. Everyone jumped aboard with great difficulty. After awhile we realized the lorry was going into the villages to collect its load – the wrong direction for us. Hundreds of bags of maize, drums of oil and other things were loaded. There was barely room to stand. There were many small children and pregnant women on the lorry, some suffering from diarrhoea, some going to hospital. The lorry owner treated us like animals but no one raised a word of protest. When we got to the train station the train was delayed for nine hours. This might be considered a normal journey in Tanzania!

When travelling one must be very patient, polite and quiet and endure all with a smiling face. Africans themselves are like this, very cool, very tolerant, acting always as if nothing has happened. People live in great poverty but never complain. There are no medicines in many of the hospitals. Children die every day. Salaries are insufficient to feed even one person yet people are calm, thanking God and bearing their suffering with smiling faces. Most families have a small amount of land to cultivate food. Those without land have a very difficult time.

We do sometimes have travel teachers in Tanzania but few pass through Tanga, unless we make a special effort to arrange a programme. As a whole, Tanzania receives fewer travel teachers than the neighbouring countries of Kenya, Uganda and Zambia.

The best thing about day-to-day living here is moving around, meeting people, being friendly with them and teaching. Almost every evening we visit different families. We have some very interesting firesides. I have found a good way to meet people and make friends: I have opened an aerobic exercise class for women which I hold for one hour a day, five days a week. Even those women who cannot attend are friendly to me as they regard me as a teacher.

I find the life of the villagers very interesting. They have no time to themselves. They arise early and do their cleaning. Then they go to their land without eating anything. In the afternoon they return, wash themselves and start cooking, which takes a very long time. In the evening they do more work in their homes. They sit and talk with neighbours and go early to bed. They usually eat but one large meal a day.

I really enjoy my life in this quiet town. I have time to pray, meditate and read the Writings in a quiet atmosphere. This is a bounty.

31

The Pioneering Bug

Nettie and A.J. Bristow-Stagg

A.J. Bristow-Stagg writes of homefront pioneering:

My wife Nettie and I received the pioneering bug a year
into our Bahá'í life as it was the topic of conversation at
nearly every meeting we attended. We sold our home,
bought a bus and took off to have a holiday before we
discussed where we would settle. Unknown to us, at that
same time, far across the country on the other side of
Australia, prayers were being said – an appeal for
homefront pioneers. It seemed as though some unknown
force was compelling us to travel 6000 kilometres in just
two weeks so that we would wind up in Townsville, North
Queensland. It was soon to be Riḍván 1986. The local
spiritual assembly needed two more Bahá'ís to maintain
itself. Our pioneering life was off to a radiant start!

Once this community was strong enough and had
sufficient numbers to warrant our going, we left for another
homefront area, again bringing the number of Bahá'ís to
the requisite nine. We asked a dedicated Bahá'í, 'When will
we know we have reached the area Bahá'u'lláh has
destined for us?' Her reply: 'Your heart will tell you. If your
heart doesn't tell you, you will probably be so broke that if
you wanted to move, you couldn't.'

We were happy where we were but our hearts did not tell
us this was the place. Indeed, it seemed too good to be true

340 AND THE TREES CLAPPED THEIR HANDS

- living there in a beautiful natural environment, good climate, with no problems. What? No problems? We should have known that was the time to worry. A Bahá'í must be like a raging river, rushing towards its goal, meeting on the way a lot of obstacles, waterfalls and rapids so as to remain alive and full of life. If you end up in a pool there is the danger that you will become stagnant. This is where we were, in a peaceful pool. It was time to get back in the current. The Bahá'í who had inspired us to move in the first place had originally wanted us to go to a more remote area, but because of minor obstacles, we stopped where we were. We now realized that the place we belonged was not here where life was so pleasing and easy, but some 75 kilometres down the road, where the change in environment was drastic. Wet seasons with high humidity, temperatures of 47 degrees Celsius indoors, and many difficulties. So we made the move and are still here. Our hearts tell us this is the right place, and besides, we are so broke we could not move if we wanted to!

We had been living here for six months when the first travel teaching team came through. The arrival of travel teachers when you live in a remote area is a great occasion. Deprived of the stimulation of contact with other Bahá'ís, the travel teams bring much spiritual upliftment and the courage required to continue to work for the Cause. Not only that, but as happened in our case, the team does a job which immediately requires consolidation and much more work. By the time the team left, our community, which had comprised but four Bahá'ís, had 54!

We celebrated our ninth wedding anniversary here at this post as well as the birth of our son. We have had many difficulties but many confirmations as well. There can be no true progress without the challenge of difficulties. When we first arrived there was much prejudice against us and opposition to any function we proposed. Local priests warned their congregations of 'this new religion'. It took over three years before people became friendly towards the Faith. Now there are more friends of the Faith than those who are antagonistic to it. Our community has expanded to the point that we have a Bahá'í centre. Although income is low here, we have managed to purchase two blocks of land and transform them into a garden and we are working on the buildings. Progress is slow. We have not had any contact with travel teachers for well over a year now. We badly need the infusion of life and vitality such teachers bring. We are struggling to continue our work. In all of Australia there are but seven thousand Bahá'ís. But seven thousand transformed souls can accomplish great things. The work of transformation, of preparation and of service is the challenge presented to each and every Bahá'í throughout the world.

32

An Iranian in Laos

Heshmet Taeed

Heshmet Taeed wrote from his home in Cairns, Australia, of pioneering in Laos during the Ten Year Crusade:

I spent most of 1954 teaching the Faith in Bangkok and four months in Chiengmai, up north. But after a full year of service, I no longer had any money and there had been no declarations. Thailand had a single Bahá'í, Mr Pramote, a gentle friendly chap. Occasionally I had short meetings with him, but it had been primarily a year of difficulties and loneliness. Then my visa expired. I did not know what to do.

A friend suggested I go to Laos, which had no believers, although it was not mentioned as a virgin territory in the Ten Year Crusade. Laos had just become independent and the French had moved out. It was still a turbulent time for the country. I was told by reporters that for months they had not been able to get a visa. I applied in a cable to the Lao government. To my surprise, within a week I had a two weeks' visa and a return on the money I spent on the cable. I learned later that this was a mistake as the government thought I was from the United Nations.

A friend had given me some money but it was not enough for a room in the dilapidated hotel in the capital, so I stayed in a sort of motel for prostitutes. Communication was difficult. My poor English was of no use and my sparse

French did little better. I felt I was in a dangerous position, in fact, and could only pray about my situation. Yet I felt that perhaps it had been the will of Bahá'u'lláh that I should be allowed into this country when reporters were not. I wanted to make it count for the Faith. No one could understand my presence there. One man asked if I had committed a crime and was a fugitive in Laos. My explanation was insufficient. A man took mercy on me and allowed me to stay in his kitchen at night. It was very small, with hardly enough room for me to lie down. During the days I simply wandered around praying. A couple of monks noticed me and said they would share the food they begged in the streets with me if I would teach them some English. They had many doubts about me as my pronunciation was not all that good; but as I was the only person who knew English, they had no alternative. Within four months I was known as an English teacher and an influential man asked if I would teach him. After about a month he asked what he could do for me. I explained my predicament – that my visa had expired and the police were asking me to leave. I kept getting temporary 15-day visas but the pressure was on for me to go. This man telephoned and got me a six month visa.

One day an American appeared who asked if I could go with him to the health ministry to translate into French. The country had only one doctor and that was the health minister himself. The American soon discovered my limitations in both English and French but he decided to hire me anyway. He asked what I wanted as a salary and I told a higher rate thinking we would bargain as we do in Iran. I asked for $150 in American money. To my surprise the personnel officer arranged for me to have $500 a month. I was so grateful that I sent my entire first month's salary to the Guardian, leaving us with next to nothing to live on for the month.

The 'us' were myself, my wife and two tiny children, due to arrive within the week. They lost some of their goods and their passports. When my wife saw my humble and rat-infested home, she was reduced to tears. We had a very difficult time until I found better quarters.

For the next two years we worked hard to promote the Word of God but no one became a Bahá'í. Then two pioneers arrived from the United States. At the same time, we had our first new Bahá'í when a man from the post office whom I had been teaching declared. We stayed in Laos for six years and saw the Faith become officially recognized. However, we were forced to return to Iran when the war in Laos, during which our house was riddled with bullets, escalated.

33

From East to West

Pauline and Isaac de Cruz

Isaac de Cruz is an Indian Malaysian and his wife Pauline is a Chinese Malaysian. Both served for many years in their own country before going to pioneer in, of all places, Liverpool, England. Isaac writes:

Thirty-one years ago, in August 1960, I attended my first Bahá'í summer school in Port Dickson, Malaysia. About 70 Bahá'ís and enquirers were present. I had been invited to attend the school by Theresa Chee, the oldest of the five daughters of Yan Kee Leong, the first believer of West Malaysia. He had embraced the Faith in 1953 and after many years, one of his daughters had at last agreed to investigate the Faith and to attend a summer school. She in turn had managed to inveigle me into agreeing to follow her for a so-called holiday by the sea. That seemingly innocent event was to enchant and captivate me for the rest of my life. Theresa declared at the summer school and I remember her parting words to me: 'I hope in a few years' time you will realize who Bahá'u'lláh is and why He has come!'

I was then an 18-year-old Catholic, quite satisfied, not having any desperate need to change the world nor my own way of life. I was not even curious. And yet, thinking back to all that, my gratitude to Him knows no bounds. Why did He choose to confer so inestimable a bounty, so precious a gift on so unworthy a being? I did lend a hearing ear to words about the Faith but it still astonishes me that I had no particular questions to ask. I was born and bred in a Catholic family and kneeling in front of the altar at home every day at dusk to recite with the family the Lord's Prayer and Hail Marys was a regular part of my daily life. I attended church as regularly as I could and had tried with all sincerity to carry out the sacraments of the church. To me, Christmas and Easter were the greatest spiritual events in the world. All Islamic-sounding things were anathema.

And yet the first book I read was *The Dawn-Breakers*, a book which I instantly recognized as presenting the truth. None of the names sounded strange to me. I immediately felt I was privileged to be able to read the greatest historical narrative of all times – about the Day of God – the promised time being made known to the peoples of the world.

One month after the summer school, on the 24th of September 1960, I declared at the Bahá'í centre which, incidentally, had been presented to the Bahá'ís as a gift by Yan Kee Leong.

After Theresa had accepted the Faith it was only a matter of time before the other four sisters began their journeys of investigation and declaration. They were such a closely-knit family that the impact of Theresa's acceptance of the Faith was bound to influence the others. The youngest of the sisters was Pauline, who accepted the Faith in 1961. She became my wife in 1966.

For years we wanted to leave Malaysia and pioneer. In 1978, when we had two children, I left for a six-month travel teaching trip to Africa. While in Nigeria I wrote to Pauline that it looked like I might get a job there. In hasty enthusiasm, she gave up our rented house, sold off everything, and moved to her mother's house with the children. I wrote telling her, 'I am ready.' But Bahá'u'lláh had yet other things in store for us. I returned to Malaysia empty-handed and resumed teaching. The next seven years were the most traumatic of our lives, fraught with constant tests. In retrospect, however, we realize that at the darkest moments He stretched forth His hands and lifted us out of the abyss. Feeble, He strengthened us. Poor, He enriched us; sinful, He forgave us. Words are powerless to describe our gratitude.

In May 1988 Pauline and our (by then) three children came to join me in England. I was about to complete my law studies. This was one of the great periods of mass teaching throughout the world, and in 1988, while serving on the National Teaching Committee of the United Kingdom, I heard about the commitment of the national spiritual assembly to this process of teaching. Our offer to serve on the teaching project set up in Liverpool as full-time coordinators was accepted. The national assembly kindly sorted out our visa problems and we have been serving on the project ever since.

This has been an educative and chastening period in our lives. Tests and trials come in abundance. We came from the East to settle in a run-down inner city of the West and to bring His Message to Liverpudlians. In the process we have had to set our own inner lives in order and evaluate our own responses to the many who come to the Liverpool Bahá'í centre – some sincere, some merely out of curiosity, some because they have come to the end of the road, and yet others for the love and warmth they know comes from the Bahá'ís. We encounter persons of all ages in Liverpool. Many have no idea of what the word 'reverence' means and many have a real disdain for even the slightest suggestion of anything that appears to be an 'organized religion'. There are so many who apparently feel it is fashionable to show disrespect for any kind of authority. At first, the attitude of these people really jolted our senses. We were challenged as never before to move beyond our narrow parochial views of human nature and to begin to comprehend, however dimly, however falteringly, the great diversity of human realities that abound on the face of this planet.

Our eastern heritage did not prepare us for the shock of encountering this culture, most especially the phenomena of today's street kids. So many of them have no proper homes, no loving parents to guide them, and are hurt by their experiences in a very tough world. This is so different from the close family groups, the respect for parental authority found in the East. To reach forth in loving-kindness and not be rejected, to allow these youths time and space in which to comprehend that concepts such as kindness, reverence and honesty are two-way responsibilities, not just something they can expect from us, but also something that we expect from them – all this takes much time and patience.

Learning to understand others who appear to have such different values, having compassion towards all, these qualities had to be relearned. I look back to the days of the early '60s when in Malaysia we found so many youngsters eager to learn, to attend deepening classes, study institutes and spiritualization courses. But the youth in Liverpool are a different kettle of fish. To get them to sit down and participate in a discussion for even half an hour is a tremendous achievement. It is a challenge that calls for much patience. We have had to learn to listen more, rather than to talk, to realize that these youth come to the centre for a variety of reasons and that their needs have to be acknowledged and given due attention.

Even the manner in which I speak assumes much importance. One day a young lady with her two children visited the centre. I spoke to her in a loving and gentle tone, urging her to come as often as she could to the centre and to take advantage of the resources available – the books in the library, the opportunity to consult with Bahá'ís, etc. I learned later that my words had totally turned her off because she had such a profound resentment for 'authority' figures and she had felt I was bossing her around. Thus the need constantly to deepen ourselves, to immerse ourselves in the Writings, to teach ourselves – first of all – every aspect of Bahá'u'lláh's Revelation, is apparent to us every day.

More than a hundred believers have now come into the Faith in Liverpool and Merseyside as a result of the setting up of this project in the spring of 1988. Thousands have heard of the Faith throughout this region through a ceaseless programme of exhibitions, local radio and national television shows, advertisements in papers and on buses, performances of dance and musical groups in shopping centres, public talks and firesides, informal dinners, teaching on the streets and in parks. The dignity of the Faith has always been maintained, although some of these teaching methods seemed at first extreme and perhaps too flamboyant. Some newcomers in the Faith have become a source of tests and trials for the community but have provided all of us with a vast learning and deepening opportunity.

34

Conversation with My Brother

Shirin Sabri

Bahá'í poet, writer and pioneer Shirin Sabri of Queensland, Australia, writes that she was five years old when her family pioneered to Papua New Guinea. Her younger brother was born there and always regarded it as his homeland. After eleven years, the family left Papua and eventually went to serve at the Bahá'í World Centre. Her brother always planned to return to Papua New Guinea and did so for a time. He then returned to Haifa, again to serve at the World Centre. When Shirin visited him there he expressed his longing for the land of his childhood. This inspired Shirin to write this poem.

Yes, it was beautiful, where we used to live,
Where bright brown boys of headlong grace
Leapt over waterfalls,
Splashed out of pools shining,
Sprang like living branches
From a fallen tree below.

We would walk, after rain,
Barefoot, the mud in sunlight steaming, slapping
Wet and pungent leaves aside
With sticks:
At dawn, reached up to prop
Elbows on the railing, rubbing toes
On the verandah's worn wood floor,
Mist unfolding
From the smooth brown river
Curving round the hill's edge.

Once, we heard
A bird of paradise call, perhaps
From the far, dense trees.
It could have been.

And there we ran,
Balancing on the earth, fingertips
Brushing the butterflies
That dipped and swung in heavy air,
Wingspans wider than our stretching hands;

And some days it rained, rained
All day, the bridge submerged,
School out of reach,
Rained warm and sweet, filled the water tanks
Till we could stand,
Hair drenched dark and slick
Beneath the tumbling overflow.

But here, now far away, remembering,
You build a small fire, in a flat earthen pot,
Sitting on the tiled floor, turn out
The kitchen light, face lit in hinge
Of cheek and jaw. You talk of islands,
The slow wallowing boat
To Salamaua, where dolphins
Plunged athwart us, and say
'Will you come back with me?'
I only answer, 'No.'

But understand, understand
I know the loss, and remember
Another departure – were you awake then?
The night the horses got away,
Hooves battering the grass,
My room dark as a drum's belly,

Hooves loud on the taut window pane.
They could still be heard
Whole minutes later
Going to roadless places,
The night echoing
Around my shoulders while I sat
Straight and still in bed.
As though my heart had then escaped me.

35

The Dance

Kathleen A. Le Mone

Kathleen A. Le Mone dedicated her poem to the Pygmy people of Mugambiro, Zaire, who tried 'to teach me the reality of Joy'.

I

It is wrong to say it is ballet, this dance
of the forest people. It is not controlled,
not premeditated, it is pure and it is African

and comes from centuries of the hunt and life
times of observing the dance of gazelles and
wildebeests, of lions and antelopes. I know

laughter filled the city long ago and is a refugee
in the forests. This dance celebrates the
refugee and declares the mystery of what

others call the primitive man. Man civilized only
to the haunting rhythm that banana trees sway
to and my heart beat has changed to.

II

They laugh and swoop down, crouching
down, an excited sound rises from between
their teeth, like a beast passing

passing quickly, but not in fear. No
song to this dance, no words, but it speaks
loudly, by rhythm, by movement, by drum

beat. It snakes through the village
slowly with a leader who moves deliberately
like a child skipping, a gazelle

in flight. He holds his fists tight,
grasping air, up and down he pumps, up
and down. His muscles shine in the

moonlight, tight, loose, tight again,
loose again. The villagers follow him
in devotion, fluid as water, unrestrained

as wind, flowing over rocks, through trees
the beat changes, hands clap and they pirouette
into the next step. The leader moves in

slow motion, reaching to his star, leg extended
he leaps and there suspended, he stops
as if to tell me something, then lands.

III

O star catchers, O forest dancers, your
heads only reach my breasts, but your vision
takes in the universe. Your laughter

echoes in my head, your joy is a
suspended crystal, reflecting light. You
give me a new name, Kahinda, the one

who rouses the people to move, you
teach me to see in the dark, you
teach me to move to the rhythm of

my heart, by moonlight.

36

Death from Luggage

Esther and Bill Bradley-DeTally

Esther Bradley-DeTally and her husband, Bill, are pioneers in the Ukraine. She struggled to write these few pages on 'an old and stiff typewriter' and sent it from Dnepropetrovsk with Bill, who was going to Kiev, in the hope he would find someone there who was leaving the country and could mail it. Her script arrived, postmarked Ottawa, Canada, a bit over a month after she first received our request for her to write it. This is typical of the wonderful response of pioneers who give of themselves every day in the service of the Cause.

Bill is shrinking and I have become orangutan-like with hands permanently curved to carry things. 'I am Bahá'u'lláh's porter,' Bill responds to my fretful queries about 'death from carrying too much luggage'. Bill and I have become pioneers. We are perhaps the latest kids on the pioneering block in what is the former Soviet Union. Here, everything must be hand-carried or lugged.

Like most Bahá'ís, we have wheels on our feet. Since I met Bill in 1985 our place called home has increased in boundary.

In 1985 I was divorced, a university student busily handling life. I was fighting remnants of several bouts of mononucleosis. I worked part-time for law firms and had one eye on our cat, Kitty, who practised the Zen of Urp. My other eye was constantly on my son, Nick, who was in his rebellious phase. He could have, at this time, cheerfully driven an army tank through our student housing walls. I had graduated with a degree in English and was in the midst of teacher training. I was so tired most of the time all I wanted was a sidewalk to lie down on and rest. But I persevered in my training courses, coping as well as I could with problems and saying daily the obligatory prayers and the Tablet of Aḥmad.

Suddenly, life changed radically. I had to leave teachers' ed. and stuff furniture into storage. Kitty went to a friend's house. Nick went to his dad's. 'Come and stay with me,' Peg urged. 'Find a job here.' So I moved to Manhattan Beach, met Bill and we married two-and-a-half months later.

Nick and Kitty rejoined us. We increased our family with a young man, Elias, from Ethiopia. We moved to a less affluent community. Finally, children grown, Bill and I moved to Seattle where pure air could aid in restoring my failed health. Bill could find no work. We had just bought a small house nestled in the woods. While I drank hot chocolate and took long walks, Bill delved into the writings of the Guardian. From that time, Bill could no longer do computer defence work. He wanted only to serve the Faith full-time. We decided to live off our savings for a year and simply to teach the Faith and serve in whatever capacity we could. Then came the call. 'There's a group going to Russia, all young adults. They need an older couple to balance things out.' We said 'yes' within 30 seconds and within a month, twelve of us, called the Marion Jack Teaching Project, were in Moscow at an Intourist hotel.

We began long, exciting, gruelling days of constant travel and teaching for two months. We travelled to Siberia and the Ukraine. The group was composed of musicians. Bill and I were part of the frog chorus when extra voices were needed. We had brought ten thousand copies of the

Promise of World Peace with us and we met thousands of people.

'I'm not going back,' I announced to Bill on the Yugoslavian plane home. And I could almost hear his brain grinding away, planning the next trip. I had had three severe chest colds and was again looking around for sidewalks. But sun, California, rest and a great travel teaching trip through the United States changed my mind. While in California, a journalist interviewed us. I heard the excitement in my voice as I talked of Russia, Siberia and the Ukraine. I also saw a video of a train going through Russian countryside and heard Russian songs being sung as background music. I cried. I knew then my soul had been claimed.

We consulted with our national pioneering office which helped us with airplane tickets. Manhattan Beach gave us our literature. Then an unexpected financial wrinkle entered our lives. But we could not be deterred from our trip. We sold our house and furniture to clear us of all debts, packed our Volkswagen bus and drove with the remaining boxes to Bill's mother's house in Jamestown, New York. Puggy, our velvet frog of a dog, was given safe haven with Bahá'ís in Ohio. Nick is in Southern Orange County, California, and Tory and John, Bill's children, live with their mother near Los Angeles. Bill's mother watches our books and thinks we're crazy. We write her frequent food reports so she will know her son is being fed.

We decided on Dnepropetrovsk, which I call Dneper because we could not spell or pronounce the name. The tourist brochure reads: 'If you look at a map of the Ukraine, the blue ribbon of the Dneper River, cutting the republic in two, will catch your eye first. Strung together upon it, like pearls, are tens of towns and villages, old and new, which constitute the Dneper necklace a thousand kilometres long. In one of its curves, the Dneper cradles the beautiful city of Dnepropetrovsk.' Another Ukrainian magazine, published in English in Canada, carried an article headlined 'Hell is at Our Heels'. It names Dnepropetrovsk as one of the ten cities in the Ukraine condemned to die from pollution. Dneper's main industry is metallurgy. It is a worker's town, a city of one million or so, closed since World War II (which they call the Great Patriotic War) until three years ago – no foreigners were allowed to visit.

Bill and I are among the first Americans here. Everyone wants to speak English with us. We speak everywhere: at English clubs, institutes of mining, railway institutes, libraries, and we are invited to many homes. We are filled with images. Like the buses, trams and trolleys which overspill, our emotions rise and fall and perceptions crowd us. We think that in Dneper spiritual hunger and disdain compete. As I write this in April 1992, Poe-like doors invisibly close around the newly-independent Ukraine. Dneper has ten institutes, ten museums, theatres, a symphony orchestra. This city is, however, also called the 'birthplace of stagnation' and is the mafioso hang-out in the Ukraine.

Victor, last autumn's interpreter, is a potpourri of information. His brown eyes flash as he spills out facts, disparate, like a Soviet bag fresh from the bazaar. 'There are no parts to repair the streetcars. Dneper has the largest insane asylum in the region.' Replying to my question about the dark streets and houses, he responds, 'All light bulbs are in Romania or Poland.' Then he warms to his favourite subject. 'Aliens', he says, 'are due to take over the world in 1993.' Another fellow, with similar magical views, wants to know our opinions. 'Will the Vikings experience a return of their religion?' he asks. 'Only in Los Angeles,' I mutter to myself. 'What have you heard of pockets of evil women in the Ukraine and in the Amazon?' he asks next. We leap to a more abstract view of evil. We discuss women

and men. Our heads clear. We step carefully down the path
of knowledge.

The Bahá'ís are newly declared here. Some were waiting
for us; some declared after our arrival. There is Nella whose
eyes shine with intelligence and who after months of
caution, of erasure of fears, declared a flaming belief. Julia,
our secretary, is young, widowed, practical, hardworking.
She spends her life on trains to and from Riga, carving out
a living selling goods in Latvia. Vasili, with gnarled hands,
gentle eyes, 85-year-old Vasili is a survivor of 17 years'
imprisonment and exile. Stalin's stamp could not change
his soul. Marina, his wife, separated from him for almost 30
years, reunited by an accidental meeting. Marina, who
lived through the blockade and starvation in Leningrad
and who survived the exile of her husband, declared last
year after we arrived. Marina and I, like two happy short-
order cooks at Howard Johnson's, sling out broken English
and Russian. We have other members in our Bahá'í
community, 16 in all. Valery, 'young Valery' we call him to
distinguish him from Valery-with-the-beard, who looks like
a maple syrup ad – young Valery trembles and shouts with
eagerness about the Faith. He is our librarian, our delegate
to the convention to elect our first historic national spiritual
assembly. He is our flame. Then there's Dima, 'Sleevki
Dima', Bill and I call him. We met this tall, handsome and
sincere university student at the open market through the
purchase of a defective Sleevki (cream) bottle. He read a
pamphlet, came to a meeting and declared his faith. Our
local spiritual assembly was formed with the presence
and wonderful help of Counsellor Patrick O'Mara from
Ireland.

Dneper is a combination of old and new. Madam
Blavatskaya, founder of the Theosophical Society, was
born here. Village ways and '90s television discover one
another. I have seen unattended facial wounds congeal;

dogs ride trolleys unticketed; mothers wait in lines for hours for unwholesome children's milk. We have spoken to hundreds, maybe thousands, of cynics and believers. Hundreds of people have extended their all to us. Dneper is a city of contrasts like the rest of the Ukraine.

In the summer of 1991, on a quiet day in Kiev, we walked through silent, closed moments – days of the coup. We were resolute. 'Don't go,' Mrs Munsiff had told us in Los Angeles. 'It will be the hardest thing you've ever done, but don't leave.' So we didn't. As the months go by, I am strengthened by many things. Lately it has been by a deeper understanding of Adib Taherzadeh's *Revelation of Bahá'u'lláh*. I begin to welcome difficulties. The more we feel, the more we give, the stronger the foundation for this Faith. My core grows stronger. I miss my son and I miss my Pug, but my core becomes stronger.

We will return home for a month or so this summer and then hope to come back here. We can only do this one year at a time. The Ukraine assaults your senses and claims your soul. Nationhood and increased deprivation of all kinds gnaw at the soul. Yet we must come back.

We must come back, back to see Inna, laughing-eyed Inna who opened her home to us. Twenty-seven-year-old Inna says of us when we are away, 'Where are my children? Come home. We are waiting.' Inna's love and dearness have wrapped around us forever. We must come back to trudge, to lug, to carry. We must come back to our community, now friends, now family in Odessa, Donetsk, Poltava, Kiev and of course, the unpronounceable Dnepropetrovsk. Will there be lamps? milk? matches? heat? sugar? hope? laughter? We do not know. All I know – and Bill agrees – there seems to be no other call. We hope we can be worthy of such a time.

37

Pointers for Pioneers

Barry Clatt

The Office of Pioneering of the National Spiritual Assembly of the United States publishes Pioneer Post, *a newsletter with stories and photos that goes out to pioneers around the world. The June 1990 edition included some observations about pioneering written by Barry Clatt who pioneered in Kenya:*

1. Take it day by day and try to stick it out to the end if you are having difficulties at your post. Later on, you may be amazed at the inner qualities which developed during your pioneering period. The other side of this coin is that if all the signs point to a premature departure from your post, don't let pride or ego get in the way. Consultation with many close Bahá'í friends, in addition to prayer and sincere inner reflection, will provide the answer.

2. Try to enjoy a well-balanced lifestyle as much as you can. Enjoy life and especially enjoy what life has to offer locally. You are in a perfect position to begin living an integrated life.

3. (This was written for Americans, but the warning against nationalism is pertinent for all) Please refrain from America-bashing. This behaviour, at best, represents boredom and lack of creativity and it is offensive and confusing to local people many times. The other extreme is to extol America as the greatest place on earth. Either

behaviour is tedious and serves no purpose in promoting the Cause.

4. Make an effort to learn something new. This will also help you maintain a perspective and lead a more balanced existence.

5. What Bahá'í would not like to learn the secret of a 24-hour-a-day automatic teaching without effort? Here's my idea: Form deep, abiding friendships with local people. You may find the vast majority of people have formed friendships or associations for reasons of business or functional convenience. But not you. You are a lover of humanity and you are God's leavening agent, and your friendships with local people will transcend ages or barriers and will so impress others that they will ask you what your secret is and why you are so happy.

6. Never, never assume even the slightest degree of superiority or advanced evolution in any aspect of life. Chances are you have much to learn about life and some healing to do.

7. Leave all your stereotypes behind. This is more difficult than you may think. Old attitudes can stick like glue!

8. You cannot run away from your problems by relocating across the ocean. Many have tried to solve problems this way but invariably it backfires. The bottom line is that it is more satisfying to meet problems head-on and it takes less energy to do so too.

9. Try to do with less and less. See how local people live. Be happy.

10. Pray devotedly with new sincerity and meaning. You may find yourself utterly astonished at the transforming power and beauty of prayers especially for you in the Tablets of the Divine Plan.

11. Learn the local language, at least to the extent of conversational fluency and to be able to teach the basics of the Faith.

12. Be open, friendly, loving, caring. Dare to be the whole person you have been striving to become.

13. If your work happens to be in the realm of social and economic development and is specifically in a non-Bahá'í environment, you may have to prepare yourself for massive disillusionment and negative expectations. But remain close to God and to the Bahá'í community and remember that even a negative learning experience can be of lasting positive value.

14. Continue to maintain your correspondence with loved ones back home especially if there is any misunderstanding or tension about your moving halfway around the planet.

15. Be prepared for the experience of a devastating crash landing upon return to your homeland. May I suggest you read an intelligent, compassionate, right-on-track October 1988 nine-page publication by the US Office of Pioneering prepared for returning pioneers.

16. Bow down as lowly and humbly as possible before Bahá'u'lláh and thank Him for this most blessed opportunity of pioneering in this most blessed era. No matter the degree of difficulty you suffer, whatever pain or depression you may experience, you will grow and develop and serve beyond any expectation. You will have a much greater capacity to love and your heart will exult with overflowing gratitude for the magnificent bounty you have been given.

38

The Pioneering Game or One Dull Night in Kinshasa

Louise Mould

Many people in Canada said I should contact Louise Mould about her experiences in Zaire. She sent this game which will, I am sure, entertain pioneers when they most need a good laugh.

Part I

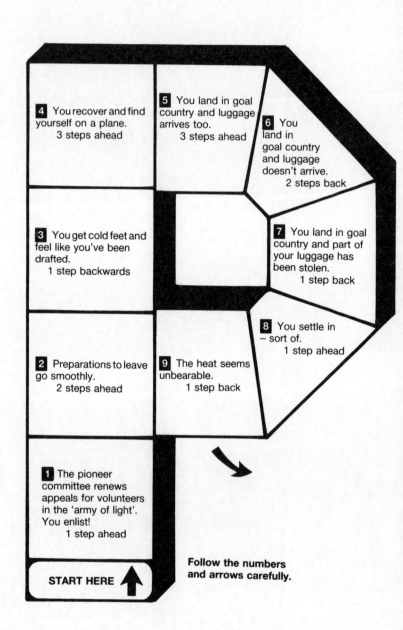

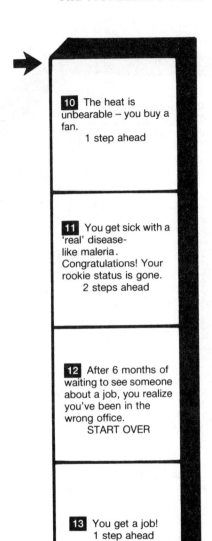

10 The heat is unbearable – you buy a fan.
        1 step ahead

11 You get sick with a 'real' disease-like maleria. Congratulations! Your rookie status is gone.
        2 steps ahead

12 After 6 months of waiting to see someone about a job, you realize you've been in the wrong office.
        START OVER

13 You get a job!
        1 step ahead

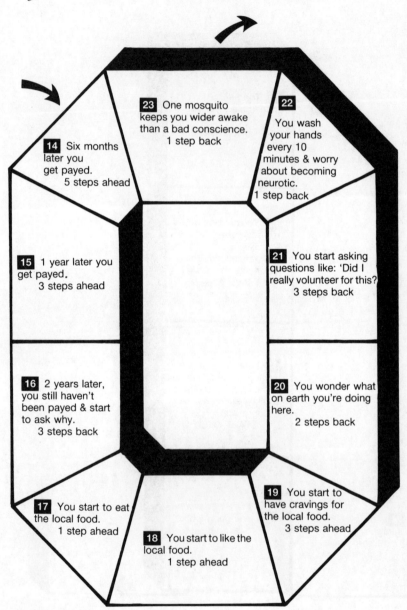

14 Six months later you get payed. 5 steps ahead

23 One mosquito keeps you wider awake than a bad conscience. 1 step back

22 You wash your hands every 10 minutes & worry about becoming neurotic. 1 step back

15 1 year later you get payed. 3 steps ahead

21 You start asking questions like: 'Did I really volunteer for this? 3 steps back

16 2 years later, you still haven't been payed & start to ask why. 3 steps back

20 You wonder what on earth you're doing here. 2 steps back

17 You start to eat the local food. 1 step ahead

18 You start to like the local food. 1 step ahead

19 You start to have cravings for the local food. 3 steps ahead

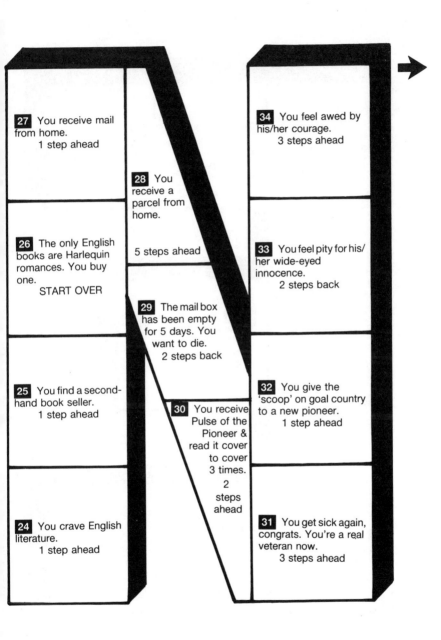

27 You receive mail from home.
1 step ahead

28 You receive a parcel from home.

5 steps ahead

26 The only English books are Harlequin romances. You buy one.
START OVER

29 The mail box has been empty for 5 days. You want to die.
2 steps back

25 You find a second-hand book seller.
1 step ahead

30 You receive Pulse of the Pioneer & read it cover to cover 3 times.
2 steps ahead

24 You crave English literature.
1 step ahead

34 You feel awed by his/her courage.
3 steps ahead

33 You feel pity for his/her wide-eyed innocence.
2 steps back

32 You give the 'scoop' on goal country to a new pioneer.
1 step ahead

31 You get sick again, congrats. You're a real veteran now.
3 steps ahead

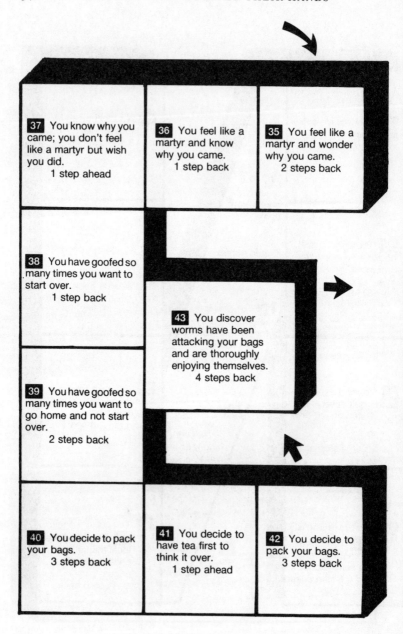

37 You know why you came; you don't feel like a martyr but wish you did.
   1 step ahead

36 You feel like a martyr and know why you came.
   1 step back

35 You feel like a martyr and wonder why you came.
   2 steps back

38 You have goofed so many times you want to start over.
   1 step back

43 You discover worms have been attacking your bags and are thoroughly enjoying themselves.
   4 steps back

39 You have goofed so many times you want to go home and not start over.
   2 steps back

40 You decide to pack your bags.
   3 steps back

41 You decide to have tea first to think it over.
   1 step ahead

42 You decide to pack your bags.
   3 steps back

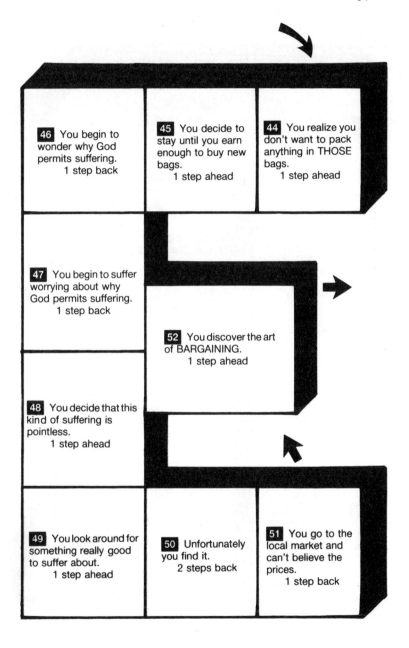

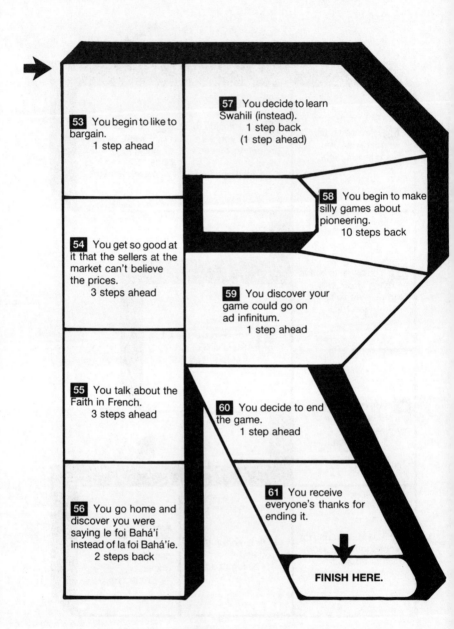

53 You begin to like to bargain.
1 step ahead

54 You get so good at it that the sellers at the market can't believe the prices.
3 steps ahead

55 You talk about the Faith in French.
3 steps ahead

56 You go home and discover you were saying le foi Bahá'í instead of la foi Bahá'íe.
2 steps back

57 You decide to learn Swahili (instead).
1 step back
(1 step ahead)

58 You begin to make silly games about pioneering.
10 steps back

59 You discover your game could go on ad infinitum.
1 step ahead

60 You decide to end the game.
1 step ahead

61 You receive everyone's thanks for ending it.

FINISH HERE.

Part II

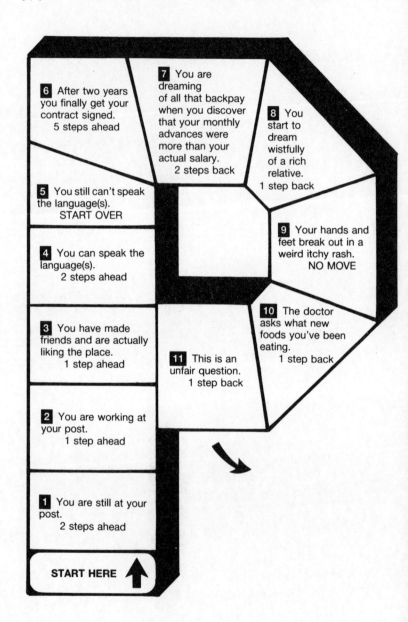

12 You buy creams and ointments but . . . the itch goes on.
1 step back

13 You decide to scratch and bear it.
2 steps ahead

14 You have lost your temper 8 times in one week.
2 steps back

15 You wonder if you are becoming extremely irritable or extremely fluent in the language.
1 step ahead

16 You decide to forget it all and pick up a spy thriller.
1 step ahead

17 You are enjoying every page when someone poses the question: 'Do books like that help one to progress spiritually?'
NO MOVE

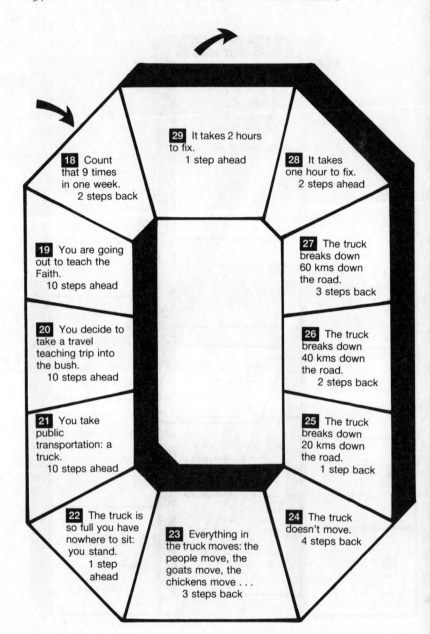

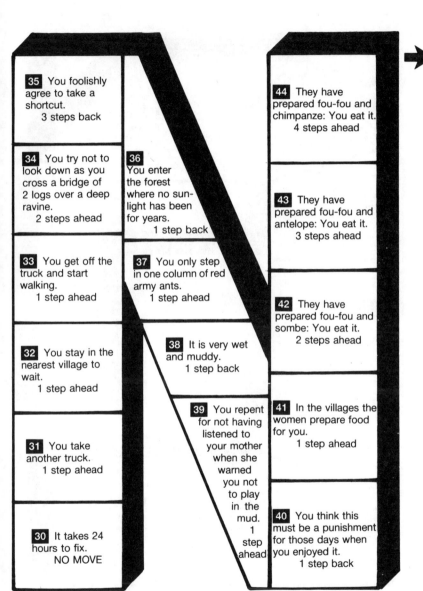

35 You foolishly agree to take a shortcut.
3 steps back

34 You try not to look down as you cross a bridge of 2 logs over a deep ravine.
2 steps ahead

36 You enter the forest where no sunlight has been for years.
1 step back

33 You get off the truck and start walking.
1 step ahead

37 You only step in one column of red army ants.
1 step ahead

32 You stay in the nearest village to wait.
1 step ahead

38 It is very wet and muddy.
1 step back

31 You take another truck.
1 step ahead

39 You repent for not having listened to your mother when she warned you not to play in the mud.
1 step ahead

30 It takes 24 hours to fix.
NO MOVE

44 They have prepared fou-fou and chimpanze: You eat it.
4 steps ahead

43 They have prepared fou-fou and antelope: You eat it.
3 steps ahead

42 They have prepared fou-fou and sombe: You eat it.
2 steps ahead

41 In the villages the women prepare food for you.
1 step ahead

40 You think this must be a punishment for those days when you enjoyed it.
1 step back

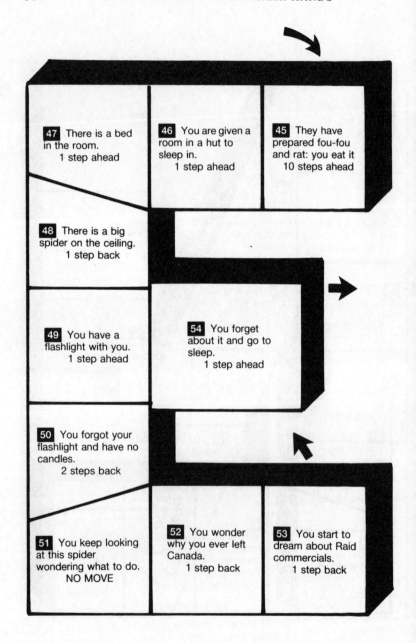

47 There is a bed in the room.
1 step ahead

46 You are given a room in a hut to sleep in.
1 step ahead

45 They have prepared fou-fou and rat: you eat it
10 steps ahead

48 There is a big spider on the ceiling.
1 step back

49 You have a flashlight with you.
1 step ahead

54 You forget about it and go to sleep.
1 step ahead

50 You forgot your flashlight and have no candles.
2 steps back

51 You keep looking at this spider wondering what to do.
NO MOVE

52 You wonder why you ever left Canada.
1 step back

53 You start to dream about Raid commercials.
1 step back

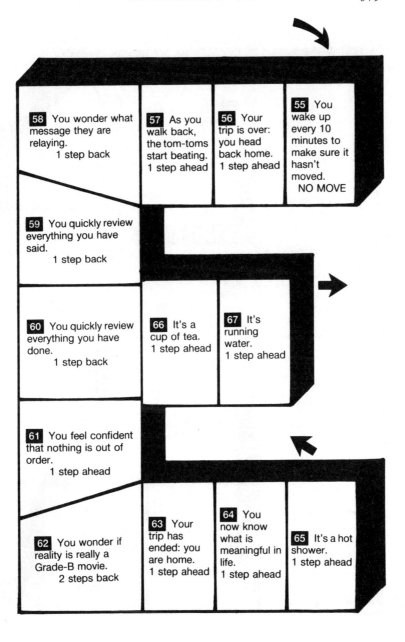

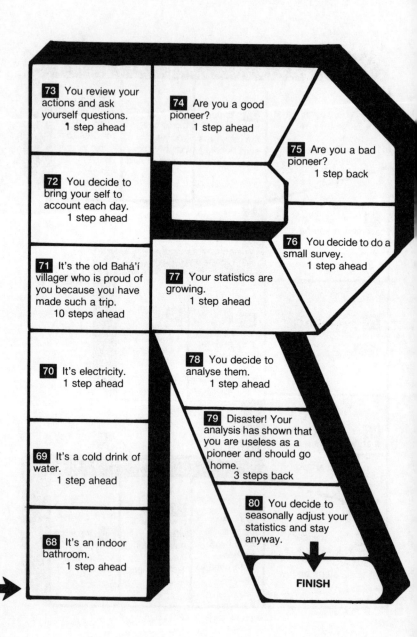

73 You review your actions and ask yourself questions.
  1 step ahead

74 Are you a good pioneer?
  1 step ahead

75 Are you a bad pioneer?
  1 step back

72 You decide to bring your self to account each day.
  1 step ahead

76 You decide to do a small survey.
  1 step ahead

71 It's the old Bahá'í villager who is proud of you because you have made such a trip.
  10 steps ahead

77 Your statistics are growing.
  1 step ahead

70 It's electricity.
  1 step ahead

78 You decide to analyse them.
  1 step ahead

79 Disaster! Your analysis has shown that you are useless as a pioneer and should go home.
  3 steps back

69 It's a cold drink of water.
  1 step ahead

80 You decide to seasonally adjust your statistics and stay anyway.

68 It's an indoor bathroom.
  1 step ahead

FINISH

39

And Now, Can You Go Home Again?

United States Office of Pioneering

The Office of Pioneering of the National Spiritual Assembly of the United States sends a letter to returning pioneers to help them with what, for many, can be a difficult transition to the life they once knew. In reality, however, they are not returning to the same life, for people and places change, and many of the changes for the returning pioneer will be those he finds have taken place within himself. Everyone anticipates culture shock when leaving home for another culture, but to experience it so profoundly in a return home after an absence of several years can be shattering. Excerpts from the letter follow:

It might sound funny, but one step in preparing to return would be to re-read any articles on culture shock that you may still have with you.

Changes in your daily living patterns, of which you may not be conscious, have become instinctive, ingrained habits. A good example of this is that you have, perhaps, finally learned to look to the right for oncoming cars when you step down off a curb rather than to the left. One pioneer, when asked why he stared at the ground when he walked replied, 'watching for snakes' before realizing he was continuing a habit no longer necessary in a city here. A lengthy stay at a post where local transport is by foot, bicycle, slow bus or four-cylinder cars can make sitting in a stateside shopping mall parking lot or driving in rush-hour traffic a traumatic experience. One of the reasons that culture shock for returning pioneers is often greater than that which they experienced on arrival at their post may be that the pioneer headed for the field *anticipates* cultural differences that will require adjustments. New pioneers are fresh and eager to meet the challenge and are thus able to maintain a better sense of proportion and humour. The returning pioneer is often tired and, rather than anticipating changes needing adaptation, expects to return 'home' to a place that is familiar and understandable. This expectation is the cause of several problems.

The 'home' you remember was a localized one – a community, in fact, parts of a community, several friends and an established routine. You were isolated from the complete environment you lived in by local and regional boundaries. Then, too, the 'home' you remember is one that has been tampered with by your memory, which selectively retains all the good things about home and forgets all the others. As a crowning blow, 'home' has changed. In some ways it's better, in other ways it's worse, in many ways it's simply different. Almost certainly it is not the 'home' you left.

So, before you even get back to the United States, you must recognize that there is a gap between what you expect and what is really here. Changes in yourself widen the gap even more. This gap and your reaction to it are two of the features of the reverse culture shock experienced by most returning pioneers.

Often, a pioneer has been so successful at detaching himself from the culture of the United States and becoming a part of his new country that on returning here, very familiar culture shock patterns appear. North American coffee is AWFUL; the kids are totally undisciplined, no one knows how to be polite; where you were, at least people were sane. You may become frustrated, angry, confused, because the set of 'signals' you learned at your post isn't working here.

When you were away perhaps you constantly wished, each time you washed your hair, for the wonderful hot, running water you had 'back home'. However, if you have been living in an area where the native people must struggle to live; where homes have little or no furniture, no running water, no electricity, where rats and disease are so commonplace they are not thought about, and where food itself is perhaps a luxury, then there will be times when you are appalled by the luxuries that in the United States are considered necessities, and by the apparent preoccupation of all Americans with the luxuries and material goods. When you are newly returned, the situation can seem so out of touch with reality as to cause severe disorientation. Even after you have been back for some time, this characteristic of American life can, on occasion, be heart-breaking, insulting and repugnant. You may react as would anyone in the state of culture shock by facing the purchase of a 99 cent cheese slicer or a 79 cent egg slicer with 'why pay for something like that when a knife will do?' While such economy could definitely be worth-while with the cost of living as high as it is, in your case, it is more likely a sign that you're in culture shock. It is at such times that you realize how profoundly the experience of pioneering has changed you. You are not the same person you were when you left. It will be a heart-wrenching realization that, while the United States was your embryonic home, in your post you struggled and realized hidden capacities and gained a vision of the world which is now your real home. 'Abdu'l-Bahá's words pertain especially to you:

O ye homeless wanderers in the Path of God! Prosperity, contentment, and freedom, however much desired and

conducive to the gladness of the human heart, can in no wise
compare with the trials of homelessness and adversity in the
pathway of God; for such exile and banishment are blessed by
the divine favour, and are surely followed by the mercy of
Providence. The joy of tranquillity in one's home, and the
sweetness of freedom from all cares shall pass away, whilst the
blessing of homelessness shall endure forever ... (*Selections
from the Writings of 'Abdu'l-Bahá*, pp. 280–1)

There are also culture shocks in returning to your Bahá'í
community. You expect that this is more of the 'going
home', that here at least, things will be the same. But
change is an integral part of life and growth that both the
community and the individual Bahá'ís will have changed.
You cannot expect communities and friends to be just
as you left them. The biggest changes to meet on your
return to the Bahá'í community are not those in the
friends here, but rather those that *you* will make. Your
role in the national Bahá'í community will be very
different from the one at your post, where heavy responsibilities were yours and demands were made on you daily.
To be the only pioneer within hundreds of miles, the only
pioneer on an island, or the only pioneer who could
untangle an administrative mess at the National Centre
guarantees a tremendous load of work and responsibility.
You were, of course, under the guidance of the national
assembly and the counsellors, but for you and for most
pioneers, personal initiative has been undoubtedly an
important part of your work. A job needed to be done and
you did it.

Back at home, the demands and responsibilities are still
there but they rest on a complete range of functioning
institutions and you share the obligation of fulfilling their
plans with many other believers. This can be a tremendous
relief, but on occasion, you may, for example, do something

on your own, out of habit, which should have gone through your local assembly and misunderstanding may result.

In your post you worked in close alliance with the national assembly, with the board of counsellors, perhaps were even on the auxiliary board or on a local assembly, and you were in close contact with these institutions, were privy to all of their bulletins, but now back at home, you are as an unknown newcomer in a community. You will miss the interaction you had with these other institutions. As a pioneer you had a feeling of closeness to the Universal House of Justice but when you return to your homeland, the Universal House of Justice becomes less visible, less a part of your daily life and this relationship can seem filtered, farther away.

There are other factors that can affect the way you integrate into your new community. The scope of your vision and awareness has become worldwide in both Bahá'í and non-Bahá'í terms. The great needs of the world and the urgency of its problems stare the pioneer in the face daily. The Guardian's words, 'The field is indeed so immense . . . the workers so few, the time so short . . .' voice a reality that is seared on your soul. Now, you are not confronted daily with this feeling of urgency and most Bahá'ís seem to be unaware that doors are being closed hourly. It is easy for you to interpret their seeming unawareness as unconcern; an emotional gap can begin to develop between you and your present community. People ask you about pioneering, but it seems they want a pat, two-minute reply about how wonderful it was to pioneer, and it may seem that none really wants to know of the difficulties, the needs, the nitty-gritty realities. And so, the gap between you and the community widens.

The clash between the situation at your post where there were too few books, too few pioneers, no money in the Fund, perhaps even no freedom to move about or to teach and the situations back home where there is an abundance of books, an abundance of time, ease and freedom of travel, freedom to teach, numerically strong communities and vast material resources also widens the gap. You may feel that the Bahá'ís here are too unaware of their bounties, are wasteful of their time and opportunities. You feel the situation is unreal. You feel you are in a vacuum, disoriented and unable to integrate into the community. Also contributing to the feeling of disorientation is the feeling that members of the community, in general, are, as yet, unaware of the difficulties of adjustment that returning pioneers experience. You may be, however subtly, conveying your feelings of what appears to be their lack of awareness and they may see that as a judgement. They may become defensive and think you feel they are not doing enough. Also the community may expect things of you simply because 'you were a pioneer'.

Then there are the well-meaning remarks or attempts at conversation which can insult or hurt you. For example, a pioneer returning from an area where there is trouble may hear, 'Got out just in time, eh?' or 'Heard you were coming back, but that you had to, not that you were running away . . .'

By not understanding the trauma you are going through, the Bahá'ís may interpret your desire to withdraw as inactivity and they will wonder how someone with sufficient dedication to pioneer can become so inactive. They cannot understand your need to withdraw a bit to regain perspective. And you, in turn, cannot tell them some of what is hurting you. The gap widens.

Here you have come home to what you expected would be 'sanity' and 'order', hoping for someone to sit down and have a good talk with, thinking that now you are home again you will get a chance to rest. Few pioneers return expecting a difficult adjustment, and friends and families also have no idea that such an adjustment is necessary and that it takes time. One factor can also be the state of your physical health. Being worn-out and run-down from exhaustion and illness can dramatically affect your ability to cope and can make even small things seem impossible to handle. Those who have been away for over two years may encounter virus strains for which they have little resistance and may go through a period of almost continuous cold, cough and flu symptoms until their bodies develop resistance to the viruses.

Some may return to non-Bahá'í families who feel that now you will stop 'running all over' and will 'settle down'. They will keep telling you they are glad you got out 'of that terrible place in time'. You feel debilitated, let-down and your discouragement is compounded as you realize that your very own family members may have no concept of the significance of what you have tried to do.

From what we have learned from returned pioneers, we can say that the strongest emotions that assail them are those of guilt and failure. These emotions are felt even before they reach their homeland. Many, many factors form the seeds from which these feelings spring. Even pioneers who remain have these feelings. We wish there were some way to reach the inside of you where these feelings are and to assure you that there is no need for them. Returning is difficult enough without adding a burden for which there is no foundation. The act of pioneering, of leaving your home to serve Bahá'u'lláh was one from which there will be great results no matter how meagre the 'results' you have seen, how much work remains to be done or whether you are coming back sooner than you had planned. The stress appears greatest among those pioneers who left feeling they were never coming back and less for those whose stay was for a definite period of time. But all pioneers know how much they are needed at

their posts and how much work remains to be done. Some
returning pioneers say they have difficulty in praying.
Often these are the same pioneers who always relied
heavily on prayer.

If a returned pioneer had nothing else to cope with but
the feelings of guilt, failure and difficulty in praying, it
would be enough. But there are also, at various times,
feelings of loss, disorientation, frustration, anger, loneliness
and alienation. You may well want to withdraw into
yourself. You may feel helpless, absent-minded, touchy,
sleepy, tearful, and some of your actions may be tremen-
dously out of character.

Wanting to withdraw is one reaction that is almost
universal. You may want to isolate yourself, to rest your
body and soul, to stay by yourself to get it all together.
Returning brings you to the realization of the depth of
changes you have undergone while at your post. You
become more and more aware that you are different from
the person who left and somehow this person does not seem
to fit in and there is the feeling that in order to adjust you
will need to change even more. There is a natural resistance
to this adjustment and a fear that the person you have
become will be swallowed up and lost in this society, that
you'll become just like everyone else. Part of the struggle is
that of incorporating your spiritual growth into a strong
person able to function back home.

It is ironic that one of the greatest needs you may feel is
to have someone understanding to talk with yet you might
have a fear and a reluctance to tell anyone that something
is 'wrong'. You feel you should be saying wonderful things
yet you do not feel at all wonderful. You feel that after all
you have learned to cope with, you should not be having
these difficulties now. The feeling that you cannot tell
anyone this for fear they will not understand is a common
feeling.

Stress Within The Family Unit

Families that pioneered together often undergo additional problems on returning. Each member of the family is undergoing severe tests of their own, and rather than being able to contribute towards the strengthening of the family, each member feels flung in a separate direction.

One member of the family undergoing difficulties may feel that someone else in the family should be more supportive and understanding but that other member may be having the same situation requiring support and not able to help anyone else. Children, as well as adults, suffer culture shock. And children have fewer resources of experience to call upon when trying to understand what is happening. It is not uncommon for children who may have at the pioneering post said nearly every day they wished to return home, to now calmly say to parents, 'Let's go back.'

Things That Can Help

1. Before returning, consciously try to rid yourself of expectations about what it will be like 'back home'. As members of a family, you can consult about your feelings and expectations so that when you get back the channels of communication are already open to the subject.

2. Consider the alternative of coming back for a vacation rather than deciding to come back permanently. 'Burning your bridges' makes coming back a step very difficult to reverse. If you are certain you cannot stay in one particular post, consider consulting with the International Goals Committee about going on to another post rather than coming back to the United States.

3. If possible, arrange for a visit to Haifa on the way back to your homeland.

4. Arrange your travel so that you travel through Chicago and Wilmette for a meeting with an International Goals Committee representative. (This advice for returning Americans can be applicable for others. Meeting with your home country's goals committee on your return can be most beneficial.)

5. Look at the return as a pioneer move to a new post. Try to identify with the struggles and sacrifices the believers in your home country make for the Faith.

6. If possible, return to a different community than the one which you left.

7. See your negative reactions as a further exercise in removing prejudice.

8. Be active. Try to balance your low-key days with activity, especially if you are feeling depressed. Bahá'u'lláh, in *Epistle to the Son of the Wolf* (p. 49), states that, 'He that secludeth himself in his house is indeed as one dead.' Activity is one of the best weapons against depression. Become involved with a project you consider worthwhile. Be active physically. Go for a walk. Ask the local assembly or District Teaching Committee for specific tasks. Ask them, don't wait for them to ask you.

9. Although looking for a job is one of the priorities of all returning pioneers, don't let this cause an inordinate amount of anxiety. Some people manage to land a job right away. For others it takes a little longer.

If you have been deputized, you may feel you will want to contribute to the Fund to replenish it, but this is not always possible immediately. Be prepared for the fact that the cost of living has risen considerably. If your contributions are not as generous as you would like to have them, remember, there is a spiritual law at work through participation to whatever extent you are able.

10. Realize that only Bahá'u'lláh can judge the merit of your services. You cannot see the ultimate fruits of your labours at your post. But your service has not ended with your return. Quoting Bahá'u'lláh: 'The movement itself from place to place, when undertaken for the sake of God, hath always exerted, and can now exert, its influence in the world.' (*Advent of Divine Justice*, p. 84) Your return to your home community brings new strength to that community.

11. Be patient, kind and understanding with yourself. There is no right way nor wrong way to feel. What you are going through is a process and the way you feel will change when your perspective changes.

12. Pray. The noonday prayer is very helpful for a returned pioneer in trauma. 'I testify, at this moment, to my powerlessness and to Thy might . . .' This acceptance of our state of helplessness is very positive when coupled with the acclamation of God's might. If you are having trouble praying, ask others to pray for you or with you, and keep trying to pray yourself.

13. Know that the national spiritual assembly of your country lovingly welcomes you and is in need of your continuing service for the Faith. If the going gets rough, physically, financially, emotionally, don't hesitate. Contact the Office of Pioneering. Its responsibility to you, in fact, that of the entire Bahá'í community, includes helping you settle back in the United States or to prepare for a new post.

14. Attend a Pioneer Training Institute and share some of your experience. It will be most helpful to those just starting out.

Another thing to remember is, that just as did adjustment to your post and resolution of many difficulties there, adjustment to your return and its attendant difficulties requires much time. It does not all happen overnight.

40

To the Pioneers of the Future

'Abdu'l-Bahá

O that I could travel, even though on foot and in the utmost poverty, to these regions, and, raising the call of 'Yá Bahá'u'l-Abhá' in cities, villages, mountains, deserts and oceans, promote the Divine teachings! This, alas, I cannot do. How intensely I deplore it! Please God, ye may achieve it.

Tablets of the Divine Plan

41

A Prayer for Pioneers

'Abdu'l-Bahá

O Thou Incomparable God! O Thou Lord of the Kingdom! These souls are Thy heavenly army. Assist them and, with the cohorts of the Supreme Concourse, make them victorious, so that each one of them may become like unto a regiment and conquer these countries through the love of God and the illumination of divine teachings.

O God! Be Thou their supporter and their helper, and in the wilderness, the mountain, the valley, the forests, the prairies and the seas, be Thou their confidant – so that they may cry out through the power of the Kingdom and the breath of the Holy Spirit.

Verily, Thou art the Powerful, the Mighty and the Omnipotent, and Thou art the Wise, the Hearing and the Seeing.

Tablets of the Divine Plan